Michael Weidle

# Mind your colour

Monographs from the African Studies Centre, Leiden

# Mind your colour

The 'coloured' stereotype in South African literature

## V. A. February

Kegan Paul International Ltd
London and Boston

*First published in 1981*
*by Kegan Paul International Ltd*
*39 Store Street,*
*London WC1E 7DD and*
*9 Park Street,*
*Boston, Mass. 02108, USA*
*Set in Press Roman by*
*Hope Services*
*Abingdon, Oxon,*
*and printed in Great Britain by*
*Redwood Burn Ltd*
*Trowbridge & Esher*
*© African Studies Centre, Leiden, 1981*

*British Library Cataloguing in Publication Data*

*February, Vernie A*
*Mind your colour. – (Afrika – Studiecentrum.*
*Monographs)*
*1. South African Literature – History and*
*criticism*
*2. Coloured persons in literature*
*I. Title    II. Series*
*820'9        PR9354.2.A8        80-41620*

*ISBN 0-7103-0002-6*

# Contents

# Preface

This book is essentially about stereotypes as found in the literature and culture of South Africa. It deals specifically with those people referred to in the South African racial legislation as 'coloureds'. The book is also an illustration of the way in which stereotypes function as a means of social control and repression. One of the direct consequences of colonialism and racism is that the colonized or the discriminated invariably become the dupe of a series of rationalizations whereby the power-holders (i.e., the whites) justify their dominant position in society. Balandier, the French scholar, has given ample demonstration of this phenomenon as it operated in the former French colonies in West Africa and the Antilles. Here, the major channels of imposing French values were the French administrative officials and expatriates in the colonies, the school system and the policy of assimilation. Such a policy led to a reverence for the metropolis, Paris, an over-evaluation of French customs and norms, and a rejection of their own culture. This illusion was soon dispelled the moment the colonized set foot in France. Most blacks discovered that they were still looked upon as le nègre, even by the lowest of Frenchmen.

The Dutch economic historian, D. van Arkel, has, on the basis of his work on the Austrian Jews, come to the conclusion that stereotypes arise when the following conditions are fulfilled: (1) there must be stigmatization, (2) social distance and (3) terrorization. The black man, then, becomes lazy, over-sexual, a ne'er-do-well, an ignoramus, fit only to provide the comic note in novels and short stories. Not surprisingly, these stereotypes prompted Ezekiel Mphahlele to rail against Joyce Cary's *Mister Johnson*: 'I flung away *Mister Johnson* with exasperation ... I had seen too many journalistic caricatures of black people and bongo-bongo cartoons showing Africans with filed teeth and bones stuck in their hair.'

The stereotype facilitates the task of the power-holder and makes it possible to stipulate a code of conduct for the blacks on the basis of characteristics imputed to them by whites. This process is nowhere more apparent than in South Africa, where blacks are allowed upward social mobility only within the institutionalized and ascribed pattern. The major emphasis in this book is on those people labelled 'coloured' within the South African racial hierarchy, and the way in which they are stereotyped in the literature and culture of that country. The term 'coloured' is, in itself, in need of explanation. Since, however, this is extensively dealt with in the introductory chapter, it is sufficient to state here, that the term is largely inspired by racist thinking. It is, for this reason, that it is placed in inverted commas, to express my rejection of it as it is used in South Africa.

Sometimes, the term 'so-called coloured' is used, and, of late, the general tendency is to refer to 'coloureds' as blacks. This is very much a post-Soweto phenomenon. There is, however, no consistency in the usage of the term black.

The picture which emerges of the 'so-called coloured' people within the South African historical and literary context, is an unpretty one. In fact, one has incontrovertible proof that Afrikaner political attitudes must have inevitably been shaped by some of these stereotypes. It is, therefore, not so surprising to find an Afrikaner cabinet minister, Dr E. Dönges, quoting from the works of Sarah Gertrude Millin and Regina Neser (in casu, *Kinders van Ishmaël*), in support of his proposed law to forbid sexual relations between white and black in 1948. Special attention is given to 'Coloured'–Afrikaner relations in literature. One is confronted with a picture ranging from ambiguity and almost near-kinship to total rejection and hatred.

The stereotype of the 'coloured' as found in literature, is contrasted with that of the *Indo* in the former Dutch East Indies (now Indonesia). References are made to the creolized situation in Surinam (former Dutch Guyana). This comparative treatment of the subject served to provide further illuminating insights into the whole process of stigmatization.

The literary and cultural scene reveals that stigmatization has helped in the process of dehumanization, the effects of which are clearly visible at times in the anomalous behaviour of the so-called coloured people. At the same time, it reveals that the process of black conscious-ness has forced many a 'coloured' into an orphic descent. There seems, at last, in the words of the Guyanese novelist, Wilson Harris, a 'charting of the hollowness to set up a new echoing dimension of spatial resources for the liberation of community'.

Sadly, however, my insight would have been severely restricted had it not, ironically, been for those years of exile in Holland. I was afforded an opportunity to abstract myself from the holocaust and develop, at the least, a comic ironic sense. Periods of teaching African, Afro-Caribbean and Afro-American literature at universities in Sierra Leone (Fourah Bay College), Surinam, Leiden, Amsterdam, Antwerp and Wisconsin-Madison further helped me to understand certain social processes.

In Amsterdam, I had occasion to come to grips with 'Cape society' from time to time. I am grateful to Angus Leendertz and his father for anecdotal evenings spent in Amsterdam. I am thankful to my institute at Leiden, the Afrika Studiecentrum, and in particular, to Dr G. W. Grootenhuis, the general secretary, for his appreciation of my activities. The historian, Dr R. Ross, was always willing to lend an ear and share his research findings on South African historical issues with me. I would be failing in my duty if I did not mention Professor Jan Voorhoeve, who supervised my research, and who allowed me to share his insights into Surinamese culture and literature and which finally culminated in *Creole Drum*. Above all, I owe my insights to my late mother, who taught us to remain sane in a race-orientated society and whose 'wisdom passed all understanding'. Hopefully, this work will contribute to the process of undoing the 'self-deception in self-definition' among the 'so-called coloured' people of South Africa.

Vernie February
Leiden

# Introduction

# Not a race of slaves[1]

The point of departure in this study is the stereotyped image of the 'Cape coloured' (person of mixed origin),[2] as found in South African literature. Several studies have been carried out in an attempt to deal with the 'coloureds'. Most well known of these studies are those by Marais (1957), D. P. Botha (1960), MacMillan (1927), Patterson (1953) and Cilliers (1963). Some South African scholars have also attempted to abstract the picture of the 'coloured' as found in Afrikaans literature. Most notable of these was the study by F. E. J. Malherbe (1958). This stereotyping has further complicated the special role ascribed to 'coloureds' within the South African context. If one observes carefully, then the picture of the Khoi as it unfolds in travel literature in the seventeenth century already contains some of the stereotypes of the 'coloureds'. It is no mere accident that certain attributes are ascribed to what is known, in the mouths of white users, as 'Hottentot',[3] and that these are then, later on, neatly transplanted onto 'Cape coloured'.

## Early stereotypes

The picture which emerges of the original inhabitants of South Africa (i.e., the Khoi and the San)[4] is an unpretty, and a comically distorted one. The inhabitants are enshrined in the following pattern. They are lazy, they love to drink, they swear and fight at the slightest provocation and are generally immoral. These characteristics are clearly visible in the literature of the early Afrikaans language movement. It is precisely in these early portrayals that one already senses something of the ambivalent Afrikaner attitudes towards the latter-day 'Cape Coloured'. In English literature of the early 1920s, the dominant theme, as

1

represented in the works of Sarah Gertrude Millin, was that of 'colour being a disease',[5] or in the words of Cedrick Dover (1937), 'smelling strangeness'.[6] Small wonder that the first literary products of 'coloureds' themselves aped the whites in this respect. Thus, Peterson and Small failed at times to escape the Afrikaans and Afrikaner tradition, whereby the 'coloured' was looked upon with ambiguity and paternal affection and regarded as a sort of 'brown Afrikaner'.

## Playing white, ambiguity and colour consciousness

If one looks at the history of the 'coloured' in South Africa, then it is hardly surprising that the above-mentioned factors all play a role among this group. Because of the various racial policies of successive South African governments, the colour of one's skin determined one's status in society. Thus, where possible, some 'coloureds' initially tried to seek their salvation with the whites rather than with their fellow oppressed. Many tried to be 'play whites'.[7] Secondly, in view of especially the rural 'coloureds' involvement with *Afrikaansdom*, if not *Afrikanerdom*, there developed between the Afrikaner and a large section of the 'coloureds' a relationship of ambiguity, and a feeling of almost near-kinship. Since colour was the sole criterion at times, 'coloureds' too started evaluating themselves in terms of pigmentation. Thus, gradations of lightness (whiteness) and brownness were noticeable to 'coloureds', which would normally not be so apparent to the non-coloured.

This study is an attempt to expose the horrible stereotyping 'coloureds' have traditionally been subject to, and to show the growth of a greater political consciousness and a rejection of white stereotypes among the 'coloureds'. Many youngsters from the Cape started sympathizing with the African National Congress (ANC). Some even left the country to undergo guerrilla training abroad. A handful died as guerrillas. Finally and ultimately, this new-found political consciousness among 'coloureds' led to a certain amount of black consciousness among the youth in Cape Town and its environment. Whereas in 1960, with Sharpeville, the 'coloureds', for various reasons, stayed outside the political campaigns of the Pan African Congress (PAC) and the ANC, the reverse obtained in 1976. The youth rose against the system of apartheid, thereby pledging full support to their compatriots in Soweto. In a sense, then, the stereotyping of the 'coloured' as found in the literature and the culture of South Africa is also a good mirror of the treatment, or mal-treatment, of this group called 'coloured', from 1652 onwards until the publication of the Erika Theron report in 1976.

## Statutory definitions (or what 'coloured' is not)

The legal attempts to define what 'coloured' is, within the South African context, have further complicated the picture. More often one only abstracts a picture of what 'coloured' is *not,* inside South Africa. Unconsciously, the practice of playing white, the cultivation of one's own artificial racial barriers and the harbouring of ambiguous attitudes towards Afrikaans and Afrikaansdom, found further sustenance in these legal definitions. Instead of providing clarity, the law brought confusion.

Generally, the statutory terms used to define the various 'racial' groups in South Africa are: 'Europeans' (i.e., whites); 'natives' and 'Bantu' (i.e., Africans); 'Cape coloured' (i.e., persons of mixed ancestry) and 'Asiatics' (i.e., various groups of Asian descent). 'Natives', 'coloureds' and 'Asiatics' are again lumped together and called 'non-Europeans' or 'non-whites'. Suzman (1960) comments that the term 'native' was largely confined to statutory use in the period before the formation of the Union of South Africa (1910). It later came to be replaced by other terms because of its opprobrious connotation, although these substitutes were no less obnoxious. The term 'African', Suzman observes, never found statutory recognition, although he advances no reasons for this. Quite clearly, it must be sought in the Afrikaner fear that, if the word 'African' is translated into Afrikaans as 'Afrikaan' (as happens in Dutch), then it would lead to confusion with the term 'Afrikaner', which they had appropriated for themselves. Thus, comically, the term 'Bantu' came to be used by the whites, and since it means nothing else but *people,* the Afrikaans term 'Bantoevolk' constitutes the greatest linguistic and tautological nonsense.

According to section 1 of the *Population Registration Act of 1950,* all South Africans must be classified as members of a particular group. Broadly speaking, then, one would have the following table:

| A *Whites* (non-black) | B *Non-whites* (blacks) |
|---|---|
| Whites are subdivided into | Non-whites are subdivided into |
| 1 Afrikaans-speaking | 1 Coloureds |
| 2 English-speaking | 2 Asiatics |
| 3 immigrants, e.g., Italians, Greeks *et al.* These tend to identify with the second category | 3 Bantu |

3

With equal justification, one could have a taxonomy based on the division of *black* and *non-black*.

The non-white or black groups are again further subdivided. 'Coloureds' are, for example, grouped into seven categories, in the following order. (Here, in terms of the *Population Registration Act of 1950,* Asiatics are regarded as 'coloureds'.) (1) 'Cape coloured', (2) Malay, (3) Griqua, (4) Chinese, (5) Indian, (6) 'other' Asiatic, (7) 'other' coloured. 'Bantu' are subdivided into eight units, i.e. North-Sotho, South-Sotho, Swazi, Tsonga, Tswana, Venda, Xhosa and Zulu.

Rightly does the Erika Theron Report on the 'coloureds' point out that very often one's classification as a 'coloured' may, in border-line cases, be dependent on the definitions of what is white or 'Bantu'. The Theron Commission was specially instituted by the South African government to investigate every facet of 'coloured' life, and possibly, during the process of investigations, to provide useful suggestions which would complement the government blue-print. That this was not so easy will be apparent at a later stage.

Before the Act of Union in 1910, these terms were rather loosely used. According to that existing tradition, an attempt was made in the *Pensions Act No. 22 of 1928* to define the 'coloureds' as a statutory group within the South African setting. The Act reads as follows:

A Coloured is someone who is neither;

    a.   a Turk or a member of a race or tribe in Asia nor

    b.   a member of an aboriginal race or tribe in Africa nor

    c.   a Hottentot, Bushman or Koranna nor

    d.   a person residing in a native location . . . nor

    e.   an American negro.

This act was amended by *Act No. 34 of 1931,* and once more by the *Pensions Act of 1934.* The *Population Registration Act No. 30 of 1950,* which made it compulsory for people to be registered as a member of either the white, 'coloured' or 'native' groups in terms of section 5(1), makes fascinating if bizarre reading. A 'white person' is defined as meaning 'a person who in appearance obviously is, or who is generally accepted as a white person, but does not include a person who, although in appearance obviously a white person, is generally accepted as a coloured person'.[8]

'Section 19 (1) provides that a person who in appearance is a white person shall for the purposes of the Act be presumed to be a white person until the contrary is proved'.[8]

A 'native' in South African terminology is 'any member of an aboriginal race or tribe of Africa'.[9]

'Coloureds' are simply referred to as persons who are neither 'natives' nor whites. The basic criteria of *appearance, descent* and *general acceptance* are very flimsy indeed. *Proclamation 46 of 1959* was declared invalid by the High Court of Justice in South Africa, precisely because it was so vaguely phrased. The various groups of 'coloureds' are defined and described in *Proclamation 123 of 1967.* Here, *descent* and the classification of the biological father are factors of importance.

In probably one of the greatest legal and linguistic tautologies, the 'coloureds' are defined in the following manner under this *Proclamation of 1967:*

> The Cape Coloured Group shall consist of persons who in fact are, or who, except in the case of persons who, in fact, are members of race or class or tribe referred to in paragraph . . . are generally accepted as members of the race or class known as the Cape Coloured.

The various definitions gave rise to such practices as 'trying for white', 'playing white' and 'passing for white'. D. P. Botha, an eminent Afrikaner theologian, makes the following very illuminating observations:[10]

> The great mass reveals such a motley character that the government is forced to divide the coloured community into various sub-groups for its purposes, of which the Cape Coloured group is the largest. From the racial point of view, the Coloured as a group defies all classification. . . . Colour can also not be applied as a criterion. The Coloureds cannot simply be labelled as 'brown people', since their colour ranges from white to black. The inefficiency of such a criterion is further emphasized by the fact that many whites are darker than a great many Coloureds and yet are not denied their place in white society because of this.

The Reverend Allan Hendrickse probably speaks for all those classified as 'coloureds' when he states:[11]

> The term Coloured is not of our own thinking, and if we look at the circumstances of the South African situation then you must ask why. We have no peculiar colour, we have no peculiar language and if other people see these peculiarities they see them not because they see them but because they want other people to see

them . . . . I do not want to be labelled Coloured . . . all I want to be known as is South African.

'Coloureds' have been variously called 'Eurafricans', 'Cape coloureds' and 'bruinmense' (i.e., brown people). This question of nomenclature is important within the South African way of life, for it will also largely determine one's ascribed role. In his survey on the 'coloureds' in Johannesburg, Edelstein came to the following conclusions, which can be regarded as fairly symptomatic of 'coloured' attitudes.[12]

| Name preferences of 'Coloureds' | Yes | Percentage |
|---|---|---|
| Black | 9 | 2 |
| South African | 265 | 53 |
| Coloured | 122 | 24 |
| Afrikaner | 1 | 0 |
| Brown Afrikaner | 1 | 0 |
| Malay | 28 | 6 |
| Coloured South African | 48 | 10 |
| Cape coloured | 19 | 4 |
| 'Bruinmens' | 4 | 1 |
| Griqua | 1 | 0 |
| Coloured Afrikaner | 2 | 0 |
| Other | 0 | 0 |

The fact that this survey was conducted in Johannesburg, where the term 'coloured' probably has a higher 'status' value amidst the overwhelming majority of Africans, may explain the rather high percentage which preferred the term 'coloured'. The Theron Commission concluded that the 'coloureds' preferred to be South Africans. The Commission, in typical white South African fashion, advocated that the various categories of 'coloured' be scrapped to make way for one category only, namely 'coloured'. It did not advocate the abolition of this racist term.

The term 'coloured, as used in the statutes and by whites in general, is largely a racist one, which is supposed to cover a more or less homogeneous group. Nothing can be further from the truth. The 'coloureds' may then be Western in language (i.e. English and/or Afrikaans-speaking), but they are fast becoming black (and homogeneous in purpose at least), because of increasing political oppression.

The justification given by the Afrikaner poet, N. P. van Wyk Louw, in a foreword to Botha's book (1960) on the 'coloureds', will find ready acceptance amongst most Afrikaners. Van Wyk Louw writes:[13]

I find the word 'Kleurling' [i.e. 'coloured'] (with or without a capital letter) a nasty word, with a plantation or colonial after-taste

— and perhaps not even good Afrikaans, an imported word; I prefer
the word 'bruinmens' which I have learnt from the mouths of the
brown people themselves when I was a child. And brown as a
colour is certainly not ugly. Else why would we try to get it by
roasting in the sun?

Van Wyk Louw is of course guilty of hypocrisy here, for while rejecting
the one term as being racist, he has no qualms about substituting an
equally obnoxious one.

## Policy statements

This ambiguous attitude towards the 'coloureds' is also found in the
policy statements of successive political leaders in South Africa. The
'coloureds', in the Cape at least, retained some political rights when the
Union of South Africa was formed. In the North, the general attitude
was reflected in the constitutions of the Free State Grondwet (1854)
and the South African Republic (1858). The Free State Grondwet
bluntly stated that, 'civic rights' and 'burgherdom'[14] were reserved for
those who were white. The South African Republic said that, 'the
people desire to permit no equality between Coloured people and
white inhabitants, in Church or State'.[15]

The early statements of Hertzog and Malan make very interesting
reading, especially in view of the role both these men played in the rise
of Afrikaner nationalism. Between 1910 and 1940 the general line by
all governments was that the 'coloureds' constituted at least a part of
the nation. Prime Minister Hertzog (1924-9) spelt out his 'coloured'
policy quite clearly in his Smithfield speech in November 1925. To him,
the 'coloured' belonged to 'a section of the community closely allied
to the white population . . . fundamentally different from the natives.
He owes his origin to us and knows no other civilization than that of the
European . . . even speaks the language of the European as his mother-
tongue . . . . Cape Coloured people must be treated on an equality with
Europeans — economically, industrially and politically'.[16]

Thus, while there was a move to control the influx of Africans into
urban areas, 'coloureds' were specifically told that they were, to some
degree, a part of the nation. Moreover, in Hertzog's speech one comes
across a sentiment which will recur in Afrikaner attitudes from this
point onwards — the 'coloureds' are of us, speak our language, have
our culture, are Western by any standards, but different only in that
they are darker. We shall see how this statement is later on literally
re-echoed in the Theron Commission Report (1976) on the 'coloureds'.

Hertzog made several attempts to extend the franchise to 'coloureds', namely in 1926 and 1929. He even thought of giving the vote to 'coloureds' in the Northern provinces. His Minister of the Interior, Dr D. F. Malan, the man who was to become the first 'apartheid' Prime Minister in 1948, was to follow his leader's views very closely at this stage. At a Malay conference in 1925, he was reported to have said that, 'the present government shall see to it that there will be no colour barrier for the Malays or the Coloureds.'[17] In 1928, Malan even opposed a private member's bill seeking the extension of the vote to white women, on the grounds that, 'the political rights of the white man shall be given to the Coloured people . . . . Personally, I should like to give the vote to the Coloured women.'[18] However, in his speech at Porterville (1938), he was to sound a completely different note, advocating the abolition of the 'native' franchise and separate representation for the 'coloureds'. Indeed by 1934, as founder of the Puritanical National Party, he stood for 'the logical application of the segregation principle in regard to all Non-Europeans' and for the introduction of 'separate residential areas, separate trade unions, and as far as practical also, separate places of work for Europeans and non-Europeans'.[19]

It may well be that Malan decided to sacrifice the 'coloured' on the altar of Afrikaner nationalism. Politically at least, the 'coloured' was brought more into the orbit of separate development from 1948 onwards. Yet, ironically, despite the vain attempts to create, for the 'coloureds', a separate identity, successive national governments in South Africa still continued their policies of ambiguity in respect of the 'coloured'.

Seen also against the backdrop of historical and political events inside the country, the *Separate Representation of Voters Act of 1951,* which paved the way for the removal of the 'coloureds' from the common roll, was hardly surprising. The 'coloured' had operated largely within the institutionalized structures of South Africa between 1854 and 1948. 'Tolerance and restraint', one is given to understand, are the twin pillars of what came to be known as Cape Liberalism. Yet, these twin concepts are more a recognition by the white man that the 'coloured' was behaving himself in playing out his historically ascribed role in society.

## Afrikaner blueprint for the 'coloureds'

The South African government is noted for appointing commissions to investigate sociological aspects of various groups in the country, and then to sweep their recommendations under the carpet. This happened with the Tomlinson Report in 1955, which dealt with the position of the African in South Africa. The same fate awaited the lengthy Erika Theron Report on the 'coloureds' in 1976. It is however prudent to recall that the volumes dedicated to the Poor White Problem, and especially some of the recommendations (Wilcocks, 1932), did not suffer a similar fate, and were readily taken up by the authorities. But then the poor white was enshrined in the imagery of the 'soap box' and concentration camp of the Anglo-Boer war: an emotional debt which had to be repaid. Resuscitation of the poor white was essential to Afrikaner nationalism; containment of the 'blacks and the browns', fundamental for the survival of the Afrikaner.

Not surprisingly, the government had no difficulty in finding several 'coloureds' who were prepared to serve on the Theron Commission. They too, had duped themselves into believing that they were working out the 'coloured' destiny at last, in conjunction with their Afrikaner brothers. The Commission came to some disturbing conclusions, at least for white South Africa. It established that 43 per cent of the children born to 'coloured' women were illegitimate, and that one fifth of the 'coloureds' were either jobless or only working part-time. It turned out that 75 per cent of 'coloured' farm workers were living below the subsistence level.

The Theron Commission came to the conclusion that there was no such thing as a peculiarly 'coloured' culture, although this was challenged by some other members. 'In practice, provision must be made for the fact that a large percentage of the Coloureds do indeed form an integral part of the Afrikaans or English-speaking cultural communities through language, religion and general orientation.'[20] This conclusion, in 1976, does not differ significantly from that of Hertzog in his Smithfield speech mentioned earlier on. The Commission continues, 'among the Coloured communities there is essentially no other culture than that of the Afrikaans-or-English-speaking Whites.'[21] The Commission, therefore advocates that, 'one should stop viewing the Coloured population as a community which is culturally different and which can be culturally distinguished from the White population.'[22]

Some members on the Commission argued, however, that there was such a thing as a 'coloured' community and 'coloured' culture. Nevertheless, all these views are indications of Afrikaner attitudes towards the 'coloureds'.

Not surprisingly, the Commission advocated the following general measures: 'coloureds' must have a direct say in the decision-making

9

policy of the country; one single term should be adopted to describe the 'coloured' people; the *Immorality Act* and the *Prohibition of Mixed Marriages* should be scrapped from the statute book; 'coloureds' should not be restricted from buying agricultural land. The major recommendations of the Theron Commission differ in no way from the pleas of Hertzog in the 1920s, the initial statements of Malan and the sentiments expressed by D. P. Botha in his book, *Die opkoms van ons derde stand* (1960). It is wholly consonant with the ambiguous attitudes of Afrikanerdom towards the 'coloureds'. They (i.e. the 'coloureds') may then be darker, but they deserve to be within the laager of at least, Afrikaansdom, if not Afrikanerdom.

Now, the interesting part of the Theron Commission was that the final report was a tacit admission by Afrikanerdom that it did not know how to fit the 'coloureds' into its concept of the nation. As such, the report is also a reflection of the fluctuating attitudes towards the 'coloureds' within Afrikanerdom. A thorough scrutiny of the report reveals some conflicting, albeit minority opinions, among the members of the Commission. These deviating ideas also reflect accurately the uncertainty of the Afrikaner towards the 'coloured'. In fact, at times, one is forcibly reminded of the late Dr Verwoerd's speech in parliament on the 13 April 1962 when he spoke as follows:[23]

> One must distinguish between citizenship of a country and . . . what the components of a homogeneous nation are. There is no doubt that the Coloureds are citizens of this country. There is just as little doubt that they are not part of this homogeneous entity that can be described as 'the nation'.

The Theron Commission advocated the removal of pin-pricks and not the institution of democracy. And, in this respect, it also reflected the dilemma of the Afrikaner. Total abolition of racial laws would, in Afrikaner eyes, mean total abdication of political power. And the aim of Afrikanerdom is to keep South Africa 'White and safe for all Whites'.

The initial reaction by the government was, understandably, negative. 'Coloureds' who were asked for comment made it quite clear that it was, 'the whites who carry a degree of expectation from the report . . .'[24] It was, however, the TLSA Journal, in an editorial entitled *Theronausea,* which expressed the popular mood even before the report was tabled:[25]

> At the time of writing (31 May 1976), we do not know and do not care whether the Report of the Erika Theron Commission on a

section of the non-citizen majority officially designated as 'The Coloured People' is to be published this year, next year or ever. Or whether it appears with or without an umbilical White Paper around its throat, strangling it at birth, as happened to the Tomlinson Report in 1955. It has no relevance either as bait or hook. The Prime Minister, who appointed the Commission, has in effect repudiated its Report in advance (because he no longer needs it) and made it plain that he appointed it not to tell him what to do but merely to tell him how to apply party policy more effectively.

# Chapter 1

# Untroubled things[1]

The history of what is now known in South Africa as the 'Cape coloured', is one of miscegenation over a period of three hundred years (i.e. from the time of the arrival of the Dutch in 1652 until today). Very many peoples and groups have contributed to this most heterogeneous of groups in South Africa. First of all, there were the indigenous groups encountered by the Portuguese and later on, the Dutch: the Khoisan peoples ('Hottentot' and to a lesser extent 'Bushmen').[2] Unable to turn these people into serfs the Dutch resorted to the importation of slaves from 1658 onwards, who formed the second group. Initially, these slaves came from Madagascar, Angola, and Mozambique. During the eighteenth century the slaves were imported predominantly from the East Indies, as we shall see later on. Then there were the Europeans — mostly Dutch and German — while in 1688, French Huguenots came to the Cape.

Intermixing took place at various levels. There was miscegenation between Europeans and the Khoi, the most obvious example being the marriage of the Khoi woman, Eva, to the Dutchman van Meerhof (chirurgyn). The earliest recorded example of a marriage to a slave was that of Jan Wouters of Middelburg, Holland, to Catherina of Bengal (slaves were invariably identified by the country of origin). Legal liaisons 'across the colour line' were, however, the exception rather than the rule.

A European woman at the Cape was a *rara avis* in the true sense of the word. In 1663 there were, for example, only seventeen white females. Prostitution flourished in this harbour port of Cape Town. Passing sailors and garrison soldiers of the Dutch East Indies Company sought sexual release with Khoi and slave women, and the results were not insignificant. Van Riebeeck records (22 August 1660) that on a visit to the quarters of constable Willem, he found, 'the self-same constable there lying in his bunk [bed] and next to him in the very same bunk, a slave named Maria, belonging to the Commander'.[3] We read further that in 1660, 'freeburgher Elbertsz was caught in the act with his slave Adouke, who lived in his house and it came to light that he had often chased her husband from his [connubial] bed in order to have sexual relations with her'.[4]

It was estimated that during the first twenty years of its existence, no less than 75 per cent of the children born at the Cape of slave mothers were half-breeds.

When Commissioner Baron van Rheede tot Drakensteyn visited the Cape in 1685, he was forced to admit after a visit to the slave quarters:[5]

the women [i.e. slaves] in order to protect themselves against the cold are clothed and covered with various pieces of old cloth and rags, that many also, especially the younger ones, were covered with tunics [uniforms] of soldiers and sailors, and that among the self-same, there were little girls and boys as white as Europeans and that there were many mothers working with small children strapped and bound on their backs . . . who seem to be more of Dutch mothers than of black women.

A European observer, Mentzel, writing in the eighteenth century, observed:[6]

the female slaves are ready to offer their bodies for a trifle; and towards evening one can see a string of sailors and soldiers entering the Company's lodge where they mis-spend their time until the clock strikes nine . . . the Company does nothing to prevent this promiscuous intercourse, since, for one thing it tends to multiply the slave population, and does away with the necessity of importing fresh slaves. Three or four generations of this admixture (for the daughters follow their mother's footsteps) have produced a half-caste population — a mestizzo class — but a slight shade darker than some Europeans.

The third form of mixing took place between the slaves and the Khoi, whose off-spring were known as half-breed Khoi. The present-day 'Cape coloureds' thus owe their origin to various groups at the Cape. The table included in Cruse (1947)[7] and which refers to the origin of the slaves and the number freed at the Cape during the eighteenth century, is an interesting illustration of some of the components within the 'coloured' community (Table 1.1).

*Table 1.1    Slaves: Place of importation (see the freeing of 893 slaves between 1715-92, of which most were born at the Cape, and 290 were definitely from elsewhere)*

| Place | Freed |
|---|---|
| Indonesian Archipelago | |
|    Ternaten | 4 |
|    Macassar | 34 |
|    Batavia | 37 |
|    Ambon | 3 |
|    Boegis | 29 |
|    Bali | 12 |
|    Passier | 1 |
|    Padang | 2 |
|    Timor | 5 |
|    Angie | 1 |
|    Borneo | 1 |
|    Other islands | 11 |
|    Total | 140 |
| British India | |
|    From the coast (Coromandel) | 11 |
|    Malabar | 7 |
|    Bengalen | 71 |
|    Nagapatnam | 3 |
|    Mandaar | 7 |
|    Sourette | 1 |
|    Tranquebar | 2 |
|    Paliacatte | 2 |
|    Peshur | 1 |
|    Kadepoena | 1 |
|    Total | 106 |
| Ceylon | 26 |
| Africa | |
|    Madagascar | 11 |
|    Mozambique | 1 |
|    West Coast | 1 |
|    De La Goa | 2 |
|    Total | 15 |
| Philippines | |
|    Sambouwa | 2 |
|    Manilha | 1 |
|    Total | 3 |
| TOTAL | 290 |

Browsing through the records, one finds that a slight incursion of Chinese blood cannot totally be discounted. The early history of the Cape is to a large extent presented as the history of Europeans and European culture, with very little indication that the indigenous peoples had a history. The indigenes were invariably seen from a Eurocentric point of view. Toynbee (1935) says that 'when we Westerners call people natives' (see the terms *indigène* [French], *eingeborenen* [German], *inlanders* [Dutch]) 'we implicitly take the cultural colour out of our perceptions of them.'[8] They then become part of the flora and fauna. From the Eurocentric point of view, we know how the Dutch looked upon the first inhabitants of the Cape before and after 1652. There are, however, few, if any, records of similar indigenes' perceptions or attitudes towards the increasing white encroachment in their territories.

Historians and other writers who write about the first Dutch contact with the original inhabitants at the Cape take great pains to prove the absence of *any* racial (colour) prejudice. This is re-echoed in the works of Marais (1939), MacMillan (1927), Cruse (1947), D. P. Botha (1960) and the Afrikaner sociologist, Dian Joubert (1974). The general picture abstracted is that the indigenes were regarded as free men, and that the great divide was between Christian and heathen, in which the spirit of Dordt is inevitably invoked to account for Dutch fairness towards people of colour. The white apologia for the Dutch is espoused by D. P. Botha (1960), when he writes:[9]

> My conclusions from the facts are that emergent colour feelings among the whites reflected rather their class consciousness. The tendency to classify children of mixed blood with the group to which the coloured parent belonged, revealed a greater measure of class than race consciousness.

He continues:[10]

> that the colour of a person's skin would emerge as the criterion for classification was due to the vast difference in the level of civilization between the whites and the coloureds. To discriminate on the basis of class in respect of social rights and privileges was not foreign to the European, because European society did likewise: This initial colour feeling in no way differed from the class feeling based on birth and origin, or on wealth and possessions. But like in Europe, this class consciousness did not lead to a rejection of the lower classes.

15

Various authors point at the humane treatment of the slaves by the Dutch, citing cohabitation and concubinage as redeeming factors during the Dutch empire. Yet, a thorough scrutiny of travel documents concerning the Khoi and San at the Cape reveals a completely different picture. By 1646, Commelin had already assembled these travel documents in book form in Amsterdam. Jodocus Hondius had his *Klare Besgryving* in print by 1652; Langhenes, a publisher in Middelburg, was responsible for two publications in 1597 and 1598 respectively covering the De Houtman voyage (Rouffaer & Ijzerman eds, 1925); *D'eerste boeck van Willem Lodewijcksz* appeared in 1598 (Rouffaer & Ijzerman eds, 1915). In all these publications, there are numerous references to the Khoi at the Cape, and these descriptions could not have escaped the notice of the Dutch, nor could they have prevented the Dutch from having preconceived notions about the indigenes.

When the Dutch arrived at the Cape in the seventeenth century, they came with the specific purpose of starting a refreshment station. They proceeded to build a fort around which grew a garrison population. By 1657, however, the first freeburghers had already been given land along the Liesbeek river. There were also the original inhabitants, the Khoi, who lived in the surrounding areas. In 1658 the first slaves were imported (the economy would increasingly be based on slave labour as time went by). During the seventeenth and eighteenth centuries, there were quite a few 'half-castes' around as a result of miscegenation between the whites, the indigenes and the imported slaves.

Initially, the Europeans called the indigenes, *inwoonderen* (inhabitants), *swarten* (blacks), *negros, strand-loopers* (beach-combers). We learn, for example, that the term 'Hottentot', which is generally applied by the Dutch to the inhabitants of the Cape, was widespread during the mid-seventeenth century and that it was also used to refer to people from the west and the south coast of Africa.

Nienaber, in his article, 'The Origin of the Name Hottentot' (1963),[11] gives a useful and concise summary of all the interpretations concerning the term. One of the theories which had a particularly long life, was that of Olfert Dapper, who was purported to have maintained that there was an onomatopoeic word in seventeenth century Dutch meaning stutterer or stammerer. As a result of this trait (i.e. impediment and stuttering when speaking), the Dutch 'called them Hottentots, which word in this sense is used at home [Holland] as a gibe against someone who, in uttering his words, stammers and stutters. They, [the indigenes] also now refer to themselves as Hottentots . . . and sing while dancing, "Hottentot Brokwa", by which they mean to say: "Give Hottentot a piece of bread".'[12]

This was eventually refuted by Hesseling in 1916, when he wrote: 'I believe that on the strength of all the reports we can safely assume that the national name owes its origin to none other than a mocking imitation by the Hollanders, and that we thus need not assume, a Dutch word, "Hottentot" for "stutterer", supposing that Dapper had such a word in mind.'[13] Nienaber concludes that the 'name Hottentot originates from a jesting carry-over of an incremental repetitive formula in a typical dancing-song.'[14] The word 'Hottentot' is also found as a surname in the Netherlands; the Dutch publicist, Ben van Kaam, first drew my attention to this. There are at least six families listed in the telephone directory in Amsterdam under 'Hottentot'. Whatever the true origin of the word, it is quite clear from historical sources that by the time of Jan van Riebeeck, it was widely known.

There are also no indications that the Dutch, or other Europeans, were hostilely received by the original inhabitants because they were white. From da Gama we learn that they danced and sang and were prepared to exchange gifts:[15]

On Saturday, there came about two hundred Blacks of greater and smaller stature and brought twelve cattle, oxen and cows, and some four or five sheep. When we espied them, we immediately went ashore. They at once started to play four or five flutes, some of them producing high notes, others deep ones, and they harmonized so beautifully such as one would not have expected of them . . . . When the feast was over we went . . . and bought some black oxen with our bracelets.

A similar note is sounded in the letter to the Company by the shipwrecked men of the Dutch ship, the *Haarlem*, in 1649. The letter states that some of the men went ashore and were 'received in a friendly manner and treated kindly'.[16]

There was also no proof that the original inhabitants in any way prevented the European from exploring the area in the vicinity of Table Mountain. We have little evidence of how the indigenes felt about this Dutch encroachment, but they were certainly not happy about it. On the other hand, we have many first and second-hand accounts of how the Europeans looked upon the first inhabitants of the Cape. The picture which emerges after the Dutch settlement is a sad reflection on the one quality the Dutch prized so highly in their make-up: tolerance (*verdraagzaamheid*). The assessments before 1652 were generally pejorative, although they also contained some positive elements.

One of the most important and illuminating sources was (and is) the account known as *D'eerste boeck van Willem Lodewijcksz* (Rouffaer & Ijzerman eds, 1915). Here we find an account of the Dutch encounter with the Khoi at Mosselbay (originally referred to as Agua (da) de Sambras). We read that:[17]

> seven black men had come to the ships . . . . Our men had given them some knives, linen [cloth] , bells and little mirrors, as also some woollen cloth, yet they did not know what to do with it and therefore chucked them away. They were also poured some wine and given biscuits, which they drank and ate.

The entry for 6 August reads as follows:[18]

> we found several tracks of human beings, cattle and dogs, as also partridges, and a little further on, found broken, the little mirrors and bells which we had given them the previous day and the pieces of linen lying on the heath; meanwhile, some of the inhabitants had been to the sloop [schuyt] whither we were also off to, but had gone past us as we returned without being detected, so cleverly could they move through the bushes.

The inhabitants are depicted in the following manner:[19]

> The people here are of stature somewhat smaller than we are at home, are ruddy brown [ros-bruin] of colour, yet the one browner than the other, go about naked, having an ox-hide wrapped like a cloak, the hair against the body, with a broad leather thong of the self-same round the waists, of which the one end hung in front of their private parts, some wore little planks [berdekens] under their feet instead of shoes. Their ornaments were bracelets of ivory and red copper, polished shells, also some gold rings on their fingers, large beads [pater nosters] of bone and wood, various tattoo marks burnt into their bodies [diversche hackelinge op haer lijf brandende ghenepen] . They were always very foul-smelling, since they always besmeared themselves with fat and grease.

Similar portrayals are to be found in the other accounts of van Spilbergen, van Warwijck, Paulus van Caerden and Seygher van Rechteren (Commelin, 1646). The Germans, Wurffbain, Merklein,

Herport, Hoffmann and Schweitzer, who touched at the Cape, painted an even more dismal picture of the people at the Cape. Schweitzer, for example, called the Khoi 'ungeheure affen' (monstrous apes).[20]

A simple list of all these descriptions would read as in Table 1.2.

*Table 1.2    Attitudes towards the earliest inhabitants of South Africa (Dutch and German)*

| Language | Physical Descriptions | Eating Habits |
| --- | --- | --- |
| clucking like male turkeys, like rattles, wheezing and whistling | of medium height, fleet-footed, ugly of pate | disgusting, eat entrails without cleaning them, gnaw on them like dogs, like liquor |
| *Adornments* | *Character* | |
| tattoos, rings and bracelets, smear themselves with fat or grease, skins and tails of animals, e.g. foxes, cattle, leather thongs or tails round private parts, little planks (*berdekens*) under feet for shoes, sometimes cloth | wild, savage, cannibals, heathens, uncivilized, animal-like, monstrous apes | *Colour* |
| | | like gypsies, mulattos, yellow like Javanese, ruddy-brown, chestnut, black |

Although historical evidence suggests that the Khoi were far from willing to give up their land to foreigners from overseas (Marks, 1972), the image of the docile, spineless 'Hottentot' continues to exist. The stereotype of the lazy, weak 'Hottentot', who was wiped out by the smallpox epidemics in the eighteenth century, or who drank himself to death, coincides with that of another much-maligned group, the Amerindians.

The opprobrium attached to the term 'Hottentot', which finds its origin in the Dutch period, will be one of the striking features of Afrikaans literature and culture. Not surprisingly, the early antagonists of Afrikaans referred to the language as a 'Hotnotstaal'. Afrikaans association with the Khoi automatically made it a language of low

19

cultural status, fit only for the uncivilized, the hewers of wood and the drawers of water. Furthermore, by implication, Afrikaans could therefore only be a language of comic proportions.

Historically, it is an indisputable fact that the Khoi, the slaves, and later on the 'Cape coloured', have all contributed to the rise of Afrikaans as a language. In the Afrikaner ethos, it was important to prove that Afrikaans was essentially a *Diets* language. Many of the theories therefore concentrated on the Germanic (Dutch and German), or Romance (French) origins. Blood-mixing of the various European groups at the Cape became linguistic determinants.

While the main concentration in this study will be on the image of the 'Cape coloured' in literary works, it is nevertheless interesting to note how the various contributing groups in the 'coloured' make-up have, from time to time, been associated with what is now regarded as the Afrikaner's proudest possession, Afrikaans.

Ironically too, notwithstanding the tremendous cultural debt of the Afrikaner to the Khoi, the slave and the miscegenated 'Cape coloured', Afrikaners are, even to this day, loth to give recognition to this, as is evident from the debates surrounding the centenary celebrations of the first Afrikaans Language Movement in 1975. The basic issue then was whether 'coloureds', who spoke the 'taal', should also be invited to the celebrations, thus being allowed to set foot on hallowed ground at the various Afrikaner monuments. Quite obviously, these debates were more pigmentocratically than culturally inspired, for apparently there was no objection to an Englishman attending, despite his non-contributory role to the Afrikaans language movement. The politically conscious 'coloured' simply advocated a boycott of what he rightly conceived as a racist festival.

Afrikaner academics, for example, Erlank, were at least so bold as to conclude that the Afrikaans cultural house could not be in order if the 'coloureds' were excluded. Afrikaner cultural standard bearers conveniently overlooked the early contributions of the Khoi. After all, Eva acted as an interpreter for Jan van Riebeeck and even married a Dutchman. It was the Dutch intention to instruct these heathen in the Reformed Religion through the medium of the Dutch language. In June, 1656, that is, only four years after van Riebeeck's arrival at the Cape, he wrote in his diary that the Khoi living in the vicinity of the fort 'spoke the Dutch (duytsche) language reasonably well, especially the children'.

In 1685, when Commissioner van Rheede tot Drakensteyn visited the Cape, he observed:[21]

It is certain that if one judges them (i.e. the Khoi), on the basis of external characteristics, one would hardly surmise any good in them, but if one has a knowledge of their lives and thoughts, one would find them different . . . . It is customary among our people to instruct the indigenes (inlanders) in the Dutch language (Nederduytsche spraek), and they speak it in their manner, rather brokenly and almost unintelligibly, so that we imitate them in this and since especially our children have taken over this habit, a broken language has come into being which will be impossible to eradicate.

The earliest plausible explanation for the development of Afrikaans came from Dr Th. Hahn, who maintained in a lecture held in 1882:[22]

The Dutch patois, can be traced back to a fusion of the country dialects of the Netherlands and Northern Germany, and although phonetically teutonic, it is psychologically an essentially Hottentot idiom. For we learn this patois first from our nurses and ayas.[23] The young Africander, on his solitary farm, has no other playmates than the children of the Bastard-Hottentot servants of his father and even the grown-up farmer can not easily escape the deteriorating effect of his servants' patois.

More important is the imputation in all these theories of a low cultural status clinging to the terms 'Hottentot' and 'Creole'. Yet, much of the first evidence about Afrikaans comes to us through the lowly and the despised, the Khoi and the slaves.

In the old archives, there are several examples of 'Hottentots-Hollands' which closely resemble Afrikaans as it eventually emerged. In 1672, for example, two colonists were threatened by a Khoi with the following words, 'duytsman een woort calm, ons U kelum' (lit. if white man one word speaks, we you kill).[24] In 1710, the following sentence was reported verbally, 'Ons denkum ons altijd Baas, maar ja zienom, Duitsman meer Baas' (lit. We think we are always Boss, but we have seen White man more Boss).[25] Marius Valkhoff (1966) gives other examples culled from the works of Kolbe and Ten Rhyne, 'Gy dit beest fangum zoo, en nu dood maakum zoo, is dat bra, wagtum ons altemaal daarvan loopum zoo' (lit. You caught this cow [in this way], and now you have killed it; is that honest? Wait and we shall all run away from here).[26] This example was taken from the work of Kolbe. The following sentence is taken from the English translation of the works of Ten Rhyne, 'Dat is doet. Was makom? Duitsman

altyd kallom: Icke Hottentots doot makom: Masky doot. Icke strack
nae onse groote Kapiteyn toe, die man my soon witte Boeba geme.'
(Lit. Come! What are you doing? Dutchman always say: I will kill
Hottentots. Well, Kill! If I die, I shall go straight to our Great Chief.
He will give me white oxen.)[27] Valkhoff is of course one of the main
exponents of the theory that Afrikaans is a Creole language, this in
contrast to Afrikaner linguists who assert that its origin is primarily
Germanic. The verbal suffix -m, -um, -om, which is no longer found in
the actual language, is, according to the Leiden linguist J. Voorhoeve,
a general characteristic of Pidgins, found, for example, in Cameroun
Pidgin English and Melanesian Pidgin English. It also formally resembles
the pronominal object in Dutch. Valkhoff has accused Afrikaner
linguists of Synchronistic Purism, the tendency to 'transfer their ideal
of purity of the White race to their mother tongue and its history'.
And of Albocentrism, the tendency to dismiss 'as corruptions' the
Hottentot, Asian, African or slave contribution to Afrikaans, 'while
similar phenomena among the White users become part of the
language'.[28]

Other non-South African scholars have taken up a similar attitude
towards Afrikaans, for example, the Surinamese, Rens, who maintained:[29]

> On the other hand, a language like the Afrikaans of South Africa,
> notwithstanding the vehement protests of Afrikaners, presents in
> its grammatical structure such a striking resemblance to the
> Creole language that, especially when one lends credence to its
> (hypothetical) way of formation, one wonders if it should not
> be included in the series of Creole languages.

H. J. Lubbe's vehement attack on Valkhoff in 1974, is fairly representative of the general attitude among Afrikaner linguists to the pro-
ponents of the Creole theory:[30]

> Since the publication of his studies in Portuguese and Creole with
> special reference to South Africa (1966), and especially since the
> appearance of his latest work, Valkhoff has ensured that his
> name will always be mentioned when the problems surrounding
> the origins of Afrikaans are discussed. Unfortunately, his
> insight as well as his motives regarding the interpretation of the
> linguistic, historical and sociological information is not
> above suspicion . . . . It is therefore regretted that Valkhoff's
> works are so often quoted by linguists abroad.

In his book, Marius Valkhoff formulated five propositions concerning the genesis of Afrikaans, of which some are very interesting:[31]

2  The importance and extension of Creole Portuguese in the world has been completely under-estimated in South Africa. In the 17th century this language must have been much more popular at the Cape than most scholars thought.

3  Consequently Creole Portuguese must also have played a much greater part in the transformation of Cape Dutch than official opinion wants to accept.

4  If we compare Afrikaans with the Creole languages we know, the former shows clearly a certain number of phenomena of creolization.

5  This partial creolization of Dutch at the Cape most probably took place among the coloured (mixed) populations, which for that matter still uses Afrikaans as its mother tongue.

Valkhoff is, of course, looked upon as a 'kaffer-boetie''[32] by some Afrikaner linguists.

The first dramatic work in Dutch-Afrikaans, *De Temperantisten,* was written in 1832 by E. Boniface. In it, one is already confronted with that quality of 'smelling strangeness' clinging to people of colour in South African literature. His Khoi characters pave the way for a set of stereotypes which, even to this very day, is still found in Afrikaans literature.

The stereotype of the present-day 'coloured' draws, I venture to say, on a fairly continuous tradition starting with the depictions of the Khoi in literature. This is clear from the critical assessments of the play *De Temperantisten,* which was written in response to a social situation at the Cape. Between Manus Kalfachter,[33] the main Khoi character in the play, and Toiings,[33] the main character in a novel of a similar name by Mikro (see Chapter 2), a literary tradition became fixed in the minds of white South African writers which was to last to the present day.

The play by Boniface had as its main object the attempts of the Temperance Society to ban the use of liquor at the Cape. It was also an attack on the negrophilist ideas of people such as Dr Philip of the London Missionary Society, who is recognizable in the play as the Reverend Humbug Philipumpkin. Another target was John Fairbairn, one of the chief actors in the fight for a free press at the Cape, who is called John Brute in the play. Boniface hands out satirical slaps to all and sundry. He also lampoons the prudent and genteel English ladies who leave the hall at the mere mention of the word chastity. And then, of course, there are the Khoi characters who supply the comic note. In the portrayal of the Khoi characters one notices how the terms 'Hottentot' and 'coloured' come to be interchangeable in white thinking. It becomes even more interesting when one realizes that the term slave, by way of derogation, was never applied to the 'coloured', as happened in the Americas. That the term slave never attained such obnoxious proportions in South Africa, is probably due to the fact that the term 'Hottentot' was already serving such a purpose for white South Africa. Hence this interchangeability of 'Hottentot' and 'coloured'. It is for this reason that the term 'Hottentot' will sometimes be used later on in discussing the play and other works which deal with the Khoi, for the usage of the latter term would only obscure this automatic transference of the term 'Hottentot' onto 'coloured' in Afrikaner culture.

Thus F.C.L. Bosman observes in his thesis:[34]

> The comical is a noticeable characteristic of the play. This is especially apparent when the Hottentot characters perform . . . generally it testifies to a sharp observation on the part of the author, with a special eye for the comic in the mutual relations of the coloureds.

At a later stage, he makes the following remarks:[35]

> In Galgevogel and Waterschuw, the first, somewhat more than the second, we can recognize the one type of Hottentot, always bellicose when drunk, from the other type, which is more peaceful and cowardly. Grietjie Drilbouten is the undefiled, average Hottentot, female thing. Common to all is, naturally, their yearning for liquor.

Bosman becomes even more explicit when he comments on the scene where the two Khoi characters, Dronkelap (Drunkard) and Droogekeel (Drythroat), are about to fight each other:[36]

> In how many villages in the Western Province do such scenes not still occur? What person who has experienced this at first hand, does not immediately recognize the living word, the expressions, the gestures, the typical coloured bragging.

He goes on to say that he knows no other dramatist who surpassed Boniface in his portrayals of 'coloured types'. 'Boniface knew his "volkies" well.'[37]

From all this, it clearly emerges that Bosman has automatically transferred the cultural image of the Khoi onto the present-day 'Cape coloureds'. He is not alone in this, as we shall see later on. Interestingly enough, Bosman's comments found their way into print in 1928, while *De Temperantisten* was written in 1832. This was just two years before the freeing of the slaves and four years before the Great Trek of the Afrikaners into the interior. In a wider perspective, there was a large anti-slavery campaign in England and elsewhere in the Western world. Interest in the 'negro' was widespread. The noble savage tradition in literature, which was at its peak during the last quarter of the eighteenth and the first quarter of the nineteenth century, did much to turn the black man at least, into a 'good savage'. In America, the Quakers were active. The European continent had witnessed the French revolution with its demands for liberty, fraternity and equality. Multatuli wrote his novel *Max Havelaar* in 1859 in which he so brilliantly exposes Dutch colonialism in what was then still known as Netherlands Indies (Ons Indië). By 1864, five thousand copies of this book had been sold.

Several anti-slavery (anti-colonial) novels were published by various authors. In 1787, Dr John Moore published his anti-slave novel, *Zeluco*. Henry Mackenzie's 'novel of social anthropology', *Julia de Roubigne,* appeared in 1777. The purpose of another play by Colman, *The Africans,* was to show that often 'The nobler virtues are more practised among barbarian tribes than by civilized society.'[38] Methodists, novelists, playwrights, poets, Moravians and Evangelists all contributed to the freeing of the slaves.

None of these serious changes seem to have filtered through to the white people at the Cape, however. Those persons who were concerned about the people of colour at the Cape, were invariably from the Christian, humanitarian stream, and British. They were products of a European liberal tradition and not shaped by the Cape landscape and cultural and moral environment. Retief's *Manifesto* cites the 'rebellious and dishonest behaviour of vagabonds allowed to cause unrest in all parts of the country',[39] as one of the reasons why the Boers trekked to the north. Further reasons advanced for the Great Trek are created by the slaves, who although treated very well (even better than the factory worker in England, one learns), are now protected by so many regulations that the farmer feels he is no longer the master on his farm.[40] Culturally too, the scene at the Cape bore no resemblance to that in England and Europe. Hooft, Bredero, Vondel and Cats were still standard fare among the educated. Roundabout

1800, the theatre in Cape Town was primarily used for amusement. Boniface's play was especially directed against the negrophilists at the Cape.

In general, then, writers portray the 'Hottentot' characters as care-free, comical, witty, loud-mouthed, fond of liquor, and prone to fighting easily. And these characteristics are just as neatly attributed to the present-day 'Cape coloured' in Afrikaner critical assessments.

An inordinate source of comic embellishment is to be found in the 'Hottentot' characters, whose names recall creatures of diverse plumage. This too, would in later Afrikaans literature be transposed onto 'coloured' characters. In *De Temperantisten*, one finds a Klaas Galgevogel (Klaas Gallowsbird), Hans Droogekeel (Hans Drythroat), Piet Dronkelap (Piet Drunkard), Dampje Waterschuw (Vapour Watershy) and, of course, Manus Kal(k)fachter and Grietjie Drilbouten[41] from the mission station of Bethelsdorp.

The 'Hottentot' characters always appear in ridiculous situations. The basic elements are distilled quite clearly. First, there is their love for liquor − giving rise to the 'tot' syndrome.[42] Second, their irascibility and hot-headedness, culminating inevitably in a fight. The third standard element refers to their moral looseness. Finally, there is the linguistic incomprehension resulting in ludicrous situations. An example of the latter occurs when Kalfachter and Grietjie arrive from Bethelsdorp to ask, in their most correct Dutch, the way to the Onion (Union) Malligheid-Gewerskaf (malligheid = madness, with implications of lunacy, Gewerskaf = activity, with implications of chaos), a wrong pronunciation of the word Matigheidsgenootskap (the Temperance Society). This is typical of the misunderstandings to which the Khoi characters fall prey when they are part and parcel of a white scheme they only half comprehend.

When Kalfachter is inducted, the entire irony is lost on him. Amidst all the trappings, he becomes a buffoon who is doubly duped. He is disillusioned when he learns that his wife, Grietjie, will not have to undergo the ceremony. He then tries everything to deprive her of liquor. He even invokes scurvy, blindness and deafness, but all to no avail. Grietjie has been busy under the table, liberally plying herself with liquor:[43]

> Grietjie shall say that you're a liar! . . . . For I've heard it all. (She climbs from under the table).
> Kalfachter, *caught with his pants down:* O father Dampie, help us then!

Grietjie, *clapping her hands:* And Grietjie shall laugh at you, and
shall not gulp a single drop of water; on purpose just to annoy
you! (*She sways*)
Kalfachter: Oh fie, Grietjie! . . .. Have you not heard the promise
I had made just now? Have you no heart in your body?
Grietjie: What do I care about your promises? . . . . I have
promised nothing! . . . No, not me.

The situation becomes intolerable when Manus Kalfachter discovers
that the other knights have been busy quaffing gin under the pretext
of drinking water. Tearing off the trappings, he drags Grietjie along
'to wet his throat'. The scene and the bout of fisticuffs pre-empt many
a similar depiction in Afrikaans literature (echoes of it being found
in the works of van den Heever, Malherbe and von Wielligh, as we
shall see later on).[44]

Waterschuw *is in a big Hottentot rage, comes on stage with his
coat off; throws it on the floor; rolls up his sleeves; positions
himself for the fight, and calls out:* Come now! . . . I am ready
for you . . . Come now!
Galgevogel, *who is held back by Dronkelap:* and what will you
do?
Waterschuw: Well come now, if you're a man!
Droogekeel, *to Waterschuw, whom he tries to restrain:* Oh!
come on. Don't fight!
Galgevogel *to Dronkelap:* Let go off me! . . . Away! (*He tries
to wrench himself free*).
Dronkelap: I don't want to.
Waterschuw *to Galgevogel:* I want to beat you that you don't
know what happened.
Galgevogel: You, beat me? . . . You?
Waterschuw, *thumping his chest with his fist:* Yes, me!
Droogekeel, *continuing to stand in front of him:* Dampie,
listen!
Galgevogel: If I lay my hands on you, Waterschuw!
Waterschuw: Come then! . . . I am ready now.
Galgevogel: I'll knock your teeth out of your mouth.
Dronkelap, *still continuing to try and restrain him:* Oh!
what madness! Don't!
Waterschuw: I'll trample on your stomach till your guts
fly through your throat.

The 'Hottentots' emerge as bunglers, fools with no conception of morality. Going to prison is interpreted in terms of free accommodation and food, and not seen as a moral dilemma. This latter aspect comes out very clearly in the novel of von Wielligh, *Jakob Platjie*. In a foreword to the book, the author himself writes in the following vein, 'May this little work give to posterity an idea of how the indigenes thought and what they did. For there is no doubt, that in the course of one or two generations, these three tribes will have lost their national character.' The author then goes on to quote a surveyor who gives expression to one of the fundamental and recurring myths about the indigenes, 'Yes, there are but two nations under the sun who are really witty, namely an Irishman and a Hotnot — they are witty without trying to be funny.' Von Wielligh further endorses this viewpoint by adding, 'True enough, there is lots of refined humour in a Hotnot, and in addition, he possesses the skill to realize both the important and serious side of a case without revealing himself as stupid.'[45]

The main characters in *Jakob Platjie* are Sina and Iedris whom we are given to understand are two thoroughbred, pepper-corned 'Hottentots', blessed with three children. Of these, the central figure is Jakob, their ten-year-old son. Conforming with the pattern of this group in literature, Sina and Iedris traipse off to the village at the end of every month to buy groceries, and, last but not least, to get stone drunk. Their homeward journey is livened up by their singing and capers. Their highest thoughts being concentrated on the bottle, as expressed by Sina: 'No my dear, you know what my dearest wish is? To be in the bar now of old Rob.' With a cheery countenance, Iedris pats Sina on the shoulders and asks: 'My old one, why must you always have a better wish than I have?'[46]

This is an operative passage echoing and re-echoing through Afrikaans literature - the 'tot' system enshrined and justified as the 'coloured's' greatest cultural heritage (vini-culture, as the 'coloured' would facetiously have it at times). Platjie sums it up when he tells his parents: 'Tata (father) and Meme (mother), let's suppose there was not a drop of gin in this world; what would you have done?'[47]

One is treated endlessly to such bacchanalian eulogies. Culturally, the 'Hottentot' characters emerge as amoral types, incapable of functioning as rational human beings. They remain buffoons right through. The emotional relationship between Sina and Iedris is reduced to comic proportions. Even when Iedris attempts to sound a serious note by referring to the rape of their possessions and their freedom, his protesting voice is neutralized by too overt an authorial intrusion and the bickering of his wife, which reduces the passage to farce. Child-like is the operative word, a quality which stretches to even include their relationship with their son. 'Merry' and 'jolly', are the words which characterize their pattern of life.

The 'Hottentots' are rather naïvely portrayed in their relationships with the whites. All the normal shibboleths are employed — ghost stories, witchcraft and other such paraphernalia. As the author says in his introduction: 'Yes, it's true, a Hotnot is short of hair and short of brains.'[48]

After the first twenty pages, one abstracts a picture of jollity, of people who have abdicated all forms of responsibility and whose greatest ambition is to get drunk and fight. Even in the courtroom, when Sina is about to be sentenced to a term of imprisonment, the tone is one of levity, which is in strange contrast to the serious implications for this Khoi family and their son, Jakob. Sina keeps on inter-rupting the magistrate who, finally at his wit's end, remonstrates: 'Meid (derogatory term for 'coloured' female), will you shut up once and for all!'[49] And when she keeps on, he turns to the policeman and orders: 'Remove this creature from the courtroom'.[50] When he finally sentences her to ten shillings or fourteen days she counters: 'Thank you mister, I'll take the ten shillings, you can keep the fourteen days'.[50] In no way is there any concern for the ten-year-old Jakob, on the part of either the magistrate or the parents.

It may well be that von Wielligh's portrayal coincides with that of a large section of white South Africa. The Khoi heads are referred to as 'klapperdop' (coconuts). Iedris and Sina are more sub-human than human. Jakob in his abandoned state is tricked by a white itinerant peddlar into accompanying him into the interior. In the process one is confronted with a row of 'coloured' characters and traits as they appear to white South Africa. The Malays are adept at witchcraft, the Bastards imitate the whites and adopt their ethnic hierarchy in respect of the Khoi.

The Jakob Platjie image is still very much alive among Afrikaners in present-day South Africa. That the cultural image must have ulti-mately affected the political thinking of the Afrikaner is clear from the critical comments on such portrayals. Thus Lydia van Niekerk writes in her 1916 thesis:[51]

The author shows that he knows the Hottentot well . . .. Siena with her sharp tongue and good-natured Iedris, both lovers of

liquor, of which they partake liberally once a month; and
Platjie, a real Hottentot child, with not a grain of bravery
in him, but exceptionally witty and in addition, always
inclined to pranks. Their way of thinking, their language and
manner of speaking, is excellently portrayed, for example,
the scene in the court room where Siena does not show the
slightest sign of respect for the law as represented by the
magistrate, and also in the conversations between the
prisoners, which testify to their lust for life and the carefree
sense of the Hottentot.

The Khoi will gradually disappear from literature, or survive only
folkloristically, enshrined in the lost innocence and glory of 'primitive' (natural) peoples. They will become 'pure and undefiled' types,
closer to the animal kingdom, as with the Hobson brothers (*Skankwan
van die duine* 1930). Ultimately, their place was taken over by the
'bruinmense' ('coloureds' or brown people), as the Afrikaner would
have it rather paternalistically, some even claim, affectionately.

In the first period of the Afrikaner language movement, the basis
will be laid for that peculiar brand of Afrikaner nationalism and ambivalence towards the 'Cape coloured', who spoke 'die taal',[52] but who
were excluded from the cultural ox wagon. An important event in
Afrikaner history was the founding of the GRA (Genootskap vir
Regte Afrikaners − Society for Proper Afrikaners) at Paarl on 14
August 1875. The cardinal aim of the GRA was 'to stand for our
language, nation and our country'. From the aims it is quite clear that
this was not just a language movement. The first germs of Christian
nationalism and Christian national education were already in em-
bryonic form.

As in the Flemish movement, the main concern was nationalistic.
The term Afrikaner is already synonymous with white. Ironically,
while the early protagonists would have agreed with Jan Frans Willems
that, 'de taal is gansch het volk' (the language is the entire people),
the 'coloureds', who spoke 'de taal', were excluded from the fold of 'het
volk' (the nation) right from the start.[52] It is understandable that the
earliest literary, or quasi-literary, efforts should concentrate on factors
such as pride and religion and the forging of an Afrikaner myth strong
enough to provide an answer to the English influence.

The early writings are thus less important as literature but fundamental in the establishment of an Afrikaner ethos and nationalism.
Scanning through these writings, one is struck by the didactic tenor,

the nationalistic and religious tone and the anti-English bias, especially towards the close of the nineteenth century (with its Boer war and the Jameson raid and the increasing attempts at Anglo-Saxonization of the Afrikaner). The 'coloured' did not loom large in the imagination of early Afrikaner writers, because of the rather bigoted (even if understandable) commitment of the latter breed to get rid of their inferiority complexes vis-a-vis the English.

The non-white as a cultural and rational being was unthinkable to the Afrikaner — outside, of course, his caricatured role — between 1875 and 1948. The Afrikaner was in the throes of cultural liberation, engaged in seeking recognition for the new language, Afrikaans. He was attempting to write his history in Afrikaans. He was wrestling with the problem of changing from being a Dutchman to becoming an indigene, from being a member of a group to becoming a member of a 'Volk' (nation). The general tone of the verses echoed sentiments such as the following found in the poem by Hoogenhout which was first published in *Die Patriot* (1876):[53]

> 'n Ieder nasie het syn LAND:
> Ons woon op Afrikaanse strand;
> Vir ons is daar g'n beter grond
> Op al die wye wêreld rond;
> Trots is ons om die naam te dra
> Van kinders van Suid-Afrika.

> Each nation has its very own LAND:
> We live on Afric's shore.
> For us there is no better soil
> In all the world around;
> Proud are we then to bear the name
> Of children of South Africa.

There is an emergent nationalism in the Cape colony, and a solidarity with the fellow Afrikaners from the Liesbeek to the Vaal rivers, all of which is reinforced by the discovery of diamonds and gold. The verse below is typical of the type of literature produced:[54]

> Waar Tafelberg begin tot ver in die Transvaal
> Woon één verenigd volk, één algemene taal;
> 'n Volk voorheen miskend, 'n taal voorheen gesmoord,
> Maar nou beroemd, geëerd, in oos, wes, suid en noord.

> Where Table mountain starts till deep into Transvaal
> There lives one unified people, one language known to all;
> A people formerly despised, a language suppressed.
> But now well-known and honoured in east, west,
> south and north.

The poetry of the first Afrikaans Language Movement is schmalzy and melodramatic. John Bull, as the symbol of the oppressive English, is the recipient of Afrikaner venom. The establishment of the Imperial Federation League in 1884 gave rise to the following poem, because the organization decided to admit 'coloured' people:[55]

> Ons nuwe Bond
> Is nou gegrond
> Van Jingoes en van Swartjies,
> Uit saam vereende hartjies.
> Een mooie set!
> o Watter pret!
> Swartmeide met rooi-nekke
> En kinders met geel-bekke!
>
> Our new League
> Is now made up
> of Jingoes and of Blackies,
> All unified in heart.
> Oh what a bunch!
> Oh what fun!
> Black female things with red-necks
> And children traps all yellow.

The image of the 'coloured' was already steeped in ethnocentricity. An interesting example in this respect is S. J. du Toit's 'Hoe die Hollanders die Kaap ingeneem het' (How the Dutch conquered the Cape). One can hardly consider it a great literary effort, let alone an historically correct one. It is important only in so far as it is an example of an early piece of writing, so fundamental to the Afrikaans language struggle. For the rest, the tone and tenor is naïve. The most interesting part of the poem is the description of the reaction of the indigenes to the first ship they encounter. This is an eternal source of inspiration to several authors. This is how du Toit describes the encounter:[56]

Eendag sit ons by die Platkop
   Jul Duusvolk noem hom nou die Kaap —
'n Ding kom uit die water op,
   Daar waar die son al aand gaan slaap,
     'n Wit ding nes 'n skaap.

Hy kom op uit dieselfde gat,
   Waar saans die son steek weg syn kop;
Eers was hy klein en laag en plat;
   Ons kyk en kyk, hy rys syn kop
     En rys al hoger op.

Die ding kom nader, hy word groot;
   Ons Griekwas kom toe bymekaar,
Ons raak al suutjies in die nood;
   Die ding die lyk mos reg-reg naar.
     Ja basies, dis so waar!

Ons hou toen raad, en ons hou raad;
   Party vlug bang-bang na die krans,
En hy wat Kiewiet was, word kwaad
   En sê: Jul's gek, dit is 'n gans
     'n Grote watergans!

Toe vou die ding syn vlerke op,
   En hy gee kleintjies af eenkant;
En ons hou toen vir hom maar dop:
   Hy gee meer kleintjies anderkant,
     Hul sak af oor die rand.

One day sitting by that flat old rock
You white folks call it now the Cape —
A thing comes from the water
There where the sun goes down each night,
A white thing just like a sheep.

He came out of the self-same hold,
Where at night the sun its head does hide;
First it was small and long and flat;
We look and look, the head does rise
And rise all higher.

33

> The thing comes closer, then gets big;
> We Griquas put our heads together,
> Slowly we are in the soup;
> The thing looks really bad
> Yes, masters, that is true!
>
> We then council keep, then council keep;
> Some flee in fear to the krantz,
> And he who is Kiewiet was then mad
> and said: 'You're crazy, it's a goose,
> A big old water goose!'
>
> Then the thing unfolds its wings,
> And lets out little ones on the side;
> And we, we only stood and watched:
> He gives off more little ones the other side,
> They go down o'er the edge.

S. J. du Toit has reduced it to a farce. James Matthews uses this first encounter between black and white to unmask the white deception.[57]

> We watched the white man's arrival
> in strange-shaped ships we did not know.
> now we have become trespassers
> on the shores of our land.

In contrast to these South African examples, there is a beautiful description by the Nigerian, Equiano, who was sold into slavery. Olaudah Equiano or Gustavus Vassa, as he came to be known, was born in 1745 and sold as a slave at the tender age of eleven. His account of his first encounter with a ship is filled with child-like wonder and awe. Equiano was shipped off to the West Indies and succeeded in buying his own freedom. He then went to England, where he became somewhat of a celebrity, as a result of his book and his activities on behalf of the abolitionist movement. The abolitionist rhetoric is reflected in his famous book, *Equiano's Travels* (1967). In a sense, his child's-eye view in simple, naïve terms, is a greater indictment against slavery. Of the white people he observes: 'and I was persuaded that I had gotten into a world of bad spirits and that they were going to kill me'.[58] He speaks of his

great astonishment [when] I saw one of these vessels coming in
with the sails up. As soon as the whites saw it they gave a great
shout, at which we were amazed; and the more so as the
vessel appeared larger by approaching nearer. At last she came
to an anchor in sight, and when the anchor was let go I and my
countrymen who saw it were lost in astonishment to observe the
vessel stop, and were now convinced it was done by magic.[58]

The interpretation of new phenomena in terms of one's own, known,
cultural tradition, can often be a source of humour in the African
novel (see: Oyono's *Une vie de boy*). Thus, the first contact between
white and black is not only exploited to show how backward the
natives are. The tragic which lurks beneath the comic, is never totally
absent.

By the time the 'bruinman' proper enters the Afrikaans novel of
the second Language Movement (1903–1925), his role is neatly pre-
scribed. In Afrikaner mythology, 'coloureds' would only perform a
functional role within the compass of the following syndromes: the
labour syndrome, the comic syndrome, the Bacchus syndrome, the
incarceration syndrome, the loud-mouthed and the bellicose syndromes.
From now on the terms 'bruinmense' and 'kleurlinge'[59] will also be
heard more often.

Afrikaans literature was, and still is, to a large extent characterized
by its earthiness and rurality. This is not surprising, since Afrikaans was
essentially entrenched in rural areas. The farmer, for example, lived in
close proximity to his squatter-labourer (ons bruinmense). It is therefore only logical that a monumental theme in Afrikaans literature
should be the farm-hand and his 'baas'. Fransie Malherbe in his article
on the colour problem in Afrikaans literature comments:[60]

That the Coloured labourer, the farm-hand, has hitherto enjoyed
the greatest attention in our literature is understandable in view
of its rural nature. Thus, also the relationship, 'baas-boy', with
its 'Ja, Baas', and 'Nee Baas' in every form of address, which
should not necessarily be interpreted as denigrating — this also
applies to the terms 'outa' and 'aia',[61] the earlier forms of respect.

Malherbe then, magnanimously advises the educated 'coloured'
not to worry about such matters, for their objections arise out of
feelings of inferiority. The Afrikaner, he continues, was plagued with
similar problems and overcame his, as will the 'coloured' in time to
come.

Afrikaner intellectuals have almost invariably found fault with Alan Paton's *Cry the Beloved Country*, on the grounds of sentimentality. Their basic criticisms were that the novel was lacking in nuances, biased and not truthful. Yet, Afrikaans literature is studded with sentimental, vaudevillesque scenes in which 'coloureds' act out their servile role and continue to supply the comic note. In reading through Afrikaans novels, it is amazing to observe how many scenes are found in reduplicated form. This is excellently revealed in a comparison of two novels, one by D. F. Malherbe, called *Die Meulenaar* (The Miller), the other, by C. M. van den Heever, called *Somer* (Summer). Inevitably, for instance, rivalry on the land between 'coloured' characters is used to relieve the preceding tension and animosity between the white characters and, by implication, to suggest in this contrasting fashion, that the white rivalry is of a morally higher and cleaner order.

The pattern of the novel is generally as follows. A nice young man falls in love with a nice, young and attractive girl, whom he had always known and secretly admired. His romantic aspirations are rudely disturbed by the arrival on the scene of another suitor. The latter is usually from the big village or the city. The basic elements in such novels consist of a beautiful evocation of the landscape, Hardyesque in quality, and fully consonant with the Afrikaans literary tradition. Interwoven is the farmer's dependency on money-lenders, the fate of the white people caught up in forces beyond their control. And finally, there are the farm-hands.

Now it is interesting to observe, how in both Malherbe's novel, *Die Meulenaar,* and van den Heever's *Somer,* the white relationships and the tragic implications of their personal involvements, are toned down by immediately following and contrasting depictions of the coloured relationships. However, where the white ones are involved, the relationships are heart-rending and of an ethereal quality. The 'coloured' ones are endowed with humour. This contrasting technique is extended to include the ever-present rivalry on the land.

In van den Heever's *Somer*, for example, one of the main characters is Wynand, a wanderer, an outsider with just sufficient a romantic attraction for the farm girl, Linda. His opponent, Hannes, is from the area and secretly in love with Linda. Hannes dies as tragically at the end as does Faans in Malherbe's novel. The reader is presented with a passage where the two white rivals are competing with each other on the land. In *Somer,* the superiority of the intruder Wynand over the local boy is immediately neutralized by a depiction of rivalry between the 'coloured' labourers, one of whom is usually a smart Aleck from the

Boland (an area in the Western Cape which implies worldly-wise, clever and forward in the derogatory sense). The other is from the rural area and therefore a better type.[62]

Here is just such a typical scene between 'coloured' farm-hands, the one known as Stefaans being from the Boland, the other, April, a farm product. The two farm-hands revile each other, to the delight of the whites on the farm. Stefaans, the smart one, for instance laments:[63]

'Oh, where are the Boland days when we worked the farm-hands so hard . . . that they collapsed on the land like young bullocks!' And April retorts sarcastically:    'What do you talk of the Boland, Bushman! . . . . When you volk [labourers] were still playing marbles over there, we were already standing with our heads between our legs chasing the corn off the field . . . . Drink, yes, that you're good at!'

The man from the Boland becomes someone whose, 'lips . . . are . . . glued to barrels of wine'.[64] In a further comic scene in the novel, Stefaans and April play out their self-demeaning roles immediately after the reader has been allowed a peep into the feelings Hannes has for Linda:[65]

Stefaans turns violently to April as if he wanted to smack him with the palm of his hand over his mouth. 'If it wasn't for Katryn, Bushman, I'd smack you.' Katryn who is present replies: 'Oh, sis, you . . . I don't keep company with such loud mouths.' Stefaans shouts to her: 'Tonight, this Hotnot . . . will walk to the minister. Oh, you nice thing Stefaans, who would not gladly dance with him tonight?' Mockingly Katryn retorts as she waltzes away with April. 'Sis, the thing is smothering in his collar! Let go off me!'[66]

Similar roles are played out by the 'coloured' farm-hands in D. F. Malherbe's, *Die Meulenaar* (The Miller). They, too, answer to such unfelicitous names as Velbaadjie (Skin coat) and Gareopa, thereby continuing a tradition starting with the Grietjie Drilboutens, the Galgevogels and Droogekeels of Boniface.

*Die Meulenaar* shows many parallels with *Somer*. The main white characters in Malherbe's *Die Meulenaar* are Louw, Koos Bester and Faans, who are all infatuated with the attractive Leonore. There are her parents Oom Tys and Tante Betta Theron, who suffer when they are forced to auction their farm. The 'coloured' labourers are

37

represented by Velbaadjie, the clown with the big mouth, Korneels, who falls foul of Velbaadjie, Gareopa and Saartjie. We follow the fluctuating fortunes of the Theron family, who mortgage themselves to Louw in order to save their farm. It is, however, all to no avail, for in the end they still lose.

In both *Die Meulenaar* and *Somer*, the 'coloured' labourers are used to supply the distraction, or the comic note. When, for example, Faans and Louw fight each other, we have a scene where Gareopa and Saartjie are at each other's throat. Saartjie shouts at Gareopa who has been trying to gain her favour: 'Oh, sis, you! Go away from here. Why are you following me around! Wait until Piet gets hold of you!'[67] Significantly, Velbaadjie humiliates Korneels on the land, immediately after the fight between Louw and Faans. In a titanic struggle, witnessed by all the other labourers, Velbaadjie works Korneels to a standstill: '"Bring a little water for Korneels. He has lost his breath!" Then he glided past Korneels . . . and the world began swimming in front of Korneels and he became so dizzy that he stopped in his tracks.'[68]

When Velbaadjie decides to leave the farm after the death of Mrs Thereon because he believes he saw her ghost walking around, Leonore, the daughter, comments: 'Are they not terrible creatures?'[69] And a little later, she says: 'It's true, the brown people saddens one.'[70] Korneels is also a tell tattle and shows no loyalty to his own breed. When Faans is beaten up, the first thing Mr Theron suggests is 'Volk?' (Labourers?/Coloureds?).[71]

In both novels, there is the ever-constant contrast between the urban and the rural, whereby it is suggested that the urban types are forward and disrespectful, and the rural ones are the salt of the earth. In Malherbe's novel, *Die Meulenaar,* Korneels and Velbaadjie are constantly at each other's throat, edged on, naturally, by the whites. The teasing becomes very rough at times and over-personal, resulting in Korneels referring to Velbaadjie's legs as 'piksteelbene' (Pick axe legs).[72] The whites in these novels can poke fun at the labourers at will. The whiteman Tys teases: 'How come Gareopa's forelock is lying just like a damara bull?'[73] And Velbaadjie, playing out his obsequious, clown's role, answers: 'Obstinacy Baas, to please Saartjie'.[73] Leonore, the white girl in Malherbe's novel, in reproaching Faans, uses words which are directly reminiscent of those in another novel by the same author, namely, *Hans die skipper.* 'We have not taught you such manners. Look, the volkies [coloureds] do that to each other, attack each other, but white people don't, decent white people don't do that.'[74] However, it is the white woman, Betta, who quite early on in the novel writes the Afrikaner epitaph for the 'coloured'. 'Untroubled Things',[75] says Betta, as they walk away. If hitherto, the 'coloured' was only decoratively functional, then he was soon to come of age in Afrikaner/Afrikaans literature with the arrival of *Toiings* (Ragamuffin) on the scene.

# Chapter 2

# You taught me language[1]

Few people outside South Africa will have heard of, let alone read, the works of the Afrikaner novelist, C. H. Kühn (pseudonym: Mikro). However, many will have heard of Joyce Cary's *Mister Johnson*. Mikro's novel, *Toiings,* which deals with 'coloureds', was, and still is, regarded as one of the supreme comic efforts in Afrikaans literature. Cary's *Mister Johnson* is also praised for its humour. The two novelists had totally dissimilar backgrounds.

Cary, born in 1885 in Londonderry, was to become well known for his novels and writings on Africa. In 1913, at the age of twenty-five, he applied for a job in the civil service in what was then Northern Nigeria. He was to remain there until 1920 when ill health forced him to return. Cary was in Africa during the period when Lord Lugard was governor of all Nigeria and was thus part and parcel of the Lugardian system of indirect rule. While he endorsed the policy of delegating power to the indigenes through chiefs, he was level-headed enough to realize that a dictatorial local potentate could easily abuse his powers. Joyce Cary wrote *Aissa Saved* (1932), *Mister Johnson* (1939), *The Case for African Freedom* (1944), *Britain and West Africa* (1946) and *The African Witch* (1936), all of which dealt with Africa in one way or another. Of these books his novel *Mister Johnson* is fairly well known among scholars of African literature.

Cary came from the British tradition of the Empire. Mikro, born in 1903 in the country district of Williston, the Cape, was from a rather stern Calvinist background. Through his entire youth he was plagued with illness. We know that he was an avid reader of Dutch, English and Afrikaans authors, that he started writing in 1930, and that it was his involvement with the 'coloureds' which turned him into one of the most celebrated Afrikaans authors. He himself sums up his involvement when he says: 'I wanted to educate my Afrikaner people to have an ear and an eye for the "coloureds".'[2]

Mikro wrote his famous novel, *Toiings* (Ragamuffin) in 1934. A sequel appeared in 1935, namely *Pelgrims* (Pilgrims), followed in 1944 by *Vreemdelinge* (Strangers). The novelist continued his interest in 'coloured' life with the publication of *Huisies teen die heuwel* (Cottages against the Hills), and *Stille Uur* (Silent Hour), jointly published in 1942.

If one now looks at the scant treatment of the 'coloured' in Afrikaans fiction up until this point, then Mikro's novels and stories, which were filled at least with empathy, were a radical departure from the general pattern. And Afrikaner critics were not slow to recognize this.

Cary's *Mister Johnson* is centred on the colonial Africa of 1913–20, when Cary himself was part of the colonial apparatus. Mikro had been a part of Africa ever since young Bibault uttered the, by now, famous words, 'k' ben een Africaander' (I am an Africaander),[3] in the town of Stellenbosch, during the reign of Willem Adriaan van der Stel in 1707. This defiant phrase was spoken in the heat of the moment, in response to a political situation. Then, for the first time, the word 'Africaander' was used to mean 'white'. Previously, in the seventeenth century, only blacks were taken as being from Africa. Afrikaans-speaking whites may well look upon this incident as the earliest UDI on the African continent. To them, this statement embodied the struggle of the freedom-loving Boers against the bureaucracy of the Company. Bibault's statement is therefore also looked upon as the earliest expression of Boer (Afrikaner) nationalism.

*Mister Johnson* was written during the hey-day of British colonialism. Achebe had not yet appeared on the literary scene. The Yoruba writer, Fagunwa, whose influence on that other Nigerian novelist, Tutuola, was said to have been profound, was unknown to the Western literary critics, although he was writing in the 1930s.

*Toiings* appeared at a time in South African political history when the non-white was still very much a non-person, politically and in literary terms. And this despite the assertion of the South African PEN publication, reviewing fifty years of English literature, that Sarah Gertrude Millin, with her *God's Step-children* (1924), and Stuart Cloete, with his *The Turning Wheels* (1937) had blazed the trail to a greater South African realism. *Toiings* was published in Afrikaans in 1934, at a time when only some twenty odd years previously, that very language was still regarded as a patois, a mere 'Hottentot's' prattle.

41

In depicting non-whites, both Cary and Mikro used as their metaphor, the 'distancing art of comedy'. Cary portrayed Africans who were subject to English colonialism, Mikro a people who were of Africa and Europe, both in the acculturative and genetic sense.

Cary intended his *Mister Johnson* to be taken seriously. Each of his novels maps out the way individuals find themselves in conflict with their environment. The conflict may be external or internal. Cary tried to show 'certain men and their problems in the tragic background of a continent little advanced from the Stone Age, and therefore exposed, like no other, to the impact of modern toil'.[4] Mikro himself admits:[5]

At the time of writing *Toiings* [Ragamuffin] and *Pelgrims* [Pilgrims] , I was about as uncivilized as Toiings himself, and asked [myself] , rather naively, whether you knew the people who lived here amongst us . . . . I despaired everytime someone said he had laughed so heartily at Toiings. I did not want you to laugh . . . Yes, they [the Coloureds] , also suffer, also strive, hope, laugh, live and mourn. And they are at our portals. We must not be light-hearted about their future. Toiings was a beggar at your door-step, hands out-stretched for a bit of love and understanding. In my mind's eye, I saw all Coloureds, all of them standing thus beggars among you . . . I saw them as pilgrims who were journeying with us to the same destination.

In a fairly lengthy review of the novel by Francois Malherbe in 1934, which appeared in *Die Huisgenoot,* he writes as follows:[6]

We live among a large Coloured population. They are as old as our nation. From the earliest times, our existence has been closely intertwined with theirs. They have built our houses, cultivated our land . . . shared our sorrows and joys. They have carried us in their arms, they were our first play-mates; we had love and respect for outa and aia. Their language is ours also, so also their customs and habits. They have no other country . . . . Culturally, however, we have regarded them as too brown (and left them) to English institutes like 'Zonnebloem' to teach them Shakespeare and Galsworthy . . . Yes, the Coloured remains a problem.

All the Afrikaner ambivalences were contained in this evaluation of the 'coloured' within the South African context. Malherbe went on to laud the 'child-like' and 'spontaneous' *Toiings.* Later on, he was to sound a more critical note. There is a noticeable tendency among Afrikaner critics to slightly, not radically, change their views, as the situation demands it. Yet *Toiings* still remained, for Malherbe, the story of a neglected boy who learned to love a good girl (goeie meid).[7]

In 1958, however, Malherbe was prepared to concede that *Toiings* was still seen too much from the 'viewpoint of the Baas'. Malherbe admonished the 'coloured' reader not to take exception to the terms 'Baas', 'jong', 'meid' and 'skepsel',[8] which are liberally strewn throughout Afrikaans fiction. In magnanimous vein, he recognized that the educated 'coloured', and especially the teacher, would find it difficult to make such fare palatable to his 'brown' pupils. But, said the learned man, such objections arose out of feelings of inferiority — something which had also troubled his people (the Afrikaners) for so long, and which they eventually overcame. Dekker (1947) also constantly referred to the 'coloured boy' and his 'meid' and to the child-like nature of *Toiings*.

To all these critics, Mikro was the realist who observed the 'coloured' and who 'portrays him in his way of life, his attitudes, his gestures, his mentality and his language'. Beukes and Lategan (1959) call Mikro 'the most artistic portrayer of the "coloured" soul and life in literature'.[9] Notwithstanding the attempts at a more honest and critical evaluation of the way in which the 'coloured' is portrayed in Afrikaans literature, *Toiings* and the like remain well within the physical and mental landscape of the Afrikaner.

Most 'coloured' readers will, in so far as they will ever read or get hold of Mphahlele's *The African Image* (which is banned in South Africa), readily agreed with his critical assessment when he fulminates:[10]

> Like South African fiction of the nineteenth century, this was
> a gloating literature. More recently, a few novelists began to
> concern themselves with contemporary 'problems', but still
> with a defensive and wounded manner about them: the
> 'colour problem', the 'Jewish problem', the 'poor-white problem'.
> Mikro the novelist, like Sarah Gertrude Millin, depicts
> grovelling, degenerate 'Coloured' labour squatters (Uncle Toms
> among them), and like Mrs Millin, he dislikes mixed blood.
> Jochem van Bruggen[11] is a sort of one-eyed Dickens: he sees
> only poor-whites and not in the complete setting . . . . The
> Hobson brothers[11] think of Bushmen as sub-human . . . .
> There is Frans Venter's novel . . . . In him the Afrikaans has
> just caught onto the black man come to the city.

One may question Mphahlele's attempts to impose his artistic vision on that of the artist, but one cannot fail to recognize his objections, if the historical and socio-cultural situation is taken into account.

Both Cary and Mikro were didactic in their purposes, both somewhat of the sociologist *manqué*. Cary was more of an outsider than Mikro. If there was any saving grace in his involvement with Africa at all, then it was that English colonialism allowed its participants and perpetrators, finally and ultimately, to withdraw. Cary could openly decide 'to avoid the African setting which demands a certain kind of story, a certain violence and coarseness of detail.'[12] Mikro, as an 'Africaander', could not ever dream of avoiding Africa.

Historically, Cary was part of an Africa where the Lugardian system of indirect rule was in operation, a system which, in the words of Christopher Fyfe, 'at its best envisioned the development of African territories by slow easy stages towards eventual self-government' — a political code which made the 'idealistic administrator feel that he was helping Africa forwards by introducing new ways gradually in forms Africans could easily accept'.[13]

Mikro was part of a South Africa, which, by the very act of Union (1910), had placed all non-whites beyond the rule of law — had turned them into non-citizens. Between the covert apartheid of the 1930s, the latter more overt forms of the fifties, and the system of indirect rule as applied by Lord Lugard in Nigeria, there was, and still is, a remarkable similarity in intent and purpose.

In *Toiings,* the reader is confronted with the 'Cape coloured' shepherd, who finds unexpected happiness in his friendship with his master Fanie, and later on, Siena, who becomes his wife. His love for Siena is referred to as something 'noble'. It is placed in inverted commas, for the very word itself, and the situation surrounding *Toiings*, has a comic ring. One is reminded of Volkelt's formulation that 'alles Komische ist Auflösung eines Wertanspruch in sein Nichts'[14] — a claim to have a certain value, wisdom or truth, which fizzles out in reality into a mere nothingness. Now, it is a fact that often what passes for humour is nothing but comic. This danger happens especially when the European writer depicts groups of peoples culturally and somatically different from themselves. Thus, F. E. J. Malherbe, in his otherwise stimulating study of humour, could use as an example of the comic, the illiterate African with his double-breasted suit pocket littered and illuminated with imitation gold pens and carrying a satchel stuffed with books (a classic example of a white-envisioned stereotype black, the townsman as opposed to the tribesman). The incongruities of the black and illiterate, as opposed to the civilized and the Christian, is for Malherbe an illustration of the claim to something higher which fades away into nothingness. One could, of course, counter by taking an illiterate poor-white, who puts on tails and striped trousers, but keeps his clogs on. But such an exercise would be pointless and prove nothing. Malherbe has, however, added, within the context of his cultural situation, an element to the Volkelt formula, which I would like to classify as a touch of 'comic ethnocentricity'.

The practically illiterate Toiings has such an ethereal view of love and life — if indeed such a concept can be applied to such a person — that he refuses to kiss his simple, trusting and God-fearing wife at night, and can only bring himself to shake hands with her. He becomes an object of sniggers among Mikro's countrymen, the Afrikaners, and one of anger among the 'coloureds', who suspect that the author is only making fun of them. This portrayal totally conforms with the image of the 'coloured' as experienced by the Afrikaners, which is fraught with condescension and 'benevolent paternalism'. While the Afrikaner does not view his attitude as such, the 'coloureds' do. The English were, of course, not averse to paternalism in their relations with the blacks. But theirs was of a type which cannot fully be dealt with in this chapter.

Yet, both *Toiings* and *Mister Johnson* are remarkable in that the emphasis is on the individual, and not on the ready-made situation which is dramatically always at hand in racially heterogeneous and culturally diffuse societies. Mister Johnson is child-like in his ambitions, his grandiose schemes of wealth, his endeavours to be popular. Toiings lacks Mister Johnson's imaginative flair, is more stolid, but no less child-like at times. Mister Johnson is constantly in trouble, largely through his own doing. Toiings' own world blows up from time to time, partly through external factors: the death of his first wife, drought on the farm, a little bit of wanderlust. Mister Johnson's existence is a constant flight into unreality. He lives what Hall (1958) calls a 'Walter Mitty' type of existence. Every disaster or near-misfortune only lends added glamour to his precarious pattern of life.

The Toiings who strays and then gets temporarily involved with a city woman, is a sad figure, one enlisting our sympathies. When he gets involved with Drieka, the woman from Eppenton (the 'coloured' version of the English word, Eppington), a suburb outside Cape Town, he is still occasionally afflicted with remorse and a sense of morality. 'Toiings wanted her with his entire being. He would have her come what may . . . . At first, his excesses worried him. There

45

are still Baas Fanie, nôi Miemie and Siena who might hear about it. At such times he was surly and wandered around in the veld'.[15]

The Mister Johnson who is so bold as to take money from the native treasury, has no remorse. Waziri, the moving spirit behind it all, forces Johnson to procure a confidential report from the district officer, which in typical Johnson fashion is nearly bungled. When the natives jeer at him on his way home — they had heard that he was caught in the act — he can only interpret their attention as an added feather in his cap:[16]

> Benjamin, stepping out with slower dignity, says, 'I hear,
> Mister Johnson, he nearly catch you. Are you not afraid of
> that prison?' He looks at Johnson with a kind of wondering
> curiosity.
>
>     Johnson laughs and tosses his hat to Sozy, hovering round
> him as usual at three yards' range, afraid to come nearer, but
> unable to take her eyes off him. 'He no catch me — I do what
> I want I see everything in dem safe'.
>
>     'What de good of dat — you no catch nutting?'
>     'I no try to catch him. You tink I fool?'
>     'What you do den, Mister Johnson?'
> Johnson has no idea. But he opens his mouth to utter
> something and at once his imagination provides him with a
> plan, glorious and impressive.
>
>     'I go take 'em when Mister Rudbeck not dar'.

To Joyce Cary, the author, Mister Johnson was 'the artist in life, creating his life . . . one of those who scarcely notices whether he has friends or not; he gives friendship but has no time to ask whether he gets it. He is too busy.' Cary goes on to make the point that Johnson need not forgive. 'You notice how children don't need to forgive: they forget . . .. He couldn't live in resentment; because life was too exciting, he was whirling on.'[17]

I think it was this child-like, ever-smiling and innocent quality in Mister Johnson which prompted Mphahlele to rail in his *African Image:*[18]

> I flung away *Mister Johnson* with exasperation when I tried to
> read it for the first time, in South Africa. I had seen too many
> journalistic caricatures of black people and 'bongo-bongo cartoons'
> showing Africans with filed teeth and bones stuck in their hair —
> too many for me to find amusement in Johnson's behaviour, always
> on the verge of farce.

Not surprisingly, Cary becomes a very difficult author to teach in West Africa. The charges range from racialism to total disrespect for the African, a biased portrayal of the blackman by a white author who could only see Africans as noble savages, buffoons or bungling fools suspended acculturatively. The main point is that we are confronted with a reaction against a European 'historical' and 'literary' vision of the blackman, who is in the process of demythologizing himself after colonialism, who is in the throes of, or has just emerged from, a violent nationalism and is groping towards an African way of life. Here, it is once more clear that, art for arts sake, or the interpretation of a text outside its sociological context, is a mere academic exercise.

Toiings too is found to be objectionable within the South African context by those people who, on the basis of their level of consciousness, reject a taxonomy which relegates them to being 'coloured'. Right through he remains the simple, trusting person, who falters only occasionally. Karreeplaas (the farm of his master) is the cradle of happiness. When Toiings leaves this valhalla, the reader expects him to falter and undergo a process of degeneration. Likewise, one expects him to return after he has come to his senses — a process accelerated by the illness of his son, David. And, in returning to Karreeplaas, he is logically ready for the ultimate culmination of his newly-found happiness in the person of Jannetjie.

Toiings at least is preserved by a supercilious, but master-child affection, from his master and madame; more important, by his love for Siena and, after her death, by Jannetjie's love, which is an extension of the Siena love. Like Mister Johnson, Toiings is characterized by a certain *naïveté*. But, whereas the Bamu-Johnson relationship strikes one as discordant and not fully worked out, that of Toiings and Siena, and later on Jannetjie, has no such false note. Bamu will never cease to be a conservative bush pagan, Johnson will always be a tragic victim of the process of acculturation. Bamu's African world is real, Johnson's will always remain unreal. Mister Johnson has set himself apart from his environment, has taken to wearing English suits and using formal English. Toiings at least operates within his limitations. When Johnson takes the English woman, Celia, to meet his wife, the ensuing encounter is superb for its comic portrayal of the two worlds existing side by side:[19]

> Before Johnson can speak, she comes in, sees Bamu and cries,
> 'Oh, you're Mrs. Johnson'.

She shakes hands with Bamu and says to Johnson, 'I think you
are very clever to get such a pretty wife'.
Bamu stares at her with a look of penetrating contempt and
says nothing.
'She wear a cloth this morning, small small for clean de house',
Johnson explains.
'Oh, but it suits her beautifully — I hope she always wears the
native dress. It is so much nicer than those terrible mission
frocks.'

Tooings and Siena have a credibility which is lacking in *Mister
Johnson*. Although critics try to prove the opposite, Toiings and Mister
Johnson remain types which conform, especially to the European
vision of the 'coloured' and the 'native'. Where Toiings is portrayed
comically, the 'coloured' interprets it as the white man laughing at the
non-white. Where the white critic talks of Mikro's love for Toiings, the
non-white can only see a benevolent paternalism. Where Toiings is
portrayed with humour, the 'coloured' can only see him as a buffoon,
someone who is liberally plied with liquor, and who constantly eulogizes
wine as an essential component in his life, as is also evident from
Mikro's *Huisies teen die heuwel* and *Stille uur* (1942). One of the
characters says: 'Pete you know me. Chrisjan knows me. Salute knows
me. You all know me. Take me and drink as an example. Drink I say,
for what else is there to do on this world?'[20]

Fully in accordance with the custom observed hitherto, F. E. J.
Malherbe comments on the passage in the following vein: 'In this way
does Mikro portray his naïve children of nature, in their shy, super-
stitious and passionate nature.'[21]

Similar notes are sounded in the work of Boerneef (pseudonym:
I. W. v. d. Merwe), where the relationship between the farm 'coloured'
and the farm white is described as being 'not too intimate like two
white people, yet very much familiar, like a young white master
(duusbaas) can sometimes be with just a "plaashotnot" (farmhotnot).
Each knew his place'.[22] Andries Harlekyn's (clown) eulogy to
'vaaljapie',[23] in the works of Boerneef, is only a continuation of a
peculiarly Afrikaans literary tradition. In his state of inebriation, the
'coloured' becomes a further object of ridicule and laughter for the
Afrikaner public.

Like Toiings, Mister Johnson also has a white man cum god-father,
Rudbeck, who is tied to him by a bond of paternal affection. The
clerk had stolen his heart by enthusiastically supporting his road

scheme. For Rudbeck, the road is an obsession. Johnson on the other hand, is so emotionally attached to him and so eager to please, that Rudbeck finds it difficult to be his executioner at the very end, and ironically, Johnson wants Rudbeck to shoot him. Yet Johnson's exit is entirely in keeping with his performance throughout the book and therefore the only realizable and acceptable one. Johnson 'triumphs in the greatness, the goodness and the daring inventiveness of Rudbeck. All the force of his spirit is concentrated in gratitude and triumphant devotion; he is calling on the world to admit there is no other god like his god. He burst out aloud, "Oh Lawd, I tank you for my frien' Mr. Rudbeck — de bigges' heart in the worl' ".'[24]

Toiings is charmingly naïve at times. In his moment of greatest happiness, he kneels down in the field and prays to God: 'Dear Oubaas. It's me Toiings. I look after the sheep on Baas Fanie's farm, and I love Siena. Yes, Master, Amen.'[25] Generally however, he plays out his comic-ascribed role. He prepares his son, 'Dawid Goliat Filistyn',[26] very carefully for his obsequious role on the farm. The farm-hands answer to the names of Woer-woer and Windvoël. The village is full of pitfalls, and by implication, the farm stands for peace, order and purity. Toiings had no such dramatic exit as Mister Johnson. After all, he never aspired so high, and could, therefore, never fall so low.

A remarkable feature, then, of humour in a white–black situation is that the black can so easily become a buffoon of some sort or another. This image is sometimes dictated by the social roles in colonial society; for example, the arrogant superiority of the white and the servility and subservience of the black (and the necessary interaction of the two groups), all of which forces the non-white character to play out his expected comic role. Invariably, the illiterate or semi-literate is also forced, through a process of acculturation, to use a language which is a corruption of his own and that of the white man. This, and his incomprehension of the subtleties of the European language, further makes for a linguistically comic farce. No doubt African students found this one of the objectionable features of *Mister Johnson*. My experience at Fourah Bay, Sierra Leone, certainly showed that Evelyn Waugh's *Black Mischief* could not count on much sympathy from African students.

Cary's *Mister Johnson* had 'most of the qualities the native traditionally has in romantic fiction'. Yet Cary 'does not romanticize him or his fate: Johnson dies sadly, not heroically, becoming tragic only in his pathetic desire to retain his dignity.'[27]

Comments by white critics have, at times, only complicated the picture. The comment in Beukes and Lategan on *Toiings* is certainly not calculated to endear the book, or the main character, to the 'coloured' public at large: 'Just as the wild animal of our country . . . had to give us the animal story, so also the Coloureds and the African intimately connected with Afrikaner life were bound to find their way into Afrikaans fiction.'[28]

The Englishman, Kettle, has taken Cary to task for showing a lack of realism in *Mister Johnson*. 'Rudbeck shoots Johnson as he would a suffering dog to whom he feels a special responsibility and although the horror of the act is conveyed, it is somewhat blunted by the underlying paternalism of Joyce Cary.'[29] Kettle questions the Cary portrayal against the emergent forces of nationalism. Hall finds *Mister Johnson* a 'social tragedy in which a man's fate is shaped by forces not only beyond his control but outside his comprehension . . . the jetsam cast up by opposing tides of African and European cultures.'[30]

African students, we have noticed earlier, have difficulties with the portrayal of a Joyce Cary or an Evelyn Waugh. 'Coloured' South Africans find it just as hard to swallow the white depictions whole. The realism of colonialism and indirect rule, as well as that of degradation and apartheid in South Africa, preclude mere beneficent assessments.

The artist can of course approach reality in diverse ways. He can concentrate on these outer manifestations with love, get to know them so intimately that they reveal a higher, spiritual truth to him. He can also be swept away by his own emotion and ideas and exploit the outward visual aspect as a means of reflecting his own inner life. He may not be enthralled by the things themselves, but by their value as symbols. In his art, the visual aspect will fade to give way to symbolic significance.

Realism which in everyday life reveals a true humanity is often typified as humour. But humour should never be confused with shallow laughter, mere jocosity. The humorist detects small contradictions in life which evoke laughter. But often these contradictions only serve to hide a deeper, spiritual contrast between the ideal and the real. The laughter of the true humorist is therefore often softened, or toned down, to a smile of sympathy or even empathy at times. The humorist will laugh about the incongruities, the follies of people, as well as the inexplicabilities of their fate with a conciliatory smile. Humour carries with it always a hint of the tragic, which brings with it 'complication, infinite complexity of motive and action'.[31]

The non-white objections highlight some of the difficulties in applying humour to white–black situations. One should not forget that our emotions are largely stimulated and determined by institutionalized structures. Not surprisingly, therefore, humour to a large extent boils down to the manner in which we deviate from, or play with, the institutionalized patterns of our emotions. Humour can therefore only be comprehended within its existing and peculiar situation (culture or sub-culture).

Mphahlele, the South African, and other West African critics and students have succeeded in diawing attention to an important and essential element in humour, namely the observer, the audience, or the silent participant. In the case of *Toiings,* we are largely concerned with the effect of this work of art on the 'Cape coloured', who finds himself politically and culturally in a system of ascribed roles as opposed to achieved roles, with no tribal past or folklore ready for resuscitation by some white parliamentarians. To them, the manner in which Mikro has crossed the institutionalized borders is not funny at all. The 'coloured' public is irritated, embarrassed and not amused by *Toiings.* Rightly does Zijderveld (1971) point out in his study on humour as a social phenomenon that the way in which the observer defines or assesses the situation, will determine whether there is cause for embarrassment or irritation, alarm or laughter. All this, in turn, will be determined by the cultural values of the observer.

Realism for the dispossessed means apartheid; deprivation: physically, culturally and mentally. Realism means being a non-person, existing by the grace of the whites. Realism means entrenchment in ethnocentricity. How serious white South Africans were in portraying the 'coloured', will become even clearer when we deal with the works of Millin and Cloete. For, if hitherto, the Afrikaans author could only see his 'coloured' character as an object of fun, then English novelists like Sarah Gertrude Millin were to turn him into a leper.

# Chapter 3

# Smelling strangeness[1]

Sarah Gertrude Millin immortalized the half-caste in South African literature with her *God's Step-children* (1924). Her most interesting and important books were those dealing with the colour question. Millin was, as she so frankly admitted in her account of the life and death of her husband Phillip (*The Measure of My Days*, 1955) very preoccupied with the racial situation:[2]

> I had written about colour since I was sixteen. *The Dark River* —
> The River of Colour, The River of Life, The Dark River itself,
> the Vaal River . . . Where I lived on the Vaal River, among the
> remnants of tribes that had fought one another and the
> Boers in Voortrekker days, I saw drunkenness, disease, hunger
> and miscegenation; and to talk to these stepchildren of the vote
> would have been like offering them the cake Marie Antoinette
> suggested for the poor who had no bread.

Millin was very productive as a writer. She had written seventeen novels, biographies of General Smuts and Cecil John Rhodes and two autobiographies. Her most important novels dealing with the question of miscegenation — a theme of paranoic proportions to her and subsequent writers — are: *The Dark River* (1919), *Adam's Rest* (1922), *God's Step-children* (1924, revised edition 1951), *The Herr Witchdoctor* (1941, American edition under the title *The Dark Gods*) and *King of the Bastards* (1950). Her autobiographical works, *The Measure of My Days* (1955) and *The People of South Africa* (1951) provide illuminating material about South Africa.

Miscegenation was of course a theme not solely confined to South African literature. In English literature of the nineteenth century there was periodic interest in the person of mixed origin, the concentration being on the Eurasian, the half-caste in India (i.e. British India). Many of these Anglo-Indians have enshrined their names in the history books. For example, Derozio, who lived from 1809 to 1833 and who wrote good poetry.[3]

Mixed breeds have always constituted rather awkward biological by-products of European colonialism. In his unfortunately too little-known book, *Half-Caste* (1937), Cedrick Dover presents us with a comparative study of half-caste communities all over the world. And although the book first appeared in 1937, and is therefore outdated in certain respects, it still contains sufficient useful material to be worthy of note within our context.

Dover at one stage draws a comparison between the Eurafrican, as he calls the 'Cape coloured', and the Eurasian. He writes:[4]

And this is not surprising, for the white strains are the same:
mainly Dutch, Portuguese, German, French and British. There
are Hottentot genes in the Eurafricans, but these are not
dominant; there are Bantu genes, but the contributing Bantu groups
were themselves previously exposed to Asiatic and other
admixture; there are the genes of slaves imported from the
mixed but prominently Asiatic populations of Madagascar,
Mozambique and Java; there are recent Indian, Chinese, Goan
and Eurasian genes. So the Eurafricans have the stature, the
brown skin, the oval face, the blackish and often straight hair,
and the brown or brownish black eyes of the common Eurasian
type. Even their speech reminds one of the Eurasian accent,
the somewhat monotonous, sing-song intonation known in
India as *chee-chee*.

His rather small chapter on literature is skimpy yet no less incisive. Of the half-caste in 'prodigal literature', as he puts it, he says that he appears as 'an undersized, scheming and entirely degenerate bastard. His father is a blackguard, his own mother a whore . . . . But more than all this, he is a potential menace to Western Civilization, to everything that is White and Sacred and majusculed.'[5] The half-caste's ability to instill fear into, and send tremors down the backs of the whites, is one which we shall persistently come across in South African literature, notably among Afrikaner writers like Regina Neser and Abel Coetzee.

Rightly Dover observes that the literature concerning the half-caste was often shrouded in ignorance and subtle propaganda. He gives an extensive list of authors who, according to the critics, are sympathetic to the person of mixed origin but whose final vision of this group is no less damaging. The works of Alain Lambreaux (*Mulatto Johnny*), Eugene O'Neill (*Emperor Jones*), Sarah Gertrude Millin (*God's Step-children*), Paul Morand (*Magie Noire*), Carl van Vechten (*Nigger Heaven*), Henry Champly (*White Women, Coloured Men*), and Joan Sutherland (*Challenge*), in the words of Dover, all serve to 'stress the frustration *motif*, the futility of coloured life, the sanctity and desirability of white womanhood, the unpardonable crime of inter-mixture and the nobility of declining to extend it'.[6] Dover refers to the literature of 'race and colour as one of smelling strangeness'.[7] Miriam, one of the characters in Millin's novel *Adam's Rest*, refers to colour as a disease which she would rather not catch.[8]

Abstinence and the refusal to procreate as well as a predilection for seclusion, in some cases even monastic, are such noble motifs found in the works of Millin and Joan Sutherland. Eugenists, anthropologists, psychologists, sociologists and politicians further complicate the picture. The absurdity of the half-breed image reaches comi-tragic proportions in the anecdote cited by Dover when 'a brown dupe of aggrandisement . . . writes to England's leading welfare journal (*New Health*, June 1935), to enquire if people with his "complaint – the result of mixed marriage" can be sterilized. "I am not too dark", he says pathetically, "but I dread to think now at 30, should I get married and have children, they might be of much darker colour than I am".'[9] The reply of the editor is hilarious in that he counsels the poor man that 'unfortunately the law does not permit sterilization on these grounds. You must, therefore, in the present state of the law, be satisfied with the adoption of birth control measures.'[9]

With such a heavy premium on colour, it is hardly surprising that most half-breed communities suffer from what Freud calls, 'the nar-cissism of small differences', that is, they distinguish expertly between subtle shades of brown or light which is normally not so overtly apparent to the non half-caste.

According to Susanne Howe in her book, *Novels of Empire* (1949), the Dutch and the French colonials have never found the spawning of half-castes an undue problem. She writes: 'the French, like the Dutch, feel less called upon than the British to draw the color line in their colonial possessions'. With them, there are 'no ugly whispers or pointing fingers [to] ruin . . . peaceful little idylls with "les brunes" of whatever shade or caste or tribe'.[10] Howe's comment on the Dutch reveals her ignorance of the circumstances in the Dutch East Indies during the time of 'Jan Compagnie', as well as her unfamiliarity with Dutch colonial literature as such. And since the destinies of the

Netherlands and the Cape became so closely intertwined, it would be interesting to see to what extent the image of the Indo, that is, the Dutch Indonesian half-breed, shows any comparison with that of the 'Cape coloured' in South Africa.

The literature referring to the Dutch East Indies is studded with images and terminologies reminiscent of those found in Anglo-Saxon territories. In fact, reading through novels dealing with the Indo, at times one is forcibly reminded of the South African literary scene, and left with just a sneaking suspicion that the inhabitants at the Cape, and the Afrikaner in particular, may have unconsciously inherited a Dutch literary tradition via the East Indies. Njais, Nonnas, Djongos, Liplappen and Sinjos[11] walk large in the imagination of many a Dutch author writing about the East Indies. These recall similar terms found in Afrikaans literature, for example: Seun, Boy, Meid, Jong, Skepsel, Outa, and Aia[12].

As in Afrikaans literature, the Indo: the person of mixed descent, was portrayed rather unflatteringly. Here too, it was easy to abstract a certain image. The peculiar speech pattern, *krompraat* (lit. crooked speech, i.e. incorrect usage of the Dutch language), gave rise to giggles and became a source of constant amusement for the *totok* (white-man) in the ever-present *soos* (fraternity), in the tropics. There is also the pathetic attempt of the Indo to imitate. This heavy insistence on imitation, the process whereby children generally acquire their first knowledge, is a notable feature of 'coloured' and Indo portrayals. It is no accident that the Indos are derisively called 'half-bloedjes' (lit. half-bloods).

The 'coloured' is furnished with a guitar, the Indo sentimentally drowned in *krongtjong* music.[13] These half-breeds concentrate on imbibing white values and habits, and it is this disparity between what they really are and what they aspire to only half-heartedly, which gives rise to endless comic scenes. As with the mixed breeds in South Africa, there are heart-rending attempts to forge an alliance with the whites.

Nicolaus de Graaff had already given a rather horrendous picture of half-caste women in his *Oost Indise Spiegel* (Warnsinck, 1930), although he is no less damaging in his assessment of Dutch women in the East. To state therefore that the Dutch were so much more tolerant in portraying the indigenes in the East, or the half-castes during colonial times, is to regurgitate a well-orchestrated myth which finds its sustenance in historical comparisons of, for example, English and Dutch colonialism, in the process of which the latter appears to be more humane.

The mixed group in the East Indies was certainly not as humanely treated as one is sometimes given to understand. Rob Nieuwenhuys observes in his book *Oost-Indische Spiegel*: 'The history of the Indos, the so-called "bastards of Europeans", as they were officially called at first, has been one of suffering throughout the entire nineteenth century.'[14] He says that they were often regarded as 'unreliable, dangerous and treated as a laughing stock'.[15] Not surprisingly therefore, this group thought of itself as 'pariahs consumed with revenge'.[15] Within the East Indies context, all the Dutch writers were 'totoks', all were onlookers.

The general picture of the Indo largely corresponds with that of the 'coloured'. Like the 'coloured', the Indo also becomes an object of comic embellishment, whose incorrect usage of the Dutch language (*krompraat*), whose liberal insistence on bi-labials where one would normally find labio-dentals, and whose tendency to punctuate his speech pattern with onomatopoeic words and use the present tense and stops instead of open fricatives, never cease to amuse.

In this respect, Rob Nieuwenhuys quotes Ten Brink in his *Oost-Indische Spiegel* who remarked that, as far as the Dutch were concerned, there was 'nothing more uncharitable, more denigrating . . . than the arrogance of the Dutch towards the coloureds . . . . There seems to be no pleasanter form of amusement than to regale each other on the linguistic faults of the sinjos.'[16]

Herman, the Indo, in *Totok en Indo* (1915) by Jan Fabricius, is such a stereotype. He is good at heart, ludicrous, sentimental, responsible for all the laughs on stage, especially through the mixed prattle used by him and his friend Cornelis. The 'coloured' in Afrikaans literature is also comically appreciated for his *sê goed* (literally, say things, i.e. witticisms). Both the Indo and the 'coloured' have in the past objected to this stereotyped portrayal by the whiteman. Nieuwenhuys for instance, recalls the protest of the Indo against the play *Totok en Indo* when it was performed in Surabaya.

The Indo too is made to suffer under his mixed ancestry. The older generation emerges as docile, acquiescent, compliant and long-suffering. After years of service, an old man is usually bought off with a clock. The young ones are rebellious, yet psychologically messed up and consumed with hatred for the whites. They are duped into a situation whereby the fulfilment of their aspirations is frustrated by the one characteristic which is responsible for their peculiar position — their mixed ancestry.

Sam Portalis in *De Paupers* (1915) by Hans van de Wall, is such an obsequious, docile type. The younger generation express the feelings of many a half-caste when they fulminate: 'They say that they want to put us on a par with them, the Europeans . . . . Believe me, they despise us, because we are brown like the inlanders. Suppose my grandfather was white, then they would have given him some medal.'[17] Similar sentiments are re-echoed in Millin's book, *God's Step-children,* when the half-caste, Deborah, asks in utter exasperation: 'What is for me, then?'[18]

There are one or two elements in the South African novel which will not be found in the Dutch counterparts dealing with the Indo. The Dutch East Indies was, after all, still only a colonial possession, and the Dutch were eventually forced to leave and subsist on a longing for 'Our Indië' (Our East Indies). The paranoia which characterizes the South African portrayal is absent, as also the over-emphasis on the purity of the blood. Herman, in *Totok en Indo* is after all, still allowed to vie with the *totok,* Koeleman, for the hand of Georgina, the administrator's daughter. The mere suggestion of a 'coloured' competing for the favour and affection of a white woman, would have had South Africa up in arms, as it did when the Afrikaner writer, Brink, made the 'coloured', Josef Malan, sleep with a white woman in his novel *Kennis van die aand* (1974).

Wine does not seem to be such an essential component in the Indo make-up. But then the East Indies was not blessed with a wine-growing district, such as one finds in the Western Cape. Nor was there, in the East Indies, that peculiar relationship which existed between the farmer and his farm-hand. The 'tot' system, as we have already seen, is peculiarly South African.

The South African novel is generally characterized by an absence of any romantic associations or feelings of nostalgia or remorse. The associations are devoid of laughter, although this would be true even in the East Indies setting. The *njai* was, after all, nothing but a concubine who satisfied the sexual appetites of the *totok.* There is no folly or any form of spiritual intimacy.

The females in these novels are unprepossessing types, relegated to the animal kingdom, impelled by savagery and physical lust, the jetsam of society. The white males, on the other hand, are without exception degenerates or psychopaths with serious flaws in their characters, from the Reverend Andrew Flood and Coenraad Buys in Millin's works to Pieter van Vlaanderen in Paton's novel. They also live outside the normative structure of their group and group myths. Their offspring is doomed from the start. The attitude is one of Christian ethical norms on the one hand, and heathenism on the other. In the *oeuvre* of Sarah Gertrude Millin, there is no noble savage throwback which endows the savage with nobility, beauty and innate innocence. Miscegenation remains sinful.

The English were of course not ignorant of the stories about, for example, the old Nabobs, during the hey-day of colonialism. Susanne Howe comments:[19]

> The cheerfully earthy minds of the time were not squeamish
> about Anglo-native alliances and their resulting troops of brown
> children. There were a few such alliances in the early history
> of the Thackerays in India. But with the rise of Evangelical
> and middle class morality, the attitude changed. To be sure,
> a certain amount of liberal feeling about the dark races pre-
> vailed after the anti-slavery campaigns of Wilberforce
> and his cohorts, and after the equalitarian doctrines of the
> French revolution had swept a few dark-skinned little
> orphan boys or beautiful and virtuous Indian maidens into
> the novels of such large-minded radicals — often Unitarians
> or Quakers — as Amelia Opie, Mary Wollstonecraft, Robert
> Bage or Thomas Holcroft. But by 1834 when William
> Brown Hockley is lamenting the situation of these hybrids in the
> *Window of Calcutta*, the *Half-Caste Daughter and other Sketches*,
> it is clear that Rousseau and St. Pierre and all the 'Noble Savages'
> have lost ground.

Sarah Gertrude Millin was the daughter of a Jewish immigrant from Poland, who came to South Africa in 1888 when she was only five months old. She grew up with colour as an operative factor in her life. Her years on the Vaal River made a lasting impression on her. In her novels, various strands of South African racial life are explored.

Millin drew attention to her work from several quarters. Of her first novel, *The Dark River* (1919), no less a distinguished short-story writer than Katherine Mansfield remarked:

> Running through the book there is, as it were, a low, troubled
> throbbing note which is never stilled . . . . This low-
> throbbing note is essential to Mrs Millin's novel, and we
> must be very certain it is there, for though the story plays
> above and below it, that which gives it significance
> and holds our attention is the undertone.

The author was deeply, and one could say, sincerely, interested in race relations in her country of adoption. Her work was at least a

departure from the normal literary trend which until the twenties
largely ignored the race question. One learns that her sympathies
however, were with the 'Cape Man', of whom she says that he is:[20]

> the fruit of the vice, the folly, the thoughtlessness of the white
> man. In the old days — taking one aspect of the matter — there
> were colonists who, like the Biblical patriarchs or monarchs,
> had their official and their unofficial households, their white
> wives and their Hottentot hand-maids. But they used their
> slave-women as Abraham used Hagar rather than as Solomon
> used the Shulamite. The association was devoid of lyricism.
> No Hottentot girl ever preened herself before her white
> lord, declaiming: 'I am black, but comely'. When the
> Abrahams were done with their Hagars, they sent them
> with their Ishmaels into the wilderness.

Mrs Millin has some damning assessment of the 'Cape Man' for whom
she is supposed to have such an affection. She did not think well of the
intellectual and spiritual capacities of the half-caste. The 'Cape Man'
emerges as a pitiable creature, at the most a city dweller, comparable
to the lower classes of the East End of London, who however, in her
view, are still superior to the 'Coloured'. She writes:[21]

> And yet the less civilised white peasant of Europe is to this
> extent the coloured man's superior: the blood in him is
> stronger for advancement. Given the opportunity, the
> descendant of serfs may be a Tchekov. But the child of
> colour, unless his colour is attenuated to the verge of
> vanishing point, does not seem to have in him the ability to
> rise. It is as if the offspring of the originally mixed unions had,
> through generations, and through circumscription of life and
> interbreeding, achieved a definite, inferior, and static race:
> a race not given to wildness (its mothers were savages,
> but they were slaves); a race with something old and
> civilised about it (its fathers were Europeans); a race made
> up of weak materials and without the capacity for spiritual
> or intellectual growth. There are some who suggest that
> mixed breeds, unless replenished in a generation or two
> with the blood of one of the original stocks, tend to die out.

One would hate to think that this is the reason why 'sex across the
colour line' is so rife in pigmentocratic South Africa.

Colour was, and is, one of the major metaphors in South African fiction. At times the theme reaches almost paranoic proportions, like in the Afrikaans novel *Hans die Skipper* (1929), by D. F. Malherbe, where the white boy involved in a fight is told that only 'coloureds' do such things; not people of the white race.

Millin's first novel was appropriately called *The Dark River.* Here one is confronted with the spiritual and physical aridity of white spinsterdom against the backdrop of 'coloured' fecundity. The novel is set in the Transvaal, in the Vaal River diggings, where the authoress had also spent her youth.

An interesting facet is the white fascination with, and envy of, the blacks, who amidst all deprivation seem so much freer and happier than their overlords. Doris Lessing deals with this in her short stories, so does Millin in her novels. The African emerges as an enviable person in a situation which should conceivably call for tears.

The colour theme is an obsession with Millin. The half-caste is a tragic figure, miscegenation is mephistophelian, 'mixed blood' is something sinful. The problem is religiously pursued in her novel *Adam's Rest,* the predominant symbol once more being that of 'Smelling Strangeness'. The character, Miriam, shows a similar ambiguous attitude towards the blacks. It is partly compounded of revulsion and superiority and partly of envy. She envies the dignity of the African, the nearest Millin can get to endowing black people with at least a savage nobility. Miriam remarks of these half-breeds:[22]

> There must be something wrong at bottom. Look at their
> ancestry. It means a bad type of white man and a bad type
> of black woman to begin with. You know yourself, Janet,
> decent Kaffir women have nothing to do with white men.
> So that's one thing. Besides, it doesn't matter what it is. I
> can't work it out, but I have a feeling about colour as if it
> were a chtching disease — perhaps it is — and I don't want
> to be near it.

The offspring in *Adam's Rest*, of the Englishman and the Khoi woman, are true to the general pattern. First, the white progenitor is a misfit who is beyond caring and whose association with his woman is, to use Millin's idiom, 'devoid of lyricism'. The white man, Mr. Croft, is a 'blond, stout Yorkshireman without any inherited prejudices against colour, and he had married his half-caste woman without any love and also without any soul-searchings on questions of miscegenation'.[23]

The children are stereotyped into fair and dark, whereby the overall tragic implications of such unions are further underlined. The fair ones suffer more than the darker counterparts, being duped into thinking of themselves as part of the superior group in the system of ascribed roles. They are also more schizoid, perpetually haunted by the fear of discovery. Often this paralytic fear is responsible for their impotency, their inability to get sexually involved with women. Anthony's relationships in Gerald Gordon's novel, *Let the Day Perish* (1952), are practically purified of sexual advances and intimacy. The greater the aspiration, the harder the fall back into the cess pool of colour and of shanty towns and poverty. Again in *Adam's Rest* we read:[24]

> Miriam was sorry for everyone. For the wretched Kaffirs, —
> the hopeless bÿwoners, even the aspiring Crofts. Was it,
> after all, their fault they had black blood in them? How
> awful it was to be born damned. That boast of theirs —
> they *kept* themselves white, how pathetic!

Sarah Gertrude Millin's *God's Step-children* was the climax of this genre, a tale of miscegenation unparalleled in South African fiction. The Reverend Flood (Millin probably had the missionary van der Kemp in mind here) is an Englishman who decides to marry a Khoi woman, Silla, after an abortive love affair with an English girl. The Reverend Flood's main intention is to prove that all people are created equal in the eyes of God. Right at the beginning, the reader is confronted with one of the key themes in Millin's works (and I am not sure whether one should not even regard it as the main theme). The Reverend Flood is having a conversation with one of the Khoi characters, Calchas, which proceeds as follows:[25]

> 'We are all God's children', he said.
> 'But is God Himself not white?' asked Calchas.
> And, as the Rev. Andrew Flood hesitated for a reply, she made
> a suggestion:
> 'Perhaps, we brown people are His stepchildren', she said.

One is confronted with various generations of the Flood clan, and the effect of their mixed-bloodedness on their spiritual and moral development. The story ends with the whitest of them all, Barry Lindsell, abandoning his wife and unborn child, by way of expiation for his crime of colour; and for neglecting his people, the 'coloureds', to preach (like his first forebear) the message of Christianity to them.

In so doing, he completes the circle. Barry's atonement is also for his great-great grandfather, the Reverend Andrew Flood.

Out of this union between the Reverend Flood and Silla, is born a daughter, Deborah. Flood emerges as a bungling fool, a mockery to whites and Khoi alike, a tragic failure and an incorrigible misfit. Mrs Millin's portrayal of missionaries in no way reflects creditably on this ostensibly liberal breed. Quite early in the novel she clearly indicates that not all the Reverend Floods can stem the tide of heathenism, or expunge such tendencies from the wretched souls of the Khoi. When, for example, Silla's boy is in the throes of death, she is made to resort quite naturally to heathen practices, notwithstanding her marriage and proximity to a man of God, presumably to emphasize her savage nature.

Of the Reverend Flood, Millin writes:[26]

By the time the Rev. Andrew Flood had been at Canaan for fifteen years he was himself in many ways, a savage. He was dirty and unkempt and wild-looking; he seldom read; he wrote to no one; he knew nothing that was going on in the big world; and it embarrassed him to meet a civilized person.

The daughter, Deborah, who is slightly fairer, is placed with another missionary couple and given the opportunity to attend school. But she also falls prey to stereotyped ideas. She is described as:[27]

not unintelligent . . . . She had, as most half-caste children have, a capacity for imitation. She copied the manners and habits − even the gestures and intonations − of Mrs Burtwell. She seemed to learn quickly, too, but only to a certain extent. Inevitably the point would be reached where a solid barrier of unreceptivity would hinder all further mental progress.

Even Mr Burtwell, the white missionary, is made to think that[28]

a child with a white father might be different. He knew that native children arrived at their full capacity very early. At the age of four or five they were far in advance of white children of the same age; but at the age of fourteen or fifteen, they begin to falter, to lag behind, to remain stationary while their white competitors went ahead.

Deborah is destined for tragedy. She first has an affair with a full-blooded Khoi, much to the disgust of the Burtwells, who attribute it (as does Deborah) to the savage half in her. Later on she has an affair with Kleinhans, a white man, which similarly displeases the Burtwells and culminates in the young girl's *cri de coeur,* and what Mrs Millin sees as the extreme dilemma of the half-caste: 'You say black is not for me; you say white is not for me. What is for me, then?'[29]

Out of this chance association with the white man, Kleinhans, is born a son, who is fair, a bundle of contradictions and who eventually marries a half-caste from the Cape, whose 'father had been a German ... and [whose] mother a coloured woman, with a little Malay blood in her and a little St Helena blood and the usual incursion of white blood'.[30] Unto them is born a girl, Elmira, who is so white that the employers, the Lindsells, resent her presence. She is of course unmasked for the fraud that she is, when her parents visit her in her 'white' school during a severe illness. Poor little Elmira then carries the cry of Deborah a little further by pathetically asking her parents: 'Why did you come?'[31]

Elmira is now only good enough to consort with, or marry, the old fossil and widower, Lindsell, by whom she bears a 'white' son, Barry. She then runs away to Cape Town, only to beget another 'white' illegitimate child. Barry is left ultimately in the charge of one of his spinster half-sisters (one of the sexually deprived types in the Millin *oeuvre*).

This blood saga reaches its climax when Barry is summoned to the death bed of his mother where he is forcibly confronted with his 'coloured' ancestry. He then decides to leave his English wife and unborn child to serve his people, like the first white progenitor, the Reverend Andrew Flood.[32]

'This is my vow', he said at last.
'For my sin in begetting him, I am not to see my child.
And, for the sorrow I share with them, I am to go among
my brown people to help them.'

This horror saga is continued in the novel, *The Herr Witch-doctor,* where the chief characters are the two 'white' half-caste brothers, the sons of Elmira. Failure, frustration, tragedy and horror are the operative symbols. The illegitimate half-brother has ironically imbibed all the arrogance of his white father, as a result of which he liberally indulges in 'sex across the colour line'. His half-brother takes after the founder of their ill-begotten clan, the missionary, Reverend Andrew Flood, and like him, proves ineffectual in living out his creed.

The one character who personifies miscegenation on a large scale in Southern African (Afrikaner) history is Coenraad Buys, the first white man in the Transvaal. Millin has immortalized him in fiction in her novel, *King of the Bastards*. Buys had populated the country with a menagerie of black and brown descendants, who still live in the Transvaal to this very day as an independent clan.

In a very illuminating foreword, one of South Africa's Prime Ministers and statesmen, General Smuts, who was a close friend of the novelist writes:[33]

> The story is ostensibly the history of the origins of a very small
> coloured or half-breed community in South Africa, the Buys
> family, in the Northern Transvaal, descendants of one white
> man, Coenraad Buys, and his harem of native women. But
> in reality, it is much more. It is, in the first place, the story
> of Coenraad Buys himself, and of his progress like some demi-
> god through the welter of confusion which reigned in South
> Africa in the latter part of the eighteenth and nineteenth
> centuries. And, in the second place, we get a picture of South
> African horror such as has never been painted before.

It is interesting that a man like Smuts, who was to be Prime Minister of South Africa on several occasions, and who was generally respected in the English-speaking world, should have referred to the story as a 'South African horror'.

The aberration of Coenraad Buys is explained in terms of his mother's four husbands. 'Sleeping black' was his way of taking revenge, or so we are given to understand. The way he is whisked out of the story is as undramatic and unconvincing as the attempted psychological explanations of his flaws.

Only Maria, the old Khoi wife, is half-sympathetically drawn, if more for her animal-like attachment to Coenraad and his equally strong affection for her; very much like that of a master for his pet dog, whose unquestioning loyalty sustains when all else is silent. Buys himself is seen against the 'noble savage' tradition of the eighteenth and nineteenth centuries, a type more readily found in the novels of Stuart Cloete. In a review of the novel, the *Star* newspaper of Johannesburg wrote:[34]

> The tall imposing figure of Coenraad Buys is one that flits in and
> out of the history of the Cape Eastern frontier of 150 years ago —
> but on the whole more out than in. He was a product of the
> wild frontier between white and black, a man at odds not only
> with authority but with the community of which he at first

formed a part . . . He might have come to be regarded as the
greatest among his people but for one thing: his women were
black; his family were the coloured rabble that ended as
Buysvolk kept apart from other people in a land of their
own.

Coenraad Buys straddles the book like a colossus:[35]

> When Coenraad presently rose, he almost touched the ceiling.
> He looked − his face and body − majestic. He wore that
> expression . . . which was not so much an outward as an
> inward smile − an expression of superiority befitting a god.

The book opens with the, all too familiar, tableau of an *indaba*
(council), evoking images of patriarchal Boers during the Great Trek
on the one hand, and colourful meetings of blacks on the other. Louis
Buys is speaking:[36]

> Look, I said the day I joined the Council, 'the whites are the
> conquerors and all is theirs. A man's one hope is among the
> whites . . . . The thing for the Buys-volk to do is to get back
> to the whites'.

The novel starts with the council and ends with one. The final epitaph
is by old Michael Buys when he says: 'Coenraad de Buys. Coenraad
de Buys. White Man'.[37] The message is rather obvious and tragic, that
for the half-breed, salvation can only be gotten, if they join the white
man, who however despises them.

Millin's attitude towards miscegenation and the half-caste is re-
echoed in the works of Stuart Cloete, who was slightly less productive,
but no less wellknown. His first novel, *The Turning Wheels* (1937),
has as its major theme the Great Trek, and was on the banned list in
South Africa for a long time. The novel is essentially an enchanting
story of heroism and love, furstration and jealousy among the Trekkers.
His male Boer specimens are colossal.

However, if white South Africa was perturbed by anything, then
it was the suggestion and demonstration in Cloete's works, whether
covertly or overtly, that the patriarchal Boer Trekker was not only
lord of the jungle, but also a lusty sexual animal who sought release
with his coloured hand-maid in the process of which he fathered a
host of half-breeds. His novel was therefore forbidden fare, although
I recollect reading it, as did many others, in those few stolen hours
and then returning it to the safe confines of the mattress cover.

Most of the Cloete *oeuvre* is about Boer history. His second novel, *Watch for the Dawn* (1939), takes us back to the Slagtersnek rebellion of 1815.[38] Subsequent novels deal with other periods, for example *The Hill of Doves* (1941), set against the Boer War of 1880-1.

Stuart Cloete's male (Boer) characters have a savage, primitive strength. They are awesome, enviable creatures, resplendent in their physical superiority. The Boer Trekker in *The Mask* (1957) is such a specimen:[39]

> Every day Simon became more attached to Potgieter, who seemed to him the ideal Voortrekker, one of those who went in front, a strong, bold, resourceful pioneer, a wonderful shot and horseman [a man in whom is embodied] all the virtues of the frontier [who is blessed with] muscles that bulged under his shirt . . . great thighs that gripped his bay horse . . . the grizzled black virility of his beard . . . one who would not die but could only be killed in some terrible adventure.

The novelist sees miscegenation as an inevitable part of survival in the wilds, where 'time was out of joint and no one was his own' (the white apologia for co-habitation with black and brown people). 'Miscegenation', Cloete says, by way of one of his characters, 'is proximity . . . . What went on between Mark Antony and Cleopatra was miscegenation . . . the choice [was probably] between miscegenation and death. Death from loneliness, drink or disease, or a combination of all three.'[40]

Cloete is as damning in his assessment of the non-white as is Sarah Gertrude Millin. To him, the blacks would always be in need of 'some white direction'. He continues to say that they (the blacks) 'think they know it all, and are not ready to wait and learn the rest'.[41]

Millin and Cloete are closer to the Afrikaans novelist tradition in terms of the colour question. Afrikaans literature has generally maintained an eerie silence on this theme. Apart from novelists like Regina Neser, with her almost cherry-ripe evocations of blonde, blue-eyed, pink-cheeked arrivals in 'coloured' families, and Coetzee's poor attempt to raise the bogey of blood purity, there are few examples which even parallel Alan Paton's *Too Late the Phalarope* (1953). There is, in South African fiction, nothing comparable to the four books on miscegenation by Edgar Mittelholzer, the West Indian writer, in which the reader is panoramically confronted with 'the Dutch Adrianson van Groenwegel, with his European intellectuality, restraint and sexual mores, on the other . . . the wild intuitive and uninhibited stock of Kaywana'.[42] Possibly the subject was too painful for many an Afrikaans writer, who without exception moved within the group myth. Possibly Calvinism (and the group myth), serves as a greater instrument of, what I would like to call, the violence of uniformity and conformity, which is typical of both the right and the left.

Abel Coetzee's novel, *Waarheen vader?* (1940), is fairly representative of the fear-psychosis which infects white South Africa at the mere suggestion of a trace of colour in the family. His book is a clarion call for the purity of the tribe and the Aryan blood cult. It is no accident that Dr Dönges[43] cited an essay by Olive Schreiner, the novel *Kinders van Ishmaël* by Regina Neser and Sarah Gertrude Millin's *God's Stepchildren* in support of his proposed law against mixed marriages in 1949. All these books conceived of mixtures as tragic and sinful products of white and black, and by implication, preached purity of the tribe. Coetzee's story fits into this category.

The story follows the familiar pattern of the ostensibly white family, whose dreams are rudely shattered by the birth of their 'outwardly coloured' child. It is a tragedy which initially rumbles subterraneously, and then erupts to cause the general disintegration of the Bastiaans clan. The symbolism employed by Coetzee is gross, overplayed and banal, like, for instance, the overworking of white as a symbol. One stumbles upon the 'white glare of the light' and the 'white calm in the dining room', which becomes intolerable to the father. The message is rather crudely spelt out, uncouth at times in its grotesqueness and insistence on blood purity.

Millin, Cloete and Coetzee, are all rather conservative in their approach to the colour question, and can only conceive of it in tragic terms. The 'coloured' emerges as 'the fruit of the vice, the folly, the thoughtlessness of the white man'.[44]

But not all South African authors use this theme in support of the theory of race purity. Some are genuinely liberal in view and exploit the theme to show the wickedness of a system which attaches so much importance to colour, that people are driven to commit suicide. Gerald Gordon's book, *Let the Day Perish* (1952), is such an empathetic plea for understanding, and, by implication, an indictment against the immorality laws.

On the jacket of his novel, one reads:[45]

The problem of the Coloured population of South Africa is the most pressing which confronts the world today. Uneasily poised

between the two worlds of white and black, holding their
rights on sufferance only, the position of people born of mixed
parentage is seldom easy and can often become intolerable.

It is the story of two brothers, the one white enough 'to pass', the
other, definitely 'coloured'. But Gordon's novel is not a celebration
of the cult of the purity of the blood. Rather, the author uses his
material to expose the inhumanity of apartheid.

The whites in his book are portrayed as bigoted and steeped in
racial prejudice. Characteristically, one of the white characters is a
German with the unflattering name of Hundt. His wife, Ruby, shines
through her aridity and non-fecundity. Hundt exploits Mary, the
beautiful 'coloured' woman, when he helps her realize her dream,
that is, to get her son Anthony admitted to a white school. In satisfying his lusts, Mary becomes the symbol of the historical European
myth of warm-bloodedness.

George, the white man who spawned these 'bastards', is depicted
in a way which does not differ markedly from the portrayals of similar
types encountered in South African novels. He is the black sheep
of the family and has a weak personality.

In Anthony, his 'white son', are concentrated all the myths of white
ethno-aestheticians. He is blond and handsome, virile and popular, a
sportsman of no mean ability — a veritable Apollo. In contrast, his
'coloured' brother, Stephen, carries his darkness heavily. He broods, is
introspective, frail, and later on becomes a passionate advocate of
freedom for his people. This latter trait at least ensures him a certain
moral ascendancy over his brother Anthony.

Mary, their 'coloured' mother, is beautiful and submissive (she for
instance meekly submits to Hundt for the sake of her child). Yet
Anthony is still ultimately destroyed. Towards the end of his trial,
he undergoes the ultimate degradation a white man can undergo in
South Africa, when he admits to a trace of colour in his blood:[46]

Gentlemen, now perhaps you will understand why I lied to the
police. You see, this isn't the first time I have stood in the
dock . . . . We were tried for the acts of our ancestors, were
convicted and sentenced to live in a world of prejudice. Even
if you acquit me now, that sentence still stands. It stands
until my earthly existence comes to a close. With Job I can
truly say:'Let the day perish wherein I was born and the
night in which it was said, There is a man child conceived'.

Although two people are prepared to stand by him, Anthony ultimately chooses to commit suicide. One would tend to judge harshly on such an ostensibly melodramatic exit, were it not for periodic reports in South African papers of well-known farmers (Afrikaners at that), who after being 'caught in the act', choose a shameful death in preference to a lifetime of racial prejudice and ostracism.

Gerald Gordon with his *Let the Day Perish* (1952), Alan Paton with *Cry the Beloved Country* (1948) and *Too Late the Phalarope* (1953) and Athol Fugard with *The Blood Knot* (1963), all portray a realism in which the non-white is at least a victim of the system of ascribed roles.

Paton especially became well known through his *Cry the Beloved Country*. He is genuinely accepted as a Christian in a country where such breeds are few and far between. He is imbued with, and impelled by, a spirit of liberal humanitarianism and is the one writer in South Africa who has relentlessly preached 'adjustment and forgiveness'. He has been accused of portraying the African as a good-natured soul by African critics and has also been accused of maudlin sentimentality by Afrikaner critics, notably, P. G. du Plessis. Yet nowhere does Paton's plea for understanding come out so clearly as in his novel *Too Late the Phalarope*. Here the concentration is on the inevitable sanctions of Afrikaner society which follow such aberrations. Paton has succeeded in building up a picture of human and personal tragedy, during the course of which the insularity of the Afrikaner microcosmos is laid bare with a razor's edge.

Pieter van Vlaanderen, the main character, is both victim and hero, who transgresses his tribe's rule of sleeping with a black woman. His name is scrapped from the family Bible and he himself is proscribed into eternal oblivion. The picture of the dour Calvinist, fearful in the sight of God, but fearless and ferocious in his hatred of those who transgress the ethics of his tribe, is frightening.

The story is rather sympathetically reported through the eyes of an aunt. It is couched in Biblical terms, which imparts to the whole something of a lament, and conveys to the seduction scene a David and Bathsheba aura. Pieter van Vlaanderen, like all such characters, is a dual personality, effeminate, strong and popular, yet tragically doomed. His tragedy, it seems, should be imputed to his strict and authoritarian father, the Biblical patriarch, plucked straight from the Old Testament. Pieter's interest in philately is explained as a feminine protest against the overwhelming emphasis on virility in Afrikaner society. Martin Tucker (1967) draws attention to the phalarope as a symbol of 'sexual misplacement'.[47] All white authors provide their heroes with such psychological excuses. Their heroes can not simply indulge in their sexual urges or have affairs without having some serious flaw in their character, which is either traceable to the parents or to some awful childhood experience. Even the 'coloured' author, Peter Abrahams, in his novel, *Path of Thunder,* operates well within the tragic, violent and inevitable stereotype of the half-caste.

In the South African setting, 'trying for white', 'playing white'· or being 'a play white' and 'passing for white' are very operative terms. This is poignantly portrayed in Athol Fugard's *The Blood Knot* (1963). Since perception is all important in South Africa, the problem of whether a person is really white or 'coloured', can at times be enormous. In Fugard's drama, the crux of the problem is revealed in the scene between the ostensibly white and the openly 'coloured' brother. By way of bizarre diversion, they decide to act out their racially ascribed roles in society. In the process they get so carried away that the resultant scene is one of wry humour and biting satire. It is however when the outwardly white brother calls his darker counterpart *swartgat* (black arse), that mere playfulness turns into grim reality. For, in that term, is contained for the 'coloured' brother, all the painful and traumatic experiences of apartheid. Shocked into an awareness that they had crossed the institutionalized borders, the two brothers in a chastening scene carry on the following dialogue:[48]

> Zacharias: 'Morris?'
> Morris: 'Yes?'
> Zacharias: 'What happened?'
> Morris: 'You mean . . .?'
> Zacharias: 'Ja'.
> Morris: 'We were carried away, as they would say, by the game . . .
> quite far in fact. Musn't get worried though . . . I don't think. I
> mean, it was only a game . . . as long as we play in the right
> spirit.'

Yet, ultimately, it is the aura of 'smelling strangeness' and 'the futility of coloured life' which lingers on in all these books. The 'coloured' woman will become 'brown, bronze and comely' the day South African novelists stop portraying her as a sex object. As long as mixing is looked upon as being sinful, then one will be subjected to the type of novel discussed in this chapter.

# Chapter 4

# Little sorrow sits and weeps[1]

In the preceding chapter, we have had an indication of how painful the process of maturation must be for adults in South Africa. Complicated as it already is, this process must be even doubly painful for children and is a double-edge sword in that it also affects the white child. In children then, are to be found all the horrible and traumatic effects of the system of apartheid.

This is sadly portrayed in that oft-cited poem, *Incident*, by the American black poet, Countee Cullen, albeit in a different context.[2]

> Once riding in old Baltimore
> Heart-filled, head-filled with glee,
> I saw a Baltimorean
> Keep looking straight at me.
>
> Now I was eight and very small,
> And he was no whit bigger,
> And so I smiled, but he poked out,
> His tongue, and called me, 'Nigger'
>
> I saw the whole of Baltimore
> From May until December.
> Of all the things that happened there
> That's all that I remember.

If the adult half-caste is caught between 'smelling strangeness'[3] and colour as a 'catching disease'[4] then the white and black children are ensconced between 'painful awareness' and 'terrified consciousness'.[5] This is excellently illustrated in a passage in *Wide Sargasso Sea* (1966)

71

by Jean Rhys. The ex-slaves are burning down the plantation of the Cosgraves in the West Indies. Annette, in her utter bewilderment, runs to her trusted playmate, a little black girl, for protection and comfort:[6]

> I ran to her, for she was all that was left of my life as it had been.
> We had eaten the same food, slept side by side, bathed in the same
> river. As I ran, I thought, I will live with Tia and I will be like
> her . . .. When I was close I saw the jagged stone in her hand but
> I did not see her throw it. I did not feel it either, only something
> wet, running down my face. I looked at her and I saw her face
> crumple up as she began to cry. We stared at each other, blood
> on my face, tears on hers. It was as if I saw myself. Like in a
> looking-glass.

Childhood, initiation into adulthood, the process of growing up, are oft-recurring themes in what is sometimes referred to as third world literature. There are, for instance, numerous examples of West Indian writers who have exploited this particular theme. Geoffrey Drayton uses it in his novel, *Christopher* (1959). George Lamming's *In the Castle of my Skin* (1953) is largely about the process of growing up and an awareness of the wider world in Barbados. Other examples are Michael Anthony's *The Year in San Fernando* (1965), Austin Clarke's *Among Thistles and Thorns* (1965), Vidia Naipaul's *A House for Mr Biswas* (1961), Samuel Selvon's *A Brighter Sun* (1952) and Ian McDonald's *The Humming-Bird Tree* (1974).

It is not an accident of fiction that all these writers are from the third world, nor that they write so profusely about children. Children in third world societies constitute an important part of the population. The poor are, after all, prolific in their breeding propensities. Birth control is a moral, ethical or academic matter which weighs heavily on the white mind. Procreation is the only form of creativity and creation allowed to the poor, for in this special realm, the white world cannot impinge. The third world child is not enshrined in his childhood from birth, as is his white counterpart. He cannot at all times rely on that special form of protection from his family, his birth is largely an accident. Right from the start, he is surrounded by the socio-economic conditions of poverty, illiteracy and the vain attempts to survive it all.

From birth, the non-white child in a plural society is already on the threshold of adulthood, with all the attendant problems of the poverty-stricken extended family, crowded rooms and a complete lack of privacy. All too often he is the unwilling spectator of, and witness to, the sex life of his parents, their frequent spells of inebriation, their numerous bouts of fisticuffs.[7] He is confronted with life in the raw at a very tender age. There is no cultural divide between him and the grown-ups. They know as little as he does, and have as little chance as he does to escape it all. Adulthood and adult responsibilities are thrust upon him at a time when he or she should still be indulging in a world of youthful fantasy and dreams. The non-white child is not cocooned in some form of Reynoldsian cherry-ripeness, the romantic cult of childhood, as is the European child.

There is an immediacy about stories focusing on children. Usually these deal with a specific breed of children, who reveal themselves as very sensitive barometers of their environment. Such a child is also spontaneous in his criticism of his world and his society. He is not yet burdened with experience, an overdose of knowledge and prejudices, although little sorrow is already sitting and weeping in his sleep. The child observes things from within his small micro-cosmos and can be very accurate. His vision is somewhat of a 'God's eye-view', as the Afrikaner writer Aucamp once called it.

The author must at all times be cognizant of the child's world. Any attempt to impose his world or vision on the child will have a deleterious effect on the credibility of the child vision. As we shall see later on, the South African writer and poet, James Matthews, fails to bring off his story, *The Park*, precisely because of his overt intrusion at times, as a result of which his 'coloured' child becomes a glorified carrier of a political message. In reading through stories concentrating on the black child, one is forcibly reminded of the West Indian novelist George Lamming's warning that 'colonialism (racialism) has been as much a white experience as a black one'.[8]

In Afrikaans literature, the 'coloured' child pops up as a silent ghost in the backyard of a white mansion, hanging about until his mother, the domestic, has finished her daily chores for the madam and the master. As viewer and viewpoint, the 'coloured' child is sometimes used as a means of social protest against a system of racial denial. Of those white and non-white writers who have exploited this theme of the child within the peculiar South African system of ascribed roles, the most outstanding are Dan Jacobson with his *Beggar My Neighbour,* Elise Muller with *Die Peertak* (lit. The Pear Branch) and James Matthews with *The Park*. These three persons represent various strands of the South African pigmentocracy, namely, white Jewish, white Afrikaner and 'coloured'.

The child theme is usually dealt with from two vantage points: from that of the secure base of the white child, which gradually crumbles into a form of insecurity; or from the insecure base of the non-white child, which leads to a fuller realization of his tenuous position in society.

Ronald Segal, a white South African and an ardent opponent of the system, spells out the position of the whites when he writes: 'White children in South Africa seem to accept the implications of race as they grow to distinguish shapes and smells and sounds, so that, almost as they begin to speak, they tighten their voices to colour.'[9]

Of their 'coloured' boy, who in reality is a full-grown man, he says: 'I never thought of him as having any children; he was the Coloured "boy", ageless, whose condition and function alike were contradicted by the equality of children.'[10] He confesses that, as a child, he had tried to dismiss him from his mind but he was always there, 'a person, human beyond hiding'.[10]

Segal has, of course, only given painful expression to that shocking realization most South Africans must, perforce, make once in their lives – the black presence in their society.

Dingetjie (lit. Little Thing), the 'coloured' girl in Elise Muller's story, *Die Peertak* (The Pear Branch), contained in her anthology, *Die Vrou op die skuit* (Woman on the Boat), stands for many a servant child, and is linked umbilically to the black and brown characters of another South African short-story writer, Pauline Smith (see: *Platkops Children*, 1935, *The Little Karroo*, 1925, *The Beadle*, 1926). Smith's Classina, who is black, and Muller's Dingetjie, play out their ascribed roles as child servants, a breed immortalized in the paintings of Cape Dutch *Kombuise* (kitchens).

Dingetjie sees her world collapsing when white technology impinges on her world of fantasy and glamour. She had been, for example, accorded the singular privilege of shooing away the flies during the Sunday culinary orgies of the white family, with her pear branch. Her task affords her a peep into the white world of ritualized order, glitter and opulence. This is her dream world, belonging as she does to the dispossessed in her country. Yet, ironically, despite this seemingly humiliating and lowly role, she is still one up on the other 'coloured' children on the farm, because she is close to the fairyesque world of the whites. In her is therefore concentrated all the pathos and (by inference) the irony, the iniquity of a society which disposes of its vast favours so frugally to the poor.

But essentially this is a story of a little 'coloured' girl whose fantasy world is destroyed because the white family decides to use a spray to get rid of the flies. It is the 'coloured' mother who must once again explain white ways and who must cushion her child against the hurt of white society. The story is loaded with implications as are those of Pauline Smith.

Self-discovery for the black and brown child often involves self-destruction. The child that the non-white child discovers is himself. The initiation of the non-white child in South Africa into the adult world is a painful and harrowing process.

Muller's *Twee Gesigte* (Two Faces) in the same anthology illustrates this beautifully. But here she allows the white child's innocence also to be destroyed. And herein lies the strength of this particular story. The centre of action is the fairyesque world of children, one white, the other 'coloured'. Muller chooses the arrival of a merry-go-round as the basis for her story. The children's imaginations run riot at the mere thought of the merry-go-round in their village. Katrien, the 'coloured' child, is depicted as being precocious both in body and in mind. For white South Africa, she was fast approaching servant status. Yet, she was a mere child, as old as her white friend, Rina. Together Katrien and Rina dream about this momentous event in their lives. On the other hand, there is Rosa, who is also white and fairly well instructed in her ascribed role.

Muller has the ability to evoke the socio-political situation without ever falling into the abyss of didacticism. The children need three pence to have a ride. Katrien knows with the certitude of all her prematureness and 'colouredness' that Rina, her friend, would get money from her father. How she, Katrien, would get hers was another matter. In child-like innocence, Rina asks: '"Is your father going to . . ." She hesitates. She had momentarily forgotten that Katrien's father was dead, that for this reason, Katrien no longer attended school.'[11]

The world of Rina and Rosa is one of self-assurance and of security. They are already the ritual heirs to their protected world. The park attendant who is normally so friendly with white children, turns into a monster when he has to deal with 'coloureds'. Rina witnesses the fairyesque world of her 'coloured' friend being blown to pieces. To the attendant, Katrien was just another 'coloured' who tried to cheat by pretending that she was younger than she was. So he refuses to let her have a ride for the price of a child and forcibly chucks her off the horse. In so doing, he initiates two children, the one white, the other 'coloured', into the adult South African world of prejudice and hatred. Two worlds blown to pieces. A fantasy turned into a nightmare. Only Rosa is left unmoved, selfish as she already is.

Pauline Smith in her *Platkops Children* confronts the reader with the white child's 'God's eye-view' of colonialism. Here too one encounters a breed so facilely exploited in colonial and racial fiction — the warm, understanding and loving servant — who is, ironically, the emotional still point in the white child's life, while the mothers go traipsing around, either running useless charity organizations or simply playing bridge or golf.

One of the best symbolic portrayals is to be found in Dan Jacobson's *Beggar My Neighbour*. The little white boy, Michael, grows up as an only child in his neighbourhood, firmly imprisoned in the castle of his white skin. But through his protective vizor, two black children manage to thrust themselves, a boy and a gril, who with their pathetically heart-rending and plaintive 'a stukkie brood' (lit. a piece of bread) rupture his serene and virginal world. Michael is at first surprised at this intrusion, but then drawn to them because [12]

> the boy was holding one of the girl's hands in his . . . . He was touched by their dependence on one another, and disturbed by it too, as he had been by the way they had suddenly come before him, and by their watchfulness and silence after they had uttered their customary, begging request.

They follow him home, he orders the servant to give them bread, and is then denied the pleasure of seeing them gobbling it up. 'He wanted to see them eat it; he wanted to share their pleasure in satisfying their strained appetites.'[13] But they withdrew. The cycle is repeated. Symbolically they re-enact their racially ascribed roles. Michael weaves the children into his fantasies which are numerous. Invariably, he is their protector, their guardian angel, their shining knight in armour, rescuing them with the boundless magnanimity of his whiteness.

He gives them a torch one day, shows them an expensive fountain pen which they want, much to his disgust and horror. In the end he wants to be rid of them, tells them to *voertsek*.[14] Jacobson works it to a beautiful, haunting and symbolic ending. Michael falls ill, but cannot rid himself of the children in his half-dream world. The haunting spectre of their black presence is always there like an African tokoloshe.[15] At the end of these agonizingly poignant spells, he takes the children into his home, thereby already crashing through one of the barriers of his whiteness. And in a scene of infinite clarity and tenderness, Michael loses his fear and touches them, realizing at last what they wanted to impart to him:[16]

> Michael looked from the one to the other; and he remembered
> what he had been doing to them in his dreams. Their eyes were
> black to look into, deep black. Staring forward, Michael under-
> stood what he should have understood long before: that they
> came to him not in hope or appeal or even in reproach, but
> in hatred. What he felt towards them, they felt towards him;
> what he had done to them in his dreams they did to him in
> theirs.

Here for the first time then, the white boy crashes through his white skin. Before, the children had always squatted outside, waiting for their 'stukkie brood':[17]

> And Michael knew that what he had to give them was not toys
> or clothes or bread, but something more difficult . . . . He took
> the girl's face in his hands and pressed his lips to hers. He was
> aware of the darkness of her skin, and the smell of it, and of the
> faint movement of her lips, a single pulse that beat momentarily
> against his own. Then it was gone. He kissed the boy, too, and
> let them go. They came together, and grasped each other by
> the hand staring at him.

After his recovery, he looks for them in vain. 'He saw a hundred, a thousand, children like them; but not the two he hoped to find.'[18]

James Matthews, on the other hand, writes about the plight of the 'coloured' child in more direct, political terms. In the case of his short story, *The Park,* the 'coloured' boy's dream is frustrated by the 'whites only' sign at the gate. Ironically, the park attendant, who is 'coloured', has the painful task of enforcing discriminating laws against his own people. 'His voice apologizing for the uniform he wore which gave him the right to be in the park to watch that the little whites were not hurt while playing.'[19]

*The Park* comes close to being a political pamphlet, but is saved by the naiveté of the child. At times, the boy does achieve something of the symbolic breakthrough of a Michael in Dan Jacobson's story. But the low-throbbing note of the 'Rage against the houses with their streaked walls and smashed window panes filled by too many people',[20] is contained within the story with great difficulty. While Jacobson's story may be technically superior, it is the crude reality of the 'col-oured' boy's existence in the story by Matthews which prevails.

In contrast to these South African short-story writers, there is the Flemish authoress, Mireille Cottenje, who wrote of the plight of a child who was classified as 'coloured' while the rest of her family remained white. This may sound an inconceivable dilemma to a European, but it is very real for certain South Africans. *Het Grote Onrecht* (The Great Injustice) is the story of Sandra Laing,[21] a girl of 10 or 11 years who was found to have 'coloured' features and blood (sic), and then re-classified accordingly. This meant her leaving her parents, her white environment and white friends and living in a strange, 'coloured' environment. Cottenje traces some of the legal, psychological and sociological implications of such an act for the family and the little girl. The book is really intended as a children's story, harrowing and bizarre though the subject matter may be. Everything that happens to little Sandra Laing (her name in real life), is seen through the eyes of her 'white' brother. Cottenje avoids some of the pitfalls of straightforward politicization, largely because her language remains fairly simple (and because she does not overtly intrude when referring to apartheid laws).

She is very successful in sketching the atmosphere of captivity and fear which prevails and also the haunting spectre of colour. She fails however to sustain this, especially towards the end when the re-classification is final. She allows the little boy, who is very attached to his sister, to run away with her to neighbouring Mozambique, where they experience some fleeting, but awesome, moments at the border. Here however, officialdom seems to be more benign. The children 'phone their parents in South Africa, who tell them they have decided to emigrate. The crudity of the South African situation, cast in fictionalized form, can sometimes appear even cruder and Cottenje does not avoid this danger towards the end. The running away of the children is too contrived, too improbable to ring true. The treatment of the children at the border of Mozambique is too fanciful. However, it is a slim but laudable attempt to move away from the 'romantic cult' of the child.

Running through all these child, 'God's-eye-views', is that 'terrified consciousness' used to suggest the white minority's sensations of shock and disorientation as a massive and smouldering black population is released into an awareness of its power.[22]

The dilemma of the child is summed up by O'l Boss in Ian McDonald's *The Humming-Bird Tree* (1974):[23]

> Two other things add up the thing worse. One is colour, one is white, an' when you is chile that don't matter a ant's tit.

But grow up an' the whole thing cheapen up like the pretties' bird rotting. An' another thing too besides. I say the whole worl' is only a dam little morsel of a place . . . . When you lose you' firs' richness what have you to expan' to?

# Chapter 5

# Sons of Hagar[1]

This image of the 'Cape coloured' has hitherto largely been distilled from the writings of white South African authors. The pictures which will henceforth be abstracted will be mainly from the writings of non-white authors. Occasional excursions into the works of white authors will still however be functionally necessary from time to time. The 'Sestigers', for example, will be dealt with, but then firmly within the argument seen hitherto, that is, white Afrikaner, brown Afrikaner. Some of the 'coloured' authors will move within various shades of the well-known syndromes of ambiguity, near-kinship, the practice of 'playing white' and race consciousness. Others will indicate the path towards a more broader, non-racial path and constitute what St Clair Drake the American anthropologist calls[2]

> a considerable minority of social scientists who remain cultural
> relativists, of poets and artists who refuse to abandon the point
> of view of romantic primitivists; and of relentless social critics . . .
> the really creative type of pluralism as opposed to that arising
> from ethnic differences.

Few 'coloureds' write in Afrikaans, despite the fact that the language is fairly widespread among them. Moreover, there are definite signs that many are moving away from the language and even becoming increasingly hostile to it. Only Petersen, Philander and Adam Small have earned places in Afrikaans literary handbooks. Of these, only Petersen has a novel to his credit (although Eddie Domingo wrote one in a similar vein called *Okkies op die breë pad*).

Petersen was born in Riversdale, the Cape Province, in 1914. His first anthology, *Die Enkeling* (lit. The Lonely One), was published in 1944. Dekker (1947) devoted a very brief note to Petersen's poetry and pointed out that here, for the first time in Afrikaans (officially that is), one is confronted with 'the curse of a darker hue'. Dekker, however, dismissed Petersen's *cri de coeur* as being 'too raw'.[3] The critic did not even see fit to supply Petersen with the correct initials (they are given as S. J.). Petersen's novel, *As die son ondergaan* (lit. When the Sun Sets), appeared in 1945, two years after the radical course adopted by a large section of the 'coloured' teachers' organization at Kimberley. The poet and novelist seems to have been very careful to adopt an open political stand, although his poetry is certainly not devoid of extreme bitterness at times. But there is no indication that this bitterness was used to propagate revolutionary changes or encourage political consciousness among the 'coloureds'. The picture one abstracts, even today, of Petersen the man, is one of the loner, the romantic, who suffers in silence.

Petersen also seems to have preferred accommodation to confrontation. In a sense, his work gained some 'limited' recognition, mostly in Afrikaner literary circles. His novel was awarded a prize and also received some critical attention in Afrikaans literary critical handbooks. The socio-realism of a Petersen was sufficiently non-political to be acceptable to various Afrikaner critics. His novel, then, is fully consonant with the peculiar South African tradition. It is one of accommodation of the veld, the mountains, the imposing landscapes. The realism of a South Africa which had just emerged from the Second World War and was already on the threshold of nationalist rule, is hardly noticeable. The rumblings and political soul-searching among 'coloureds', culminating in the historic TLSA conference at Kimberley, the establishment of the NEUM and the Anti-CAD, are noticeably absent.

Petersen's novel, *As die son ondergaan* (When the Sun Sets), is interesting because it deals with the familiar theme in Afrikaans literature of the rural person in an urban setting. The only difference is that he deals with the plight of the 'coloured' in the city. Since this is an oft-recurring theme in South African literature, his novel will be evaluated against the works of one or two white and black South African authors. Commenting on Petersen's first novel, Beukes and Lategan (1959[3]),[4] after briefly referring to the technical deficiencies, speak of the author's poignant, realistic portrayal of the tragic fate of one of his own people, a young idealistic 'coloured' from the rural areas who sinks into the cesspool of the big city. Petersen's novel was but one of many dealing with this theme in Southern African literature. Usually taking the form of an innocent person from the rural areas who is unable to accommodate his or her longing for a wider horizon, and who eventually leaves for the city where he or she succumbs to vice. The end or downfall of the character is usually tragic, softened or toned down only by an eventual return (catharsis) to the fold. In the South African setting, where race plays such an important role, this has given rise to a rather repetitive and, at times, boring, cycle of the black man in the throes of the wicked city.

Basically, there are three streams. The rural African in the urban novel, of which Alan Paton's *Cry the Beloved Country* is a good example. Usually the centre of activity is iGoli (i.e. city of gold, Johannesburg), where many Africans were forced to seek work in the gold mines. Then there is the rural Afrikaner and his loss of innocence in the city (Johannesburg or Cape Town). And finally, the 'Cape coloured' from the rural area and his fall from grace, in which the centre of action is invariably Cape Town, the natural habitat of this species. Their crises are sometimes almost similar to those of the Afrikaner youngster, in that they take place within the trinity of Church, language and God.

Nadine Gordimer writes: 'It is axiomatic that the urban theme contains the classic crises: tribal and traditional values against Western values, peasant modes of life against the modes of an industrial proletariat, and above all, the quotidian humiliations of a black man's world made to a white man's specification'.[5]

Invariably, the reader is confronted with the image of the townsman as opposed to the tribesman, the challenged as opposed to the challenger. At a later stage we shall see that Gordimer is vindicated when she argues that non-white authors are beginning to wipe out such white literary stereotypes.

In writing *Turbotte Wolfe* (1925, reprint 1965), William Plomer became the first white author to break through a typically indigenous South African literary trend of ignoring the black presence. He was also one of the first to portray the 'tribal' African, within the context of the urban setting. Before this, the person of colour never loomed large in South African fiction. Pre-Union literature was generally of an inferior and coarse quality. The notable exception was Olive Schreiner's *The Story of an African Farm* (1883). But, even with her, there is what Laurens van der Post calls, in the foreword to the 1965 edition, 'a curious limitation upon her awareness: the black and coloured people of Africa who were with her from birth and far outnumbered the white are not naturally and immediately in it'.[6]

Despite Schreiner's later involvement, van der Post observes that; 'As people in their own individual right, alas! they never walked large in her imagination or understanding'.[7] For, even in her great novel, *The Story of an African Farm*, the liberalism that she preaches is heavily diluted by her brief and intermittent treatment of her African characters, who are not allowed to attend the church services on Sundays.

Before 1920, there was very little evidence of a desire to portray a greater South African reality. Plomer's product was therefore a much-needed one, or as van der Post comments in the foreword:[8]

> no less remarkable was the steadfastness with which Plomer maintained his own untried view of life around him against that taken for granted by the European community of South Africa. The attitude of white South Africans to their coloured and black countrymen had never before been challenged in depth from their own midst.

Lewis Nkosi comments on novels in the vernacular, as well as those in English as follows:[9]

> Most vernacular novels, as well as those written in English, novels upon which we were nourished in our boyhood, worked and re-worked the theme of *Jim Comes to Jo-burg* in which it was implied that Jim's loss of place in the tightly woven tribal structure and the corresponding attenuation of the elder's authority over him was the main cause rather than the result of the nation's tragedy.

It is for this reason that the educated black inside South Africa objects or at least does so partly to Alan Paton's *Cry the Beloved Country*. Paton could not escape his image as erstwhile leader of the, by now defunct, Liberal Party of South Africa. For, to the African, a liberal in the South African context meant, and still means, 'a white man who believes in redressing political wrongs by constitutional means ... [who] accommodates himself to the legislative machinery in the hope that he can use the concession by which he came to occupy a certain position inside the machinery to persuade the oppressor to change heart.'[10] For this reason, Alan Paton's novel *Cry the Beloved Country* is, according to critics, the prime example of what Lewis Nkosi calls the 'Jim comes to Jo'burg' syndrome, with all its peculiar South African imputations. The Reverend Kumalo is found to be unacceptable because he personifies the good healthy life of the reserves, an 'uncle Tom' basically. The tenor of the book recalls too vividly for the African, the white man's attempts to retribalize him in the Bantustans. Yet, it is an indisputable fact that no other work of fiction has brought home to the non-South African, the terror of the black man's existence. It is a matter of deep regret, however, that Wulf Sachs's work, first published as *Black Anger* and later on as *Black Hamlet* (1947), in which we are introduced to the conflict and the terror of the black individual, is hardly ever referred to.

The urban theme was also well exploited in Afrikaans fiction. Popular magazines like *Rooi Rose, Die Sarie Marais* and *Die Huisgenoot* ran lengthy serials by lesser authors flaunting the theme of the virginal Afrikaner boy or girl, fortified initially against any moral decay by the Bible and the Dutch Reformed Church, only to go under in the city. The tone is highly moralistic – honour thy father and thy mother; the lost sheep; the good shepherd; the forgiving parents; heart-rending, tragic.

What Petersen does, then, is in no way a departure from the rather moralistic fiction in Afrikaans. Like many an Afrikaans-speaking person (whether 'coloured' or black), he too must have been nourished in his youth on scores of such books. As a poet and teacher of Afrikaans, he in all probability dealt critically with this theme in Afrikaans literature. Being from rural Afrikaans-speaking stock, and later on residing in an urban area, he was excellently placed to exploit this theme. Yet what emerges is rather disappointing, pedestrian at times and tragic in its missed opportunities of wiping out the pitiful portrayal of the 'half-caste', as hitherto found in the works of Millin, Cloete and even Gerald Gordon. Although we are in the period of the United Party of General Smuts, the 'coloured' was no better off than he is today. He was still an appendage of the white power structure, whose presence was best ignored, whose future was best shrouded in abstruseness or incongruities, or painfully juggled by the rulers in an attempt to fit his group into their system of ascribed roles. In the early forties, there were abortive attempts to establish a Coloured Affairs Department, which was staunchly resisted by a large section of the 'coloured' teachers, as was made clear in the preamble, 'Not a race of slaves'.

Despite the early assurances of General Hertzog and Dr Malan, the way was carefully prepared for the eventual removal of the 'coloureds' from the common voters' role. In the Free State and the Transvaal, the 'coloureds' never even had a semblance of political rights. It was only at the Cape that certain fringe benefits were offered as a sop to both 'coloured' and African alike. And it is on this rather slim basis that the so-called great Cape Liberal tradition is built.

Nowhere in Petersen's novel do any of these problems surface. His book becomes even more striking when one contrasts it with the works of one or two South African authors, who also have the urban setting as the main theme.

Now, despite this historical legacy, one finds no such evidence of social realism in Petersen's novel. Instead the story is a fairly straightforward account, differing only slightly from the mainstream of Afrikaans literature. First, one is confronted with a rather peaceful and serene depiction of the village — Petersen seems to be more at home in portraying rural scenes, which are liberally strewn throughout the whole book (1971[4]):[11]

> The gold of ripe quins and purplish blue lucern, perhaps an orange tree or two, is there anything more beautiful?
> At a slant behind the village, there is a hill covered with aloes — fiery red horns which flare up when the sun touches them; yellow ones too, velvety like candle flames.

This is in complete contradistinction to the functionality of minute and detailed physical landscapes, as found in La Guma's work, which is there to enlarge the reader's understanding of the moral dilemmas confronting the individual in society, and to arouse indignation. Petersen's lyrical, but simple, prose is beautiful and different from the haunted and proscribed world of the black ghettos of Johannesburg, or the Second Avenues of Mphahlele. For the world of Mphahlele is one of slush and hardships, a world punctuated with domestic quarrels and characterized by the main character's attempts to escape and endure. A prose which Gerald Moore has described as the 'taste of blood on the tongue'.[12] Mphahlele's world is one where the 'sound of the bell floats in the air at ten minutes to ten and Black man must run home and Black man must sleep or have a night special permit'.[13] It is a place with 'dirty water and flies and children with traces of urine running down their legs and chickens picking at children's stools'.[14] Mphahlele himself admits: 'I have been moving up and down Second Avenue since I was born and never dreamt I should ever jump out of the nightmare.'[15]

The main character in Petersen's novel, Frans Hendricks, is a dreamy, 'coloured' man whose aspirations are not fulfilled and whose village is the still point in his life, a nostalgic frame of reference made up of fiery aloes and vast expanse. This tendency to idealize and romanticize the rural area (the platteland) and the veld, is especially true of Afrikaans fiction. Another is the notion that in order to describe for example, the veld, one should write in Afrikaans.

The Hobson brothers, two Afrikaner writers, express the general opinion when they maintain: 'English is the wrong language of the veld. After all, there isn't any veld in England, any Karroo and above all any Kalahari'.[16] Petersen, then, is true to the Afrikaans tradition of portraying, on canvas, the awe-inspiring and immense South African landscape.

Apart from a cursory reference to 'Die Bruinmense', the novel could have been that of a white author. And in a sense, one should at least admit that this is a departure from the normal pattern of literature conscripted for the victims. His main character is white in his aspirations, his loneliness, his unfulfilled self in the rural area. He is described as someone who already as a toddler was 'quiet and withdrawn . . . totally oblivious to everything around him . . . a dreamer who preferred to roam around in his own inner world'.[17] Frans Hendricks remains a lost soul, a-political in his aspirations, non-revolutionary in his frustrations. We are briefly reminded of the depression which crippled all hopes of achieving his ambition to become a teacher. Then follows the long-suffering role while his brother Jim, and his sister Joyce, become the inheritors of his dreams.

Only occasionally does Petersen provide a glimpse of the 'colouredness' of his characters as a component in their tragic make-up when he writes: 'For which way can they turn? They are the children of Brown people.'[18]

The journey to Cape Town is uneventful and livened up only with the introduction of the Cape Malay character —stereotyped into a roguish, comic figure:[19]

> Short of body, round of stomach, with fat cheeks and a Hitler
> moustache . . . Kassiem, a suitcase in both hands, trotting
> up to the window. He saw the African sitting and his baggy
> eyes became big. 'Nei Salie man, aafterol! There's a blienking
> djoems [a black man] in the compartment. Isn't there a
> place somwê-else?'

Here for the first time, he gives the reader a comic description of a typical South African realism. But one is also acquainted with that horrible virus of group consciousness. And all through this scene, the main character, Frans Hendricks, remains silent.

Petersen however soon relapses into his old pace, trotting out descriptive passages which are almost photographically true to life, but devoid of soul and intimacy. The tragi-comic Hanover Street of the 'coloured' ghetto, District Six, which in the works of La Guma is such a dramatically lively scene, becomes a tame alley where there is only a frightening lack of space.

Long flash-blacks to the rural environment turn Frans Hendricks into a dull and uninteresting character, overshadowed by lesser ones such as his land-lady, Mrs Lyners, who in her pseudo-sophistication, and in her monologue, maintains, 'ek is vanaand 'n ientepennit vrou . . . vra nieman niks . . . skuld niemand niks'[20] (I am Mrs Lyners, an independent woman, ask no one anything, owe no one anything) emerges as the only character of full flesh and blood proportions. She is a woman who occasionally takes unto herself a man, whom she pampers as long as he is loyal: she is pathetically sad in her quasi-respectability and is funny in her inflated appreciation and evaluation of herself.

The main character, Frans, continues to dream — at art galleries everywhere.[21]

> Last Sunday he stood in the art gallery staring with burning
> eyes at the life so immortally depicted on canvas. One picture
> in particular arrested his attention, a picture in a corner of
> the big hall; just a simple landscape, with blue sky and fluffy
> white clouds, an outstretched mountain chain, grey shrubs
> in the foreground and along the farm road, the fiery red
> aloe horns. Oh! to be able to paint thus, without pause, just
> paint.

Frans is drawn to Volkwyn without being influenced by him. He does not intrude into the lives of the other people he encounters. When he does intrude, it is the stock situation of unrequited or misplaced love — the deflation of the beautiful and ethereal by the base and the mundane. Unable to stand such lacerations, he wilts, gives in and is ready to succumb. But even in his relationship with the fallen woman, he remains something of a puritan, an emasculated saint turned sinner, yet undefiled, only soiled somewhat. In no way does this derelict of a woman contribute to the hero's understanding of the conditions which produce people like her. Even at the very end, Frans never quite succeeds in becoming truly tragic. By the time he has listlessly dreamt himself out of the novel, his parents are ready to appear on the scene to come and save him from further excesses and from drowning in his romantic illusions. 'Something in him breaks.

Helpless and small he is again. And through his sobs he complains; "Ma ...! She ... fooled me ...!" "Come my child. Tomorrow we are going home".'[22]

Frans Hendricks, the 'coloured', is tragic only in so far as tragedy is conceived of as some higher effort which ends in anti-climax and frustration. The novel capsizes in its inability to either attain the stature of the psychological novel (see *Nostromo*, Ch. IV), or that of social protest (see *And a Threefold Cord* by La Guma). *As die son ondergaan* seems to bear out Lewis Nkosi's indictment, that in the work of Afrikaans-speaking 'coloured' writers, 'there are no real full-blooded characters with real blood to spill; no characters whose fighting or love-making has the stench of living people: they are cardboard pieces and cardboard pieces don't spill any blood'.[23]

Frans Hendricks represents one facet of South African life as seen by 'coloured' authors. It is still a white-oriented picture. This is a pity, for Petersen, the sensitive poet, is deeply conscious of the injustices in his society. The characters still move within a white idiom. Petersen continues a typical South African tradition. One finds it hard to identify with the inner nightmare and conflict, if any, of his character, Frans. This is not the case when one comes across the works of La Guma, for instance. Ambiguity and near-kinship are terms which linger on in respect of Frans Hendricks. This will also be continued painfully in, especially, the earlier utterings of Adam Small.

# Chapter 6

# A voice in the wilderness[1]

In Adam Small, the 'coloured' poet and dramatist, this ambiguity towards Afrikaans culture surfaces very strongly. The poet seems to be a bit of an anomaly on the South African literary scene. Afrikaans literature has never been extremely rich in 'coloured' authors and after the police brutality in the 'coloured' townships of Bonteheuwel and Manenberg in 1976, probably never will be. Those authors who have, however, written in Afrikaans are carefully nurtured in textbooks. S. V. Petersen, the poet and novelist, has kept an eerie silence, while P. J. Philander has apparently chosen the safe confines of a Quaker school in Long Island, New York. This discussion of Adam Small will also reveal how difficult it is to maintain oneself as an artist and a human being when one's views conflict with those held by others in the society.

Adam Small has been a contentious person in the Cape setting. During the late fifties and early sixties, the politically conscious 'coloured' found his political aspirations largely reflected in the NEUM (Non-European Unity Movement) and the Anti-CAD (Anti-Coloured Affairs Department), but Small kept to himself. In fact, during those vitriolic years culminating in the massacre of Sharpeville, it was almost heretical not to belong to one of the many political groups operating in Cape Town and its environment. Apostasy was severely attacked, abstinence turned one into a quisling − a favourite term of abuse for dissidents. Another of the weapons used from time to time was social ostracism. Few people could face up to the severities and most of them capitulated. Adam Small seemingly withstood all these pressures.

He was suspect among a section of the politically conscious 'coloureds' for another reason. At a time when there was a general plea for a boycott of the specially created university institutions, Small did not hesitate to accept a lectureship at the one established for 'coloureds'. Thus, the 'brown Afrikaner' badge came to be associated with him. The politically conscious 'coloured' looked upon the establishment of the university college for 'coloureds' in Bellville, a town outside Cape Town, as an attempt to forge the 'new brown man'. And as such, any association with these 'apartheid institutions' was looked upon as a form of betrayal.

Smaîl was also a poet and a dramatist who chose Afrikaans as his medium of expression. Since Afrikaans was generally associated with the architects of apartheid, it was not favourably looked upon by the educated and politically-conscious 'coloured', especially in the urban areas.

This question of language in a colonial situation is of course of fundamental importance. In the Cape, the language question gave rise to numerous debates among the teachers who belonged to the TLSA (Teachers League of South Africa). Readers were treated for weeks on end to a series of articles in which a certain Rylate[2] (a pseudonym) took a critical look at the language question in the country. Afrikaans in particular was scathingly dismissed as a fascist language. The author was also contemptuous of the white efforts to foist Bantu languages onto the African. Of Afrikaans he writes:[3]

> The 'taal', once formed, had a most revealing up-and-down
> history. After spreading under the DEIC it fell back with the
> coming of the British in 1806. Thereafter, ITS FORTUNES
> BECAME INSEPARABLE FROM THOSE OF THE PRIMITIVE
> FEUDAL TREKBOERS. Thus, the First Taalbeweging . . . did
> not start as a language but as a POLITICAL movement.

Writing about the entrenchment of Afrikaans in urban areas and especially in industry, Rylate observes:[4]

> Afrikaans became the 'werktaal' of the platteland reflecting all its
> particular viciousness, vulgarity, coarseness, barbarism and back-
> wardness. The townward migration of the Afrikaners between the
> two wars spread Afrikaans into the peri-urban and even into the
> urban areas. Since they constituted the main bulk of the white
> labour aristocracy . . . Afrikaans tended to become a 'werktaal'
> also in the cities, thereby reinforcing the Afrikaans spoken by the
> Non-European workers who had migrated from the country to
> the town and acting as a human wall between the Non-Europeans
> and English.

A. C. Jordan, that distinguished scholar of African languages, was then given space to reply to Rylate's arguments. Being more of a linguist and therefore in a better position to sort out the straight political issues from the linguistic arguments, Jordan proceeded to point out that some of the arguments were rather inspired by the politics of Rylate. He showed how Rylate's attitude towards Afrikaans was the reverse side of the coin, that is, of white attitudes towards non-whites. Jordan also questioned the non-critical approach to English which, as the major language of imperialism and colonialism, had led to the exploitation of nations all over Africa and Asia. The general attitude was however crystal clear even in the fifties. Afrikaans was a language of contempt and of oppression. The whites were only interested in creating Bantu languages in order to retribalize the African. Linguistically then, these arguments may be full of loopholes. Yet, politically, they expressed what many a 'coloured' felt.

The Afrikaner, through his policy of Christian National Education[5] enunciated in 1948, tried to foist onto the 'coloured', what he conceived of as 'mother-tongue' instruction (generally referred to in Afrikaans as *moedertaal-onderwys*). This, in essence, meant education through the medium of Afrikaans. Many 'coloureds' looked upon *moedertaal-onderwys* as nothing but a ruse to keep them backward. Moreover, there was more than just a sneaking suspicion that this type of education was deliberately designed to keep the non-white from learning English and therefore cutting him off from a more universal culture. This was unmasked with perspicacity by Bastiaanse in *The Educational Journal* of the Teachers League of South Africa as far back as 1956, more than twenty years before the eruptions at Soweto and Bonteheuwel. In fact, his argument has a greater validity than ever since Soweto. Bastiaanse writes: '*moedertaal-onderwys* is masqueraded as "mother-tongue instruction", whereas in fact it is no more than the political enforcement of Afrikaans as a medium in schools.'[6]

The author then goes on to make it categorically clear that he is not against Afrikaans as a medium of instruction and communication as such, but opposed to the way in which the language is exploited in order to bolster up the system of apartheid. Afrikaans becomes a tool of the hated system of Christian National Education which, to most enlightened 'coloureds', is neither Christian, nor National, let alone a system of education. Bastiaanse continues:[7]

> What is being attacked is the use of Afrikaans as a political weapon
> not only for the supremacy of one section of the *Herrenvolk*

over the other section, but, worse still, for its use as an agency
of domination over the millions of Non-Whites in this country.

When one therefore reads the views of an anthropologist who has
spent possibly a year or more in the Cape among the 'coloureds', in
one specific area, namely, Woodstock, commenting in the following
vein, one seriously doubts the use of even informants in the discipline
of anthropology. The American O'Toole makes such a vain attempt
to explain why 'Cape coloureds' prefer English to Afrikaans, in his
book, *Watts and Woodstock* (1973). He invokes Fanon who wrote
that 'The Negro of the Antilles will be proportionately whiter — that
is, he will come closer to being a real human being — in direct ratio
to his mastery of the French language.'[8] Now, O'Toole would have
us believe that if we substituted 'Cape coloured' for 'Negro', we
would have 'an accurate statement of the value of language to the
Coloured people'. O'Toole continues:[9]

> Many Coloureds are insulted if a stranger assumes Afrikaans is their
> first language. Almost all Coloureds will answer a telephone and
> exchange greetings on the street in English . . . The general rule,
> according to Coloured informants, is that what is mundane,
> trivial, unimportant (or romantic) is spoken in Afrikaans.

O'Toole is guilty of generalization when he says, for instance,
that 'almost all coloureds will answer . . . in English', for a similar
survey in the Boland, an Afrikaans-speaking rural environment, would
produce the exact opposite result.

If one looks at O'Toole's analysis, it would seem more logical for
the 'coloured' to adopt Afrikaans rather than English if he wished
entry into, and acceptance by, the dominant group: the Afrikaner.
For I have yet to meet 'Cape coloureds' who try to 'play white' by
simulating an Anglo-Saxon background. In view of the historical
situation, it is easier for the 'coloured' to pass as an Afrikaner than
an Englishman. Possibly, O'Toole was too eager to swallow some
of the information passed on by his informants whole and would
have done well to invoke, or heed, Fanon's other warning: 'The blackman has two dimensions. One with his fellows, the other with the
white man.'[10]

In South Africa, where the white man is rather loth to listen to the
black man's protest, the oppressed are only too happy to find a willing
ear in liberals from overseas. Quite obviously, the real reason must be
sought in that peculiar and near-incestuous relationship that exists

between Afrikaner and 'Cape coloured'. The 'coloured' is turning away from Afrikaans for several reasons. It is a deliberate act of defiance and an expression of contempt for 'die Boere' (the Boers), as Afrikaners are abusively referred to.

This hardening of 'coloured' attitudes towards the Afrikaner as a group, came out very clearly in a study by the late Melville Edelstein, entitled, *What Do the Coloureds Think?* (1974). He concluded that the 'coloureds' put more social distance between themselves and the Afrikaner than any other race group, barring blacks of course. He also found that 'coloureds' had a very low opinion of the Afrikaner as a group. However, 'coloureds' tend to change their attitude to the Afrikaner depending on their personal experiences.

If contempt for Afrikaans and Afrikanerdom constituted one facet, then the basic question of English versus Afrikaans is the other important factor. 'Coloureds' all realize that a mastery of the English language will bring in its wake an accessibility to a greater culture, and to greater cultural values. This in itself is nothing new in a colonial situation, where a rejection of the language of the political overlord is a well-known form of protest. I have seen this type of language soul-searching at first hand in Surinam, the former Dutch West Indies, just prior to independence in 1975.

Historically, Dutch has been the medium of instruction in the schools, the language of the law courts and of government. Side by side, there was, however, *Sranan Tongo* (lit. the Surinamese Tongue), a Creole language, which has steadily become the *lingua franca* of the various ethnic groups. Before independence, and one can safely assume even afterwards, the entire role of Dutch in post-colonial Surinam came up for scrutiny. The antagonists of Dutch argued that the language was spoken by a few million people and of no use internationally. This was a very valid objection. But the political argument should not be ignored, for the Dutch language was, and still is, associated with Surinamese enslavement by some nationalist. Shedding Dutch would therefore mean shedding another layer of enslavement.

The Surinamese example clearly illustrates that the alternatives suggested pose equally serious problems. It is, after all, an established fact that there is a generation of Surinamese so steeped in the Dutch language and culture, that an imposition of another language would create serious problems. The elevation of *Sranan Tongo* to that of official language would have serious drawbacks in terms of international relations.

In the Ministerial document of 1975, it was therefore duly recognized that Dutch could not be dispensed with forthwith, although the priorities emerged quite clearly. The preference was for English, Spanish, Portuguese and (for the time being) Dutch, in this order. I have purposely used the Surinamese example to show how, in a country which had various possibilities open, the choice was no less easy.

In South Africa, there is not such a variety of European language alternatives as in Surinam. In a sense, this was a blessing, for the choice is a fairly straightforward one between English and Afrikaans. It was further facilitated by the fact that one language, Afrikaans, was associated with apartheid and Afrikanerdom, parochialism and oppression, and that English was regarded as the gateway to the wider, un-prejudiced world. Moreover, English was the language of Shakespeare and not of the ox-wagon and the musket. It is therefore logical, in view of the government measures to create small, self-contained ethnic groups, that non-whites should choose an international means of communication. The choice is not ethnically, but politically inspired.

Language as an instrument in the process of enslavement and colonialism is therefore of fundamental importance. In fact, 'coloured' attitudes towards the art of Adam Small are largely responsible for his *oeuvre* being ignored in 'coloured' schools. The article by G. Jonker, in the militant, anti-government, but well-respected *Teachers League of South Africa Journal* (October–November 1969), is fairly symptomatic of 'coloured' attitudes towards Small's literary works in general.

Even the way Small uses his language is singled out for attack. Thus Jonker scathingly comments:[11]

> A writer is of course free to use a dialect, provided the dialect
> is the form in which the writer can obtain the purest and most
> precise expression of his thoughts and his feelings. When the
> writer however uses a dialect to achieve an effect which does
> not flow organically from his writing . . . then it is not permissible.
> Then the writing is not genuine but ersatz. It is completely
> odious to *manufacture* a dialect, put it in a speaker's mouth
> in order to portray him as being different [*andersoortig*]. This
> is what Small is guilty of.

The operative word in Jonker's criticism, which must and can only be understood within the South African context, politically and linguistically, is *andersoortig*. Perhaps it is just as well to put Small's use of a particular brand of Afrikaans, which is confined to 'coloureds', in wider perspective. Small is, after all, not the first writer to exploit that particular language which he, the writer, hears among his people.

A very good parallel in this respect is the Dutch as spoken by the Creole lower classes. While the educated ones will generally speak standard Dutch, the lower classes speak what is termed Surinamese Dutch.[12] The lower class 'Cape coloured' also speaks a different dialectal form of Afrikaans which is richly interlarded with English.[12] But the Surinamese Dutch of the Creoles has, so it seems, lost its badge of shame, whereas Coloured-Afrikaans, to avail oneself of such a monstrous term for the time being, has lost none of its stigma. Even Sranan Tongo, the *lingua franca* of the Surinamese, has lost its slave stigma, whereas the dialectal Afrikaans of the 'coloured' is constantly up against the stench of colour and politics.

The 'coloured' objection to Small's exploitation of a particular brand of Afrikaans is worthy of a closer look. It has been variously called Kaaps (i.e. the language from the Cape), even facetiously Capey language, and Kleurling-Afrikaans (Coloured-Afrikaans). It is looked upon as a mark of low social status and cultural inferiority. It is said to degrade instead of uplift, thereby only confirming the Afrikaner in his prejudiced belief that the 'coloured' is culturally and linguistically a buffoon. Small himself, in a foreword to his anthology *Kitaar my kruis* (Guitar My Cross, 1974[2]), writes:[13]

> Kaaps [the term he himself prefers], is not what some Englishman
> in South Africa refers to as 'Capey' . . . also not what some
> Afrikaans-speaking persons refer to as *Gamat-taal. Kaaps* is
> a language in the sense that it carries the full fate and destiny
> of the people who speak it: their entire life, 'with everything
> contained in it'; a language in the sense that the people who
> speak it, give their first cry in life in this language, conduct
> all their business in their life in this language, expectorate
> in the throes of death in this language. Kaaps is not funny or
> comical but a language.

What Small says here does not in anyway differ from the pronouncements of non-whites on language elsewhere. We may do well to recall, within this context, the words used by the Surinamese, Koenders, in 1948 in support of Sranan Tongo:[14]

> Just as you find in other languages words that are borrowed from
> others, so also in our language, but it isn't a broken variant of
> another language. It has its own manner, makes its own words
> in its own way. A people that has neglected its language, or
> heaps insults on it for the sake of another language, whichever
> it may be, is more stupid than our forefathers.

The well-known Afrikaner poet and dramatist, Uys Krige, in a foreword to the university publication *Groote Schuur* (1960), observed:[15]

> Our *dialectal Coloured language* is a dangerous means to employ in poetry. If it is not supported by a refined sense of language in the poet, who must avoid mere 'camera' work and who knows how to effectuate a synthesis of the rough expression with a certain elegance and refinement, if it does not spring from a special poetic vision and is not backed up by a strong technical ability, it can at the most be *snaaks* [funny], and at its best *oulik* [cute].

Afrikaner critics have also accused Small of stooping to achieve effect, of using an arbitrary and confusing phonetic spelling. The answer to this must obviously be that Afrikaner academia cannot fully penetrate the 'townships' and ghettos of Windermere and Bonteheuwel. In 'Focus on Adam Small' in *Newscheck,* one reads:[16]

> By adopting as his medium the *Englikaans* patois of the Cape Coloureds, Small has succeeded in turning his poetry into a joke which nonetheless unfailingly illuminates the pathos of its subject. He has also made it untranslatable, incomprehensible to readers not familiar with South African by-ways. While thus losing internationality, Small has struck perhaps the first unmistakably all-South-African note.

Ironically then, Adam Small's exploitation of Kaaps, as he himself calls it, seems to bring him closer to the working classes than, for example, the English rhetoric of some 'coloured' political leaders. The response which his play, *Kanna Hy Kô Hystoe* (Kanna, He's coming Home, 1965), has evoked among a section of the 'coloureds' themselves, seems to indicate that in terms of literature, he is busy creating 'accomplished street poetry . . . as wide as God's eye'.[17]

In this respect, it is interesting to note that the novelist, Alex La Guma, does not encounter opposition when he exploits that peculiar brand of English common to the poor 'coloureds' of District Six. In his unpublished MA thesis presented at Leeds University in 1969, H. P. Africa comments on *A Walk in the Night* in the following vein:[18]

> The action of the novella is set in District Six, a part of Cape Town where a poor section of the Cape Coloured lives. These people are bilingual and speak both English and Afrikaans. Lexical,

grammatical and phonological interference is a common feature
of their spoken language.

He then goes on to refer to this type of language as:[19]

a form of syntax which in many ways is peculiar to District
Six, Afrikaans lexical items which occur frequently in English
sentences, and some utterances which though represented as
spoken English reveal Afrikaans substructures.

Africa then recalls Uriel Weinreich who in his *Languages in Contact*
(1954) defines interference as, 'Those instances of deviation from the
norms of either language which occur in the speech of bilinguals as a
result of their familiarity with more than one language, i.e. as a result
of language contact.'[20] What Africa says of the English used by La
Guma in *A Walk in the Night* is surely also applicable to the special
brand of Afrikaans used by 'coloureds' in the Cape. Or is La Guma's
English less objectionable, because his politics are acceptable?

Much of the 'coloured' objection to Small as a writer then, seems to
stem from disapproval of his politics. It is no mere accident that the
Moses figure in Small's poetry is singled out for special attack. The
poet, in the eyes of his antagonists, identifies himself with Moses and
sees himself as a non-racial 'coloured' Moses, who with the help of his
brothers, the Afrikaners, will lead his people, the 'brown Afrikaners',
to the promised land of Afrikanerdom. This is probably a vast over-
simplification of what Small really believed then, but fundamental
to this assessment is the fact that Small wanted change by talking to
the oppressor. The antagonists illustrate their viewpoint by referring
to one particular poem in his anthology *Kitaar my kruis:*[21]

> nou vrinne
> die Here het gabring
> an my sy wonnerwerke oek so
> hy het gavra wat's in my hand
> en vrinne
> in my hand was my kitaar
> kô, lat ons sing.
>
> now friends
> the Lord had revealed to me
> just so his miracles
> he'd asked me what's in my hand
> and friends

> in my hands was my guitar
> come, let us sing.

To the educated 'coloured', there is no irony or humour in this poem. To him, it is essentially Small's vision of the Christological role he can play through poetry. The symbol of the guitar as one of the cultural assets of the 'coloured' man becomes as tainted with ethnocentricism as, for example, the 'tot' system.

Yet, this attitude towards Small on the part of many a 'coloured' deserves closer scrutiny, for it highlights some of the problems found in Chapter 2, when humour was applied as a symbol in such situations. Again, Zijderveld (1971) is right when he argues that it is the audience which will determine whether the crossing of the institutionalized borders is a cause for embarrassment, anger or laughter.

By very definition, the ideologue, whether white or non-white, finds no room in his ideology for humour, let alone a comic ironic stance. Ironically then, the Afrikaner who believes in apartheid, and the 'coloured' who rejects the system, will both be irritated by some of Small's poetry. And their irritation is rooted in their essential non-understanding of the function of humour as an instrument of play and unmasking in their society of ascribed roles.

Jonker traces Small's role within the South African context against his utterings on socio-political issues during, and especially after, the traumatic period of Sharpeville. He comments on Small in the following vein:[22]

> Adam Small differs remarkably in two ways from his two fellow Coloured poets, Petersen and Philander. They are satisfied to be known as Coloureds. He is a so-called 'brown Afrikaner'. They are rather ashamed of their political role, he is rather proud of his political versifications. These differences are striking but unimportant. Ashamed or unashamed, the political role remains the same. If you want to cut off a section of the non-white peoples from the rest, it does not matter whether you prefer your group to be called 'Coloured', 'Bruinman' [Brownman] or 'Bruin Afrikaner' [Brown Afrikaner], which you look upon as being different [andersoortig] and unique [eiesoortig], because the fault lies not in the naming process but in the breaking away.

Jonker quotes extensively from Small's book, *Die Eerste Steen* (The First Stone, 1961). The book is dedicated, significantly at this stage in his career, to 'My People, The Afrikaners'. In a devastating comment Jonker writes:[23]

> And politically speaking, Small is right. His politics are theirs.
> His views are shaped on those of the Afrikaners. Their viewpoint
> is his viewpoint. The trouble is that his skin is brown. With Small
> this is the great reason for his bitterness. And he *is* a bitter person.
> Bitter because, 'he who is a sensitive and educated person, not
> a skollie [a street ruffian and a criminal] or a sore in the com-
> munity, but someone to whom dignity should be due, whose value
> as a human being should be rated higher than that of civil servants
> who shout at him' is cast out of the fold of 'his volk'.

Small writes in *Die Eerste Steen* as follows:[24]

> And this is precisely the greatest sorrow and the greatest sin
> of it before God; that all these things are done, whether with
> legal backing or not, are done also to people whose level and
> value of life is comparable to the best . . . . But it is a crime
> against society if one isn't light of colour. The most undignified
> type of human being, the lowest of scum is privileged above
> the rest of us — as long as he is white. A white skollie has
> greater freedom than I have.

Prior to this, he had commented on the dilemma of his people as follows:[25]

> The brown people [Bruinmense], have no natural apartheid
> territory in South Africa, have no natural *aparte* [separate]
> language, have no natural *aparte* history. The new deal is
> according to these lines and the idea of an alliance can be
> translated as the idea that the white man and the brown
> man (bruinman) are companions in adversity in South
> Africa. They will stand together in South Africa or go under
> together.

This viewpoint, as espoused by Small at this stage in South Africa, found willing response among the Afrikaners but would, of course, be totally unacceptable to the 'coloured' masses at large. After Sharpeville, in particular, the need for a united black front was seen as an absolute necessity in the struggle for freedom.

To Adam Small (at least in 1961), 'the brown man was closer to the Afrikaner than any other population group in South Africa'. He continues:[26]

I repeat: the brown man is much closer to the Afrikaner than
any other population group in South Africa, much closer
than the Jews, much closer than the Greeks, much closer than
the English, much closer than the Dutch or any other white group
in South Africa . . . . The Afrikaner welcomes the Jews, the
Greeks, all these, immeasurably far removed as these people
are from his cultural traditions. The ideal of unity with the
English is nurtured . . . . But we, who are in every meaningful
way much closer to the Afrikaner than any of these groups
of people, our name is not mentioned.

Rightly does Jonker observe that the united white front is an anti-
black one which is anti-democratic and pigmentocratically inspired.
Continuing his attack on Small, Jonker writes:[27]

He does not plead for the end of oppression in South Africa.
Oh, no! He wants to shout open the portals of Afrikanerdom
for the 'brown man' . . . . He wants to do this on the basis of an
'alliance' [Bondgenootskap] and 'partnership in adversity'
[Lotgenootskap] . And this alliance can only have one possible
interpretation: an alliance to maintain the suppression of the
majority: and partnership in adversity can only mean that their
future will be linked with the maintenance of oppression.

Adam Small reveals himself, in his writings, as virulently anti-com-
munist and in this also he is only equalled by the Afrikaner. He is also
devoutly Christian, and refers to communism as that 'soul-destroying
danger . . . which can overrun the continent of Africa as far as the
southern point through the black masses'.[28] For him, at this stage in
his life, the only effective counter was to 'appeal to the Christian conscience . . . for the cause of justice and love'.

Small did seem to live up to his 'brown Afrikaner' image when, in
1961, he wrote rather scathingly about 'coloured' political leaders:[29]

unpleasant people who fill the world with slogans in the service
of so-called democracy, who deliver tirades on free speech and
freedom of expression . . . but who themselves do not even once
live up to one democratic principle. [He continues] . The way
these people go about things, we shall finally be free— free without
any sense of responsibility; we shall be free, yea unbridled;
the kind of freedom which is the destruction of all mankind.
They too will enslave us.

One could possibly argue in defence of Small that he was warning against rigid ideologies which permit no deviations from the official line. On the other hand, the political set-up in South Africa in 1961 allowed for only one stance (and still does) — an anti-government one.

Small's problem is also that of the writer and his role in an oppressive society. By adopting an attitude at such an early stage, in a terminology which is so clearly open to misinterpretation, Small tarnished his own literary image. The African, Caribbean and Asian writer cannot expect a charitable reception from his fellow *literati* and his people, if he appears to accommodate himself in a situation of oppression. If he does not openly choose sides, he risks being classed with the exploiter. The third world writer is, after all, purporting to write about and for his people, and in the process of creation hoping to give his work of art a touch of universality. The writer cannot withdraw into his lonely garret and write about daffodils. The 'coloureds' may then be over-harsh in their dismissal of Small's poetry, yet his early political activities and pronouncements certainly did more harm than good.

One may argue that politics is no basis for literary criticism, but then there is no act which is not political, within the South African context.

The sixties proved to be a period of great destruction. Sharpeville was a watershed in South African history. Yet, notwithstanding increasing international pressure, the apartheid measures became more rigid. One by one, black leaders landed up in South African jails. Black political organizations were either banned or forced underground or into exile. This inevitably created a political vacuum. The children born in the sixties were totally of the 'apartheid generation'. The so-called liberalism of even the fifties had ceased to exist. As during every revolutionary period the seventies saw the emergence of a new breed of young people who embraced black consciousness. These were the children of the apartheid generation who owed less loyalties to the older political vanguard. SASO (the South African Students Association for Blacks) and BPC (Black People's Convention) were the two organizations largely responsible for this new thinking. The role of the deceased leader, Steve Biko, has been amply dealt with in articles and books. In the Cape, this new black consciousness was reflected in the changing attitudes of 'coloured' students at the ethnic university college of Bellville. This led to unrest on the campus and police interference. In a recent nationwide interview on South African television (1978) Adam Small recalled how he was converted to, or influenced by, black consciousness because of the late Steve Biko. Small was of course, teaching at Bellville during this period and he too was confronted with the new South African youngster. From newspaper cuttings and interviews one gets a glimpse of his involvement with, or attitude towards, black consciousness.

Black consciousness as expressed by SASO meant the search 'for a Black identity, self-awareness and self-esteem and the rejection of White Stereotypes and morals.'[30] All over South Africa, from Soweto to Bonteheuwel, a young people were proclaiming their blackness. The idea of 'stopping to look at things through white eyes and beginning to look at things through Black eyes'[30] found response in the souls of the oppressed youth.

Small also seemed to have endorsed these black consciousness ideas. In 1973 he was very much involved in the People's Free Education Front and with its aim of having a black University for blacks and run by blacks. He envisaged his ideal through the media and the arts. His activities led to his eventual resignation as a lecturer at the college in Bellville, although it would be better to say that he was outmanoeuvred and forced to resign.

In an article in the *Rand Daily Mail* (1971), Small commented on racism in the following manner:[31]

> Racism is a phenomenon of inferiority. Our blackness is a
> phenomenon of pride . . . . We can no longer care whether
> or not whites understand us. What we do care about is
> understanding ourselves, and, in the course of this task,
> helping whites to understand themselves . . . . We are
> rejecting the idea that we live by their grace (that is,
> that they have the right to decide our future). We may live
> by the Grace of God, but we do not live by the grace of the
> whites.

Again in an article in the *Rand Daily Mail* (27 June 1973), he finally seems to repudiate the 'brown Afrikaner' syndrome. 'We certainly do not want to be Afrikaners. The term "Afrikaner" is associated with narrowness and a history of discrimination . . . . The greatest problem . . . is that violence is committed in the name of religion.'[32]

But let us return to Small's literary output and see how some of the critical assessments apply to his work. One of the notable qualities in his poetry is his exploitation of a brand of humour which is peculiar to the group of people he writes about. But even an ostensibly innocuous statement like this could lay one open to a charge of believing in a special type of ethnic humour. I have already indicated how humour can be squashed by the ideologist both to the right and the left. Small's poetry has been labelled funny *(snaaks)* and a joke by whites; 'coloureds' have only detected buffoonery in it. Yet it is an indisputable fact that lurking everywhere in his poetry or drama is that special brand of humour whereby marginal groups retain their sanity in oppressive societies — that is, through the gift of laughter. The oppressed can at times play out an ostensibly comic role in the presence of the oppressor, whereby the latter becomes the pitiable one. Laughter can of course be a purifying device, or an escape valve — an outlet for feelings of frustration, hatred and hostility. The extent to which one experiences behaviour as painful, is determined by the value one attaches to it.

Anton Zijderveld puts it so clearly in his book on humour:[33]

The humorist, like the anarchist, is after all, bent on
transgressing the limitations and borders, imposed on us
by language and institutions. He shifts border-lines, reformulates
existing definitions, creates to some extent, some kind of chaos and
rejoices, in a short-lived, though often intense, feeling of
superiority . . . . When humour, for example, becomes completely
politicized, and is wielded as a political instrument, then it
changes from playful laughter into grim reality. Even in
conflict situations, humour is doomed to remain a game,
because, through the laughter that it evokes, humour is
in a position to transcend the borders between ideological
positions. Humour is, therefore, of limited significance
to those who are interested in maintaining these borders.
It is probably, for this reason, why ideologues are so
seldom humorous — they simply cannot afford to be so.

The way in which outsiders, like the American O'Toole, can, for instance, misinterpret situations, is crystal clear from an anecdote which he cites in his anthropological study, *Watts and Woodstock*:[34]

A popular story in Woodstock [an area outside Cape Town]
concerns a Coloured man who is kneeling on the floor in a
D. R. C. [Dutch Reformed Church] when the parson walks in
and says, '*Seun*, what are you doing here?' The Coloured
man replies; 'Washing the floors, if it pleases the *baas*'. The
parson says, 'Well, that's all right. As long as you aren't

103

praying.' The story is not told to elicit laughter.

Once again the observation by Zijderveld would seem to supply the correct answer to O'Toole's when he writes about black humour:[35]

> The laughter that these jokes evoke, is not laughter-with-
> the whites about the Blacks, but laughter-among-themselves
> in a group with self-consciousness and pride. In such a
> situation, there is hatred against the 'sell-out' who still
> keeps on trying to adapt to the life pattern and ideas of
> the majority. Jokes occur which warn against the 'sell-out'.
> Humour then becomes a means of social control . . . . This
> type of humour not only rejects the assimilation of the
> blacks, but also contains a second layer: the frustrated white
> is also taken for a ride.

To reject Adam Small's humorous and satirical attacks via his poetry and prose, is, therefore, to ignore or misinterpret the peculiar culture (sub-culture) in which his writings find their origin in South Africa, or to apply ideological standards to them in which laughter is not permissible.

Small himself is painfully aware of this when he quotes Sutherland on satire in his foreword to his anthology *Kitaar my kruis* (1974[2]). 'Satire is not for the literal-minded . . . . The unintelligent either do not read satire at all, or misunderstand its significance when they do.'[36] For an essential task of the satirist is to invite the reader to share his moral indignation, to unmask the deception and to preach the ideal. And it is Small's ideal which he preaches which falls on barren ground: brotherhood, love and justice in a Western Christian democracy.

Small fulminates against Afrikaners, the Dutch Reformed Church, apartheid, freedom fighters, The Non-European Unity Movement, like some lone-ranger. And in the process he seems to become a victim of the socio-political climate which expects the person of colour (and rightly so), to develop along ideological lines which plead for the destruction of the system in South Africa. Small's lone attempts to prefer, what he sees as, 'sensitivity to crudeness, intelligence to boorish-ness, honesty to deceit',[37] fall on barren ground.

Yet, possibly Small is saying, by implication, that the ideological stance precludes the comic-ironic and the satiric viewpoint. The task of the satirist is, after all, to hold up an ideal picture to his society. Nothing is sacred or sacrosanct. It may just be conceivable that Small is misinterpreted for the very reason that some students and critics fail to appreciate Evelyn Waugh's African portrayals. Karl's comments on Evelyn Waugh come to mind here: 'Too often, however, we tend to look for social enlightenment in a humorous writer whose very humour depends on his parody of those who accept and strongly believe in social enlightenment.'[38] Karl continues to remind the reader that for the comic writer, 'the terms of his comic intention must allow him free play'.[39]

Much of Small's satirical swipes centre around religion. The poet himself is a religious person, notwithstanding the doubts which assail him from time to time. In his anthology *Sê Sjibbolet* (1963), he quotes one of his spiritual mentors, Sören Kierkegaard:[40]

> I know it well, there have been mockers of religion who would
> have given — yea, what would they not have given? — to be able
> to do what I can do, but did not succeed because God was not
> with them . . . With me is the Almighty — And He knows best how
> the blows must be dealt so that they are felt, so that laughter
> administered in fear and trembling may be the scourge — it
> is for this that I am used.

Adam Small is not the first poet to attack the conservative and even racist role of the Church. The négritude poets from the West Indies were the first blacks to consciously expose this double role of the church as an institution in Western societies. Virulently anti-clerical and even anti-Christian at times, the West Indian writers unmasked religion as one of the instruments of black oppression. Exploiting biblical texts, these writers and poets use them to expose the original Christian myth through a process of inversion. An excellent example of the anti-clerical and possibly anti-Christian, stream, is Jacques Roumain who writes in *The New Negro Sermon*:[41]

> We shall not forgive them, for they know what they do. . .
> They have made of the bleeding man the bloody god,
> O Judas snigger, snigger Judas. . . .
> In the cellars of the monasteries the priest counts the
> interest on the thirty pieces of silver.

Having exposed the priesthood and the church, Roumain espouses a new myth — revolution under a red banner:[42]

> No brothers, comrades,
> We shall pray no more . . .
> We shall no longer sing our sad and despairing spirituals.

> Another song shall surge from our throats,
> And we shall unfurl our red banners.

Small too is capable of ironic depiction, of inverting the Christian myth, of using the vulgar argot, which by sheer contrast with the original Biblical passage and elevated language, irritates. But Small is in no way anti-clerical in the négritude vein. His products are not vituperative ejaculations of hatred. He does not see institutionalized Christianity as integrally interwoven with, for example, racism or imperialism. Small, rather, tends to accommodate himself within the Christian myth. He can still write in a mood of acquiescence:[43]

> The Lord has shaken
> and the dice rolled wrongly for us
> That's all.[43]

The same acceptance of one's ascribed role of suffering is found in another poem, *Lydingsweg* (Road of Suffering):[44]

> We have long ago in places
> like Windermere
> all our longings
> forsworn.
>
> Oh Lord, you can go on listening
> to our song
> without worry, we are long ago
> past sorrow's door. . . .
> So don't worry Lord
> I'm fixed up
> I am my own Lord
> and then we too are even.
> if another's gang stabs me
> full of holes one day
> I'll go and die on my own cross
> specially for me.
>
> Oh! Long ago in places
> like Windermere
> we have all our longings
> forsworn
> long ago in places
> like Windermere

> we have all our longings
> forsworn.

Small is therefore never anti-Christian, only against the perversion of Christianity by the whites who profess to believe, but who discriminate on the basis of colour. He will use the Biblical passage and transplant it onto the 'coloured' setting, which gives his protest extra emotive force. And this would seem, at least to the white Christian, to be heresy. Christian books are studded with people who were burnt for less.

The poet, for example, uses the Christmas story to show that his people are familiar with such humiliations and know such lowly places on earth:[45]

> we know such places,
> yes, we know them.
> we've got duplicates all over
> in Windermere,
> in District Six . . .

This inversion of the white Christian myth reaches its zenith in his poems *Second Coming — I and II.* The coming of the Lord is portrayed in twentieth century terms: Christ himself is welcomed as a superstar by hippies and pious types alike. He is whisked off to a white reception, while the 'coloureds' surge towards him on the white fringe. And in what is possibly one of the best and poignantly pathetic lines in his entire *oeuvre,* a 'coloured' calls out as the car drives off to the white reception:[46]

> en notice my hie agter, please
> en smile moet my.
>
> and notice me here, at the back, please
> and smile with me.

In that one line is concentrated all the force and pain of Small's struggle — and by implication that of the 'coloureds': to be noticed and recognized.

Yet, there is nothing in Small's poetry which is comparable to the biting satire found in the works of the Antillean poets. Compare and contrast, for example, the poem entitled *Je n'aime pas l'Afrique* by Paul Niger from Guadeloupe with Small's religious poetry:[47]

Christ redeemed sinful man and built his Church in Rome.
His voice was heard in the desert. The Church on top of Society.
And Society on top of the Church, the one carrying the other
founded civilisation where men, docile to the ancient wisdom
to appease the old gods, not dead,
sacrifice every ten years several million victims

He had forgotten Africa.
But it was noticed that a race (of men?)
still had not paid God its tribute of black blood, they
reminded him
So Jesus spread his hands over the curly heads, and the
Negroes were saved.
Not in this world, of course

From Small: 'O God, Thy highest test is not the fire but the humili-ation'.[48]

For him as for Kierkegaard, 'Christianity is the divine, and that instance of the divine which precisely because it is truly divine would not at any price be a kingdom of this world.' Unfortunately, within the South African setting, this type of celestially-orientated Christianity has long outlived its purpose. But then, the Small of the seventies would himself concede this.

Many of his poems deal with the political system and despite the complete dismissal of his *oeuvre* by Jonker earlier on, it is certainly worthwhile taking a closer look at it. The poem *Liberalis Gahêkkel* (Liberal Heckled) is particularly interesting because in it he attacks those do-gooders who pose as liberals, but who in essence are no different from the other whites who discriminate:[49]

They view you with their whole range
of prejudice;
we, however, really sacrifice,
It's not for nothing we're nice

The way in which Small gives form to his political and religious protest in his writings finds no solace with the Afrikaners who interpret his poems as being hostile to the white man. But, neither does his attitude appeal to the politically-conscious and educated 'col-oureds', who view his 'socialized ambivalence' towards Afrikaans culture with disgust.

And yet, the satirical poem, *Oppie Parara* (lit. On the Parade), recalls that of the Nigerian writer, Wole Soyinka, namely *Telephone Conversation* in *Commonwealth Poems Today*.[50] The parade is an open square in Cape Town, which serves as a market and platform for various types of activities (formerly, blacks held mass protest meetings here). In the poem, he lampoons whites who lack the one trait which makes for true living – the gift of uninhibited and unbridled laughter. The tone and tenor of the poem right through is half-mocking and the white woman is made to appear ridiculous. There is even a subtle reference to sexuality in the poem, but it is formulated in such a manner that it is spleened of all vulgarity. It is the wit of a superior, and not of an inferior, which characterizes this poem:[51]

Oppie Parara

Please Madam
come smile
just look
our stalls are piled full of happiness

oh come why so sour today
fie fie
is life then vinegar
And where does madam buy it
looks dear to me too

no, madam
come smile
our stalls are piled full of happiness

The white woman cannot smile
and she commands:
I want nothing,
the coollie strictly formal

But madam, paw-paw, paw-paw and bananas
and juicy grapes from the heart of Canaan
and how does madam fancy such a fig
look just how swollen it is
from top to bottom bulging out
don't blush madam
we have a leaf to go with it

And in order to re-establish the balance, the white woman angrily
retorts:

> You, you coollie
> I shall call the police now!
>
> The fruit seller's voice trails behind
> police, police?
> Oh no madam, don't be so spiteful
> say decently goodbye . . . .

At times however, Small's poetry sags rather heavily under his
Kaaps and one is then indeed left with a feeling of unrefinement and
vulgarity. It is for this reason that some of his products have a pamphlet quality about them, and can also be relegated to transient inferiority. In his play *Kanna Hy Kô Hystoe* (Kanna, He's Coming Home,
1965), however, he reveals himself as a dramatist, who can do for
Afrikaans what Soyinka has done for Nigerian (and English) drama.

For the non-South African not familiar with Afrikaans or the
peculiarities of South Africa, *Kanna* (as I shall henceforth call the
play) will be well-nigh impossible to come to terms with. Yet
it is essential to remember that 'drama has unique capacities for
social unification, in that it works through the eyes of the spoken
word. Hence, if rightly shaped and performed, it can be equally
accessible to the literate and illiterate, the educated Christian convert
and the traditionalist, or, in Elizabethan terms, to the stage box and the
groundlings.'[52]

*Kanna* is fulfilling such a dual function, according to Afrikaans
critics. Thus, the celebrated author, poet and Afrikaner critic, W. E. G.
Louw, reminds the reader that *Kanna* is a play filled with poetry and
must be performed on the stage in order for the outsider to comprehend and enjoy its full richness. He finds the play not only a wry
commentary on South Africa, but one which brings tears to the eyes.

Significantly, many reviewers use as their starting point the lines
spoken by The Voice in the play: 'This is a story about the simple
one, the simplest of simple, the poor who will always be there . . .
always.' Small himself, in commenting on a performance of his play
by white actors, observes: 'The human exchange is necessary. And in
our country that exchange is easier through art than anywhere else.'[53]

'Coloureds' themselves, who have seen amateur performances, were
similarly moved, according to first-hand information. For in the play,
there was instant recognition of facets of their own lives. Yet the play

has also succeeded in transcending a parochialism and in exciting emotions of pathos among, especially, the Afrikaners.

*Die Transvaler,* a paper catering for the Afrikaner in the North, commented on the performance of Wilna (a white) who plays the old 'coloured' woman, Makiet, as follows:[54]

> As Makiet, Wilna has created an unforgettable and moving
> female character in Afrikaans, which can hold its own any
> day with those women in world literature, like Brecht's
> *Mutter Courage,* Schiller's *Maria Stuart,* Ibsen's *Hedda Gabler,*
> Euripides' *Electra* and *Medea,* Sophocles' *Antigone.*

It must be realized at all times, that the 'coloured' has been forced into such a stage of 'socialized ambivalence' that whatever dramas were performed, in draughty church halls and schools with abominable acoustics, consisted either of Strindberg's *The Father*, Shakespeare's *Hamlet*, or worse still, the Afrikaner author Frits Steyn's *Wildsbokkie.* All these plays were of course far removed from the cultural, linguistic and socio-political realities of the 'coloured' townships of Bonteheuwel and Manenberg.

The story is a fairly simple one of a rural 'coloured' family which lives in poverty-stricken conditions and decides to move to the city. Kanna, the main character, is an orphan adopted by the redoubtable old woman, Makiet. The pattern is the familiar one of a poor family pinching and saving to enable Kanna, their one bright hope, to enjoy a good education.

In a sense, Kanna is the first real 'Been-to' in South African literature, a type so readily found in the works of the West African authors, Achebe, Armah and Soyinka. Kanna leaves for overseas and all action is centred round his scheduled return — the cargo come home. In this respect he recalls the parallel with the cargo cultists in Guinea as found in the novel *Fragments* by the Ghanaian Armah:[55]

> The main export to the other world is people . . .. At any rate it
> is clearly understood that the been-to has chosen, been awarded,
> a certain kind of death. A beneficial death, since cargo follows
> his return. Not just cargo, but also importance, power, a radiating
> influence capable of touching ergo elevating all those who . . .
> have suffered the special bereavement caused by the been-to's
> going away . . .. After all, in the unelaborated system —
> where the been-to has yet to make his appearance, and there is
> no intermediary . . . at any rate — the human being once dead is in

his burial considered as having been exported to the other world.
A return is expected from his presence there: he will intercede
on behalf of those not yet dead, asking them what they need most
urgently .... Needs dictated by instant survival and subsistence
requirements .... The been-to here then only fleshes out the
pattern. He is the ghost in person returned to live among men,
a powerful ghost understood to the extent that he behaves like
a powerful ghost, cargo and all .... In many ways the been-to
cum ghost is and has to be a transmission belt for cargo. Not a
maker, but an intermediary. Making takes too long, the intermediary brings quick gains.

In a sense then, Kanna is the 'Been-to' who was sent off (admittedly
not with a libation in West African style, but at least with a prayer),
to the other world to return with cargo, like Baako, the chief character
in Armah's novel *Fragments*. Kanna does not return permanently
(only briefly upon the death of his old mother, Makiet), but through
the technique of flashback and scenes spanning time and space, even
the grave, the reader is familiarized with Makiet and her family. Small
has also 'transformed the irritating flashback into a way of annihilating
time and space so as to raise dramatic issues about the relationship
between past and present'.[56]
While Kanna is overseas, Kietie is raped as a toddler by a street
gang, which is witnessed by her brother, Diekie. There is no over
dramatization of the horror of this act. If anything, the horror of it
is conveyed precisely through the down-playing of the incident. Kietie
is first engaged to a road-side preacher who commits suicide. Then she
gets married to Poena, who forces her to become a prostitute. Diekie,
her brother, is eventually hanged for murdering Poena. In a poignantly
simple scene, a similar effect of overall tragedy is achieved when Diekie
says farewell at the station, on his last journey to Pretoria to be hanged.
The central figure in the play is the old woman Makiet. Of the
white girl Wilna's portrayal of Makiet, the author himself says: 'in
her acting, the old woman gains a dimension, a stature which keeps
her rooted at one and the same time in the circumstances of the old
brown woman, of whom I had written ... rooted also in eternity'.[57]
Makiet then is the hardened prototype of the selfless, hard-working
and long-suffering 'coloured' woman. She is umbilically linked to Lea,
the female character in *Mine Boy,* a novel by the South African author
Peter Abrahams. Makiet realizes that reward on this earth for her children
can only come through education — and education will bring in its wake

cargo. Her role becomes even more strenuous through the limitations imposed on her by the artist. Makiet can only operate from a wheel chair, can only transmit through gestures of the hand, the body and the eyes. In respect of Makiet it is worthwhile quoting O'Toole when he so astutely observes: 'The strength of the wife role in poor Coloured society lies in the fact that a woman can always fulfil her faminine functions as homemaker and mother, while it is not always possible for a man to fulfil his masculine function as a bread-winner.'[58]

Small, in an interview quoted in the Afrikaans daily *Die Burger* (September 13, 1973) said of *Kanna*: 'The play . . . gives the best insight ever into a portion of our South African reality and, naturally, into a portion of the universal reality of poverty here among us.'[59] The line: 'Toe, Sit, Hulle Maar Die Hysgoed Op Die Karretjie' (then they dumped all their belongings on a little cart), filled with pathos and evoking images of the play *Anatevka*, could very well have been the epitaph of the poor.

There are, however, deficiencies in the play. Small does not allow one to enter into the private awareness of his characters. The constant comparison with Brecht by critics jars, for a comparison with the works of the Nigerian dramatist Soyinka would have been more profitable, especially his *The Swampdwellers*. The play is however characterized by one outstanding quality – that of visual actuality.

The discussion of *Kanna* has again revealed how difficult it is to define Small within the South African context. The aura of ambiguity continues to cling to him, notwithstanding his more political pronouncements in the seventies. Praised by Afrikaner critics for his play, he still had to have special permission by the whites to attend a performance of his own play, about 'coloureds', by a white company, in a white theatre.

And therein lies his dilemma. Perhaps his self-mockery, in one of his poems, illustrates this:[60]

> Ou bryn pêllie
> ou swart pêllie
> ek sê
> wat is daa in die wêreld in vi djou
> sê vi my?
> ek sil vi jou sê:
> fokôl man, fôkol!
> — die gatkant van die railwaytreine
> die gatkant van die êrouplyne

113

> Ol' brown pally
> ol' black pally
> I say
> what's there in the world
> for you
> tell me?
> I'll tell you:
> fuckall man, fuckall!
> the backside of the railway trains
> the backside of the aeroplanes

Poetry for Small has, in the words of John Huizinga, 'not only an aesthetic function . . . but a vital function that is both social and liturgical'. Yet his central dilemma remains:[61]

> I am not against the appellation Afrikaner [he apologizes]. I
> am only against petty Afrikanerdom . . . and Afrikanerdom is for
> me at the moment petty, generally petty. Read thus or hear,
> everywhere I say Afrikaner, actually petty Afrikaner. It is
> this that I am contrasting with Afrikaans. We must not forget
> that many people besides the Afrikaner speak and is therefore
> in one way or another Afrikaans. This is actually my dilemma
> as a 'Sestiger'.

And yet, the following sardonic lines by Small nibble at one's consciousness (Small, 1974[2], p. 28):[62]

> brownman
> why worry?
> your guitar
> is slung o'er your shoulder
> — the noose gets tighter and tighter —
> but your guitar's slung o'er your shoulder
> brownman
> why worry?

Since 'politics is fate' where freedom does not exist, Adam Small's satire goes unheeded, and he finds himself judged on the basis of political and philosophical statements which are subject to misinterpretation. Unfortunately for him, it is the 'brown Afrikaner' image which lingers on in the minds of his antagonists. The white Afrikaner, who undergoes his cultural revolution under the name of 'Sestiger', is confronted with a similar crisis. He must prove that Afrikaans is not synonymous with Afrikaner oppression and *baaskap* (overlordship/ domination).

# Chapter 7

# My brother's keeper[1]

The ambiguity and duality surrounding the 'Cape coloured' reach a peak with the group of Afrikaner literary iconoclasts who pursue their cultural revolution under the nomenclature, *Die Sestigers* (i.e. those from the sixties). The 'Sestigers' one learns, do not form a movement as such, but consist rather of a group of individuals who deviate from the accepted myth of Afrikanerdom. In a foreword to a publication on these writers one reads that: 'The literature of the "Sestigers" is a literature of exile inside their own country, and especially in the wider context of Afrikaans literature.'[2]

The 'Sestigers', one gathers, are writers who open the portals of Afrikanerdom by touching upon such issues as the oppression of the blacks and the hypocrisy of Afrikanerdom in respect of sex and religion. Formerly these issues were either sacrosanct, taboo or simply ignored. One should however bear in mind that they were not the first Afrikaans writers to draw a link between literature and society. Afrikaans poetry was (and still is) full of references to social issues affecting themselves, for example the Anglo-Boer war, the period of poor-whiteism in Afrikaner history. But the involvement was a group myopic one, or as the South African critic and writer, Ezekiel Mphahlele, puts it, 'one-eyed Dickensian' in orientation.[3] The chief concentration was on the Afrikaner tribe, with the blacks featuring only as stereotypes.

The 'Sestigers' were however different in that they seriously attempted to break through this group myopia. Understandably, quite a few of the Afrikaner writers concentrated on the 'coloured' as part of the Afrikaans-speaking community. Jan Rabie, the novelist and short story writer, represents one spectrum of the search for a common identity within the Afrikaans-speaking community. In his novel *Ons die afgod* (lit. We the Idolaters, 1958), he attempts

116

to define the 'coloured' presence within the Afrikaans community.

André Brink, the other Afrikaner writer who has largely determined the face of the 'Sestigers', even went one ambitious step further, in his novel, *Kennis van die aand* (1974), by letting his main 'coloured' character, Josef Malan, become a gross historical (genetic) and political indictment against Afrikanerdom.

Breytenbach, the arch-apostle of the 'Sestigers' before his fall from grace, attempted to destroy the cultural ox-wagon with pyrotechnical zeal while still in exile in Paris.

Admittedly then, the 'Sestigers' were openly critical of their tribe, the Afrikaners, and some came close to identifying themselves with the black cause (or at least pleading for a change of heart among their fellow white men).

Jan Rabie, in assessing the South African situation, even resorts to what appears to be a 'black idiom'. He reminds his group, the Afrikaners, that the non-whites are only used as a source of cheap black labour, that the English are at least capable of a critical voice and the Afrikaner, his people, fulfil an oppressive role. Like Adam Small, Jan Rabie's main concern is to define the boundaries of, at least, Afrikaansdom as opposed to Afrikanerdom. And he is especially concerned with the role of his 'brown brother' within Afrikaansdom.

Rabie realizes that his community of Afrikanerdom cannot function optimally if half of its speakers are eliminated solely on the basis of having a darker hue. 'The Afrikaans community', he writes, 'is but half a one. Of the four and a half million with Afrikaans as their mother-tongue, half is not regarded as Afrikaner . . . is poor and voteless . . . . Our brown brothers [bruin broers].'[4] Drawing on history, Rabie goes on to remind his fellow Afrikaners, in most forceful terms, that 'the Afrikaans language is the country's greatest multi-racial achievement hitherto; originating during the mixing of Hollander and Hottentot and imported slaves two, three centuries ago. Hottentot-bastards were the first to carry the name Afrikaner. Afrikaans and Afrikaner is therefore not synonymous with Whiteman.'[5]

But the one person who by and large constituted the vital sinew within 'Sestiger' thinking was Breytenbach. He had crossed all institutionalized borders by first going into exile, and then marrying across the colour line; that is, someone who was not white, let alone Afrikaner. While overseas, he had heaped scorn on Afrikanerdom and worse still, had openly aligned himself with black revolutionary movements. He was welcomed by black and white opponents of apartheid, who were enamoured of the idea of an Afrikaner convert against the political system. After all, had history not produced other loyal Afrikaner freedom fighters, notably, Abraham Fischer?[6]

Breyten was also of course (or primarily one should say), a poet of no mean ability, who, in style and content, had shaped Afrikaans in a way it had never been shaped before. He was not only an iconoclast but also a pioneer. If at home in South Africa, young people were rather charmed by the Breytenbach phenomenon, then overseas it was his political pronouncements which gained for him the fame he eventually enjoyed. In an article entitled *Vulture Culture,* he spelt out some of his political credo as follows:[7]

Apartheid is the state and the condition of being apart. It
is the no man's land between peoples. But this gap is not a
neutral space. It is the artificially created distance
necessary to attenuate, for the practitioners, the very raw
reality of racial, economic, social and cultural discrimination
and exploitation. It is the space of the white man's being.
It is the distance needed to convince himself of his
denial of the other's humanity. It ends up denying all
humanity of any kind to the other and to
himself.

Being an artist himself, Breytenbach realized that the white writer,[8]

cannot dare look into himself. He doesn't wish to be bothered
with his responsibilities as a member of the 'chosen' and
dominating group. He withdraws and longs for the tranquillity
of a little intellectual house on the plain by a transparent river.
He will consider himself a new 'realist', an 'anti-idealist'.

In another article, called *The Fettered Spirit,* he refers to the Afrikaner ideology as one of 'Christian Nationalism or Calvinist tribalism . . . trying to perpetuate itself (according to the image it has of itself) by monopolizing all power and dictating to the other tribes their supposed lines and forms of cultural, political and economic development.'[9]

Let us take a closer look at the tone and tenor of the two excerpts concerning South Africa. One is at once aware of a very interesting phenomenon. When Breytenbach discusses the political scene in South Africa in its totality, he is less forceful. However, when Breytenbach discusses or rails against the tribe that is Afrikanerdom, or when he interprets the tribe within the overall South African setting, he comes over very forcefully indeed. Being of the tribe and having belonged to the tribe, having subscribed to the tribal ethos at one stage, he does not have to resort to pedantry and sophistry in his depictions. For he knows the tribe inside out. Notice, for instance, the difference between the line in *Vulture Culture* that, 'apartheid is a state of being apart', and the following attack on the Afrikaner in *The Fettered Spirit* that, 'Afrikaner ideology is one of Christian Nationalism and Calvinist tribalism'. The first observation seems forced and the second is plucked straight from the heart.

It is when he is at least Afrikaans (if not Afrikaner), that he is most effective in his commentaries on the South African political scene. Then he can confront his reader with the beauty and the tragedy of his land culminating in such lines as the following:[10]

God the Bureau for the Safety of the State
God with a helmet on
in one hand a brief case full of shares and gold
in the other a sjambok.

At home, he was admired by younger Afrikaners for daring to say what they felt vaguely. Older Afrikaner academics, while recognizing Breytenbach's poetic talent and contribution, were very uneasy about his un-Afrikaner-like activities. The extent to which Afrikanerdom was disturbed by Breytenbach's extra-literary activities is evident from an interview with the Afrikaner Professor T. T. Cloete in an Afrikaans daily, *Die Burger,* in 1974.[11] When asked whether Breyten Breytenbach was really a danger to the Afrikaner nation and the Afrikaner language, Cloete made it quite clear that the poet was associating himself with the enemies of Afrikanerdom. He enumerated wellknown opponents and writers in exile, among others, Mphahlele, Brutus and La Guma. The inference was crystal clear — Breyten was also an enemy. Cloete was however prepared to concede the intrinsic merit of the literary products of Breytenbach. From Cloete's remarks it was already evident that Afrikanerdom was prepared to sacrifice Breytenbach. This aspect of his life will however be dealt with at a somewhat later stage.

There are thus very many facets to the poet Breytenbach. In the first place, he was an Afrikaner who wrote in Afrikaans, and Afrikanerdom never allowed him to forget this. But, he was also a poet living in exile in Paris, away from his immediate language community, which in the end would inevitably have imposed certain restrictions on his creative ability. In addition, Breytenbach was also playing a very active political role against the political system in South Africa.

119

The poetry of Breytenbach is indeed one of the highlights in the history of Afrikaans. It is not my intention to go into the 'earthiness of the oral and anal notes'[12] in the work of Breytenbach, nor the influence of Zen Buddhism on some of his poetry. The concern is rather with Breytenbach the Afrikaner prodigal son and his impact on Afrikaner culture as a 'Sestiger'. The poet's problem was not to make an orphic descent, but to deny the tribe and risk ostracism and hostility. A poet who writes in a language like Afrikaans is in greater need of his immediate community than someone who writes in English, or French for that matter. One needs to dip into the idiom and melody, in order to sustain the creative process. In the absence of such an immediate Afrikaans-speaking community, the risk of losing one's touch is not unreal.

Exile is an oft-recurring theme with Breytenbach. As an Afrikaner who wrote (and writes) in Afrikaans, his dilemma was compounded of several elements. He needed the tribe, the language, the melody and the landscape for his creativity. Yet, at the same time, he had learnt to despise the tribe. This loneliness comes through at times. Rejection of apartheid for a black man in South Africa means regaining dignity. For the white writer it entails isolation and negation, alienation and frustration and probably feelings of guilt. For the pressures, even from friends from within (i.e. in South Africa), are great not to over-step the institutionalized borders, as Breytenbach at times experienced. In his poem *Luistervink,* Breytenbach realizes that he can at the most become, 'a Frenchman with a speech impediment'.[13] Yet he knows that others will follow him and it is on their behalf that he wishes to intercede. He pleads that those who come afterwards should also be treated with kindness.

Yet to me it is not the poem in which he calls Vorster a butcher, but a simple and lyrically beautiful one, depicting his imaginary home-coming, which lingers on. It is filled with pathos, humour and nostalgia. It is so specifically South African (Afrikaans), and yet so simply univer-sal — the exile who dreams of seeing his hearth once more in his poem, *Die hand vol vere*:[14]

> inside ma's heart is standing still
> (and where are the glasses?)
> pa wakes up a little dazed and confused
>
> but mummy is already outside
> in dressing gown with red cheeks

and there I was larger than life
on the lawn near the cement dam . . .

a top hat on
a smart suit
carnation in button hole
new Italian shoes for the occasion
my hand full of presents
a song for my ma a little bit of pride for my pa

. . . I had thought I would be there just so
like a Coloured Christmas choir on Christmas morning mummy
I had thought how we would cry then
and drink tea.

Here Breytenbach was not trying to be just Afrikaner and man
or Afrikaner, politician and man. Here he was a *man* in exile like
La Guma, Nortje and Mphahlele, longing for home. Not *Afrikaner
man,* just *man.*

One suspects that part of Breytenbach's appeal as poet, painter
and Afrikaner, in Holland, was his political opposition to apartheid,
rather than the beauty of his poetry. In a sense however, Holland
as a country did more to provide Breyten, the exile, with a spiritual
(linguistic) climate of recognition than France, for example, ever
could.

Increasingly, Breytenbach's activities were taking on a political
turn and in 1974, he returned clandestinely, some aver out of misguided idealism, a deep-rooted nostalgia and a suicide wish, in order
to set up a series of political cells for the overthrow of the apartheid
State. He was arrested and sentenced to nine years. All Afrikaner
writers hastened to find extenuating circumstances for his crime. Some
of his poetry was movingly recited in the courtroom. Never had the
judiciary been assaulted with such an effusion of Afrikaans poetry.
He was made to appear a prodigal son who had strayed. The poet
himself apologized to the Prime Minster, Vorster, for insulting him in
one of his poems. Afrikanerdom closed ranks to help an illustrious
son, like it had never done for other distinguished blacks. The
Breytenbach case revealed one important lesson to those so-called
iconoclasts — Afrikanerdom knows no pardon for those who stray
from the fold. Even Breytenbach had to acknowledge this in his final
plea, which ended in a rather pathetic *mea culpa.*

In all the apologies made for Breytenbach afterwards by Afrikaner poets, novelists and academicians, one by Adam Small stands out. 'There are people who . . . find nine years a heavy sentence and that is true . . . but I too live behind bars in this country . . .. The bars are the colour of my skin.'[15]

Concerning Breytenbach's poetry Small continued: 'how many of the verses which can still be read as one would want them to be read, how many of the verses can still remain standing after what Breytenbach has said in court? It is as if Breyten would now have to start writing all over again, it is as if he had destroyed a large part of his own work.'[15]

If Breytenbach temporarily stood for the voice of conscience in Afrikaner literature while overseas, then at home, André Brink seemed to fulfil a similar role. As a young and very bright Afrikaner, he had given ample proof of his talents. He was rather prolific as a writer, having written several novels and articles.

However, the novel which caught on outside the confines of Afrikanerdom and Afrikaansdom was *Kennis van die aand* (translated by the author himself as *Looking on Darkness*, 1974). It dealt specifically with the situation of the 'Cape coloured', Josef Malan. It was also the most daring treatment of the colour question ever attempted in Afrikaans by an Afrikaner author. One has only to compare Josef Malan with *Toiings* by Mikro, or *Skanwan van die duine* by the Hobson brothers, to appreciate this.

Afrikaner religious, cultural and political leaders were particularly upset by the content and the tenor of the novel. The book gained the distinction of being the first novel by an Afrikaner writer in Afrikaans ever to be banned. The Dutch Reformed Minister who submitted the novel to the censorship board spoke for most of Afrikanerdom when he advanced reasons as to why the book should be banned. He objected to the novel because it tore religion apart and also ridiculed it. The novelist also vilified the Afrikaner, who was depicted as being cruel and oppressive. The police force in particular was portrayed as inhuman. Other church dignitaries called the novel filthy, vulgar and obscene. The Reverend Vorster, brother to the Prime Minister, spelt out his peculiar literary critical opinions in the following manner when he said: 'if this be art, then a house of ill-repute is a Sunday School'.[16]

Even one of the judges hearing the appeal against the banning order saw fit to prejudge the findings by declaring the book to be despicable, inhuman, sadistic and violent (*Die Burger,* 7 August 1974).[17] The following criticism was fairly general:[18]

The country in question is South Africa, with its police force
and whites portrayed as overlords and the oppressors of those
with a darker pigmentation. The people with a different skin
colour are represented in the form of the South African Cape
Coloured, who is the narrator in the book .... We have a
distorted and one-sided picture of race relations in this land
where Josef, like a Christ-like figure, is made to suffer innocently
and led to the slaughter chamber by the white man who acts
like a bully. The complicated racial situation is reduced to a
one-sided coarse contradiction, with on the one hand, the white
oppressor boorish, stupid, pale and impotent — and on the other,
the brownman — virile, refined, intelligent and civilized.

Critics overseas received the book with general acclaim. Thus the
ex-South African and novelist Jonty Driver, now resident in England,
said in the *Times Literary Supplement* of the English translation
that Brink 'has torn the nest to pieces'.[19] Driver, the exile, proved
himself to be totally ignorant of the ambiguity and near-kinship charac-
terizing 'Afrikaner-coloured' relationships when he innocently and
naively commented: 'It interests me that Afrikaner writers seem to find
it much easier to identify imaginatively with the Coloured than with
the black Africans'.[19]

The story centres upon Josef Malan, a talented 'coloured' actor,
who is awaiting excution for the murder (an unfinished suicide pact)
of his white girl friend, Jessica. He is intelligent, sensitive and moves,
despite his brownness, in an essentially white idiom. His world is one
of Molière and Tartuffe, of Shakespeare and Hamlet, of Pirandello
and Artaud.

There are few novels in Afrikaans where the 'coloured' features
so large. Brink, the novelist, supplies Josef with a neatly constructed
genealogical tree. One of the striking qualities of Afrikanerdom is
its glorification of the heroic past. All this is a necessary adjunct to
powerful myth formation in the Afrikaner group. One of the noticeable
omissions in the 'coloured' make-up is the lack of such an historical
background as a solid basis for myth-formation. Now, thanks to Brink,
the 'coloured', Josef Malan, was provided with a past and myth in the
best Afrikaner and Afrikaans tradition. In this past are found various
strands of South African history — slaves from the East Indies, Khoi
from the Cape, French Huguenots in exile, Dutchmen, Irishmen and
Xhosas. In the initial chapters, Brink constructs a collage of
miscegenation and violence unparalleled in Afrikaans literature. The

associations are also 'devoid of lyricism', as Millin would have it. Josef's ancestry disappears in an orgy of violence. They all die prematurely, never reaching beyond that Christological figure of thirty-three years of age. His 'coloured' males are martyrs in the white man's world. Here the no-past, no-myth, heritage of the 'Cape coloured' is forcibly accounted for. Josef Malan is the first 'Huguentot' in Afrikaans.

Josef's ancestry reads like a page from the Old Testament. It is studded with an Abraham, a Rachel, a Martha and finally, a Josef Malan. Admittedly, this is a creditable attempt to cast the history of the 'coloured' in fictionalized form. The historical novel as a genre draws, of course, on a long tradition in Afrikaans literature. There is the Boer war hero and spy, as enshrined in the works of Mikro. There is the Great Trek hero, as found in the novels of Stuart Cloete. The Dutch past is invoked in *Mooi Annie* by d'Arbez. The nearest one can get to this in the fiction of black writers is Peter Abrahams' *Wild Conquest* (1951).

The picture as it emerges in Brink's novel is an unpretty one. It recalls the factual accounts of Marais in *The Cape Coloured People* (1939) and those of numerous other South African authors. The novelist, Brink, uses the historical situation as an indictment against the system of apartheid. As with Breytenbach, he too is particularly forceful when attacking the tribe. Despite the book's short-comings, it is a wry commentary on South African society. Liberal critics waxed lyrical over the novel. Here was an Afrikaner writer and an academic, telling the world in fictionalized form that the Afrikaner was a monster and a brute. He was no outsider but an insider. Moreover, his novel disturbed his tribe so much, that one of the Ministers of the Church immediately submitted it to the censorship board for scrutiny. Rugby photos and pictures of scantily clad white girls, which generally adorn Afrikaans newspapers, made way for lengthy articles on the pornographic and politically damaging qualities of the book. Academics took part, the clergy wrote long tirades, even ordinary members of Afrikanerdom responded. Yet, there are definite indications that Brink did not veer so radically from the accepted Afrikaans literary tradition.

First of all, Josef is a 'coloured' who, in the words of his mother, can claim on the basis of his father's family tree that 'he has a history just like any old white man'.[20] The female progenitors are again submissive types, the men tragic misfits or mere pawns, doomed for premature extinction. Having situated the 'coloured' in this historical framework of rapine, unwilling pregnancies, relationships shorn of romance, lives without any glorious myths to prop up dreary existences, Brink then proceeds to portray Josef, the main character, in modern-day South Africa.

Much of the praise or criticism heaped on the novel stems from the author's treatment of the racial situation. Afrikaners objected to the portrayal of the white man as a predator, rapist and violator. Liberals extolled the revolutionary and anti-racist stance of the novel. Yet the interesting quality of the book is hardly mentioned in reviews — that is, Josef's relationship with his white friends. For it is in this, that Josef Malan appears to be cast very much in the South African literary tradition of ambiguity.

In no way is he free from the unconscious desire to be white. He is industrious, intelligent, a prototype of the sensitive, educated 'coloured' as described by Adam Small in *Die eerste steen.* Yet he is firmly encapsulated in the castle of his skin.

Josef's relationship with white women is even more interesting. It seems to approximate to 'a kind of subjective consecration to wiping out in himself and in his own mind the colour prejudice from which he has suffered so long'.[21]

The white women are all pre-Raphaelites, walking straight out of the paintings of Millais, paeans of beauty, golden-haired tributes to white aestheticism — for example, Jessica and Hermien. The relationship between Josef and Jessica is one big rhapsodic canticle. The same undercurrent of sex which pervades the novels of white authors from Africa to America, when white women and 'coloured' men are brought together, is noticeable here.

Hermien, the white girl on the farm where Josef grew up, becomes a Virgin Mary or a Little Miss Muffet. The childhood episode where Josef briefly sees Hermien perched naked on a rock is nostalgically recalled when he is with Jessica. In the throes of sexual activities, he has to forcibly suppress this image of Hermien, 'heraldically perched on her rock'.[22]

Josef's first meeting with Jessica, the girl from England, has a dreamlike ethereal quality. The moment lasts forever, is permeated with fragrant romance and *weltschmerz* — they become twin souls breathing as if one. Josef, 'so beautiful, so brown',[23] becomes a 'coloured' Werther. Fully conversant with Shakespeare, Molière and Pirandello, he is in effect only frustrated by his darker hue. His sexual encounters with white women have a singularly poetic quality. By contrast, his 'coloured' females are as unprepossessing or as totally insignificant as those found in the works of Millin. Josef's mother groans under life and her periodical sexual escapades. The 'coloured' women in Josef's theatre group are evaluated largely in terms of their sexual capabilities — that is, they are either good in bed or very inept. No romantic aura surrounds them. One suspects, nay knows for certain, that Brink's inability to create truthful 'coloured' female characters is due to his failure to penetrate this facet of South African life. After all, the law simply forbids such contact. On the other hand, it is easier for the white and 'coloured' male to forge some sort of relationship which passes for friendship in South Africa.

In demythologizing the South African scene, the novelist Brink himself fell prey to some white myths. In fact, Josef is much more of a product of ambiguity than would at first be apparent. He is also much more of a 'brown' Afrikaner than meets the eye in this ostensibly political novel. There is, for instance, the relationship between Josef and Willem, the Afrikaner who grew up with him, but who has become a prosperous person in town. Their relationship was very intimate in childhood, but awkward in adulthood. Yet both of them fail to wipe out that former intimacy. It embarrasses Willem at times, yet he cannot ignore Josef. It is this ambiguity and former intimacy in a shared childhood, which causes Willem to provide the financial backing for Josef's theatrical group. This duality is evident when Josef visits Willem in his office. Willem is half-apologetic on the one hand, yet forced to defend his white self. He admits; 'I am bound by my colour to the group which allows this to happen. I can do nothing about it.'[24] Josef, despite the fact that he is castigating his former friend, coaxes him into a familiarity, by recalling the childhood scene, where they fell asleep in each other's arms. The 'brown' Afrikaner brother and the 'white' Afrikaner, bound to each other in a bond of shared memories and racially ascribed roles.

Jerry, Josef's friend and fellow actor, emerges as a much more realistic type, who at least operates within the society with guile, humour and suppressed bitterness. With Josef, like with Jan Herold, in Rabie's novel, *Ons die afgod* (1958), one is still reminded too much of Mikro's Toiings, 'hands stretched out for a little bit of love . . . at the Afrikaner portals . . . marching to the same destiny'.

Self-immolation on Josef's part does not wipe out the desire to be white. The Josef who says, 'each person must choose his own territory of involvement and mine is the theatre'[25], is a far cry from the two characters, Michael Adonis and Willie Boy in La Guma's *A Walk in the Night* (1962).

In all the rumpus about Brink's book, one article contained in the

*Journal* of the TLSA (more of an open letter to Brink), was completely overlooked by white South Africans. The letter assesses the novel from the viewpoint of the 'non-citizens', as the writer puts it:[26]

> Your chief character Josef Malan is a 'talented brownman', and therefore it is necessary to obtain some clarity about the concept 'Coloured' (as also the concepts Bantu, Indian etc.). Clarity about race, colour and nation is the sine qua non for any meaningful discussion of South African affairs . . . . The 'Coloured' (or Bantu, Indian etc.) is not a human being but an artificially created classification, who exists by and in the South African legislation . . . . Poor Josef Malan. You have created him, as 'Coloured', and therefore he stands under the sign of the lie, is less of a fully-fledged human being. Just notice the relationship between Josef and Willem, especially upon Josef's return. Here one is not confronted with a man, but with what the Afrikaner intellectual *thinks* the educated Coloured would feel, think and do . . . . You have used your own experiences in creating Josef Malan . . . he makes love as you made love or as you could have done it . . . You have tried to create Josef out of two conflicting elements, man and 'Coloured' man . . . Why must Jessica and Josef die? Do you really expect me to believe and accept that the only future there is for love across the colour line is death? Come off it André! . . . Here you give in as artist to the deep and dark feelings of your tribe.

Brink's novel covers a wide political canvas, Jan Rabie's *Ons die afgod* (1958) is mainly concerned with the 'bruin' (brown) presence within the Afrikaner cosmos. When the novel first appeared, it made a considerable impact because of the empathetic plea contained in it. Rabie was thus one of the earliest iconoclasts by Afrikaner (Afrikaans) standards. This idea of an Afrikaans-speaking community which included 'ons bruin broers' (our brown brothers) came out clearly at the conference of all those writers styled as 'Sestigers', at the University of Cape Town in 1973. In a sense, it was a coming together of like and 'enlightened' Afrikaners (Afrikaans-speaking persons), who were said to be committed artists. Theirs was a Mini Trek, convened to define at least, the borders of Afrikaansdom, if not Afrikaner-dom, as they understood it.

Rabie, the Afrikaner, and Small arrive at similar conclusions in respect of the Afrikaans-speaking community. The 'brownman' is Afrikaans, if not in skin colour, then at least in language and culture.

Right at the inception of Rabie's novel, one of the cardinal themes is spelt out. Frans, the questioning and enlightened Afrikaner, is speaking to his former classmate and friend Willem, who has turned into a successful farmer and a die-hard conservative. In the course of the conversation, Willem states that 'everyone who speaks my language is dear to me'.[27] And a little later, when Frans is alone with Willem's sister Hermien, he is prompted to ask whether the 'brown people', who also speak Willem's language, are also dear to him. Here already, there is a hint of Rabie's search to prove that 'Afrikaans is not synonymous with Afrikaner and white'.[28]

Willem and his family stand for the traditional ideas and values in Afrikanerdom, enshrined in the trinity of Language, God and People. This trinity is fed by an ancestral veneration for the land and cheap brown and black labour. The Willems are the ritual proprietors of *Die Groot Trek*. Frans, the roamer, is the voice of conscience, who sees where his people have fallen by the wayside. He realizes that they have turned material possessions in the shape of huge farms, into idols. He then, is the representative of the Mini Trek.

Jan Herold is the brownman who approximates to the Afrikaner way of life and thinking. He grew up with Willem, played with him, and is imbued with a similar ancestral love for the soil of his village, Greysdal, as, for example, his white friend Willem. But Herold is destined for tragedy because he has come back to disturb the neat little equation of Afrikanerdom, by stepping out of his institutionalized role of subservience. The relationship between Willem, the Afrikaner, and Jan, the 'coloured', is fraught with ambiguities. For Jan, the brownman, this is symbolized by his attachment to an old pocket knife he once received from Willem as a present. Willem himself is awkward and defensive in discussing Herold, the 'coloured', with his friend Frans.

The whites are openly hostile to Herold. To them, he is a smart Aleck (or to put it in Afrikaans, *oorlams*). He, for instance, drives a car and refuses to behave slavishly. Both Herold and the whites of Greysdal are caught up in a mutual web of distrust and dependence. Herold's great desire to buy a piece of land in Greysdal, the town of his birth, and notably a part of Willem's farm land, is not only a direct threat to the Afrikaner heritage, but also underlines his unconscious identification with them. Herold is a typical product of cultural ambivalence.

Frans, the outsider, is similarly caught between his love for his people, the Afrikaners, and a realization that the brownman is also part of his cultural heritage. Frans is even prepared to sacrifice the friendship of Willem and the love of his sister for his beliefs. His one man crusade is destined to fail because he gets embroiled in two types of hostilities — that of Jan Herold who mistrusts his motives — and that of his fellow Afrikaners in Greysdal, who come to look upon him as a 'kafferboetie'[29] and a traitor. In stepping out of his ascribed role, Frans loses everything, including the love of Hermien.

Williams, the 'coloured' school principal, who prefers to speak English and not the language of the oppressor, is cast in the role of the communist. He, however, at least knows how to operate within the Afrikaner system without losing his self respect. Williams stands for the rejection of Afrikaans and Afrikanerdom. Jan Herold is a 'coloured' who tries hard to accommodate himself within Afrikanerdom and the cultural pattern. Yet, not even Williams is free from the taint of ambiguity. He, for example, changes his tone and attitude towards Frans after his initial hostile attitude, when he finds out that the latter meant well.

When Herold is mercilessly thrashed by Willem, the incident comes over as one of self-castigation. Similarly, when Herold lands in prison, it is Willem who feels he should save him from the indignities of the common criminal by buying him to serve his sentence as one of his farm labourers. It appears to be more of a conscience salvaging effort on his part however. Yet, this ostensibly kind deed elicits only resentment and sullenness on the part of Herold.

Such ambiguities characterize the entire behaviour patterns of both Willem, the Afrikaner, and Jan Herold, the 'coloured'. Herold's ambiguous attitude and his repeated pathetic attempts at self-immolation are a radical departure from the *Toiings* type, and a notable feature of the 'new brownman' in Afrikaans literature of the 'Sestigers'. In the end, Herold kills Willem, the white Afrikaner brother, for denying him, the 'brown Afrikaner' brother, a part of his heritage. He kills him with the very same pocket knife he once had as a gift. And in so doing, he symbolically seems to kill his other self. Again, one is back with the cry uttered by Mikro and Small about the 'coloured' when Jan Herold says: 'I did not want his land! If he had only once treated me like his fellow human being.'[30]

Jan Herold and Josef Malan, then, are 'coloureds' (bruinmense) who are the products of cultural ambivalence. In Jan Rabie's view, the Afrikaans community is incomplete, because our 'brown' brothers are rejected.

The 'Cape coloured' may then be largely Afrikaans in terms of ·language (although this too is debatable). Through the pigmentocratic factor, he operates largely in an idiom which makes him essentially non-Afrikaans. It may very well be that the Afrikaner has duped himself into thinking that he understands the 'coloured's' language, whereas in essence he is completely out of touch with the 'coloured's' idiom, as will become even clearer from the works of Alex La Guma.

Breytenbach's warning in his article, *Vulture Culture*, looms large for all Afrikaner writers who move outside their institutionalized roles: 'If you write or paint or film as an Afrikaner you have to compromise the only raw material you have, yourself, your own integrity. You become alienated from yourself which is worse than being cut off from the tribe.'[31] Few Afrikaners are prepared to defy the tribe or invite its scorn. Breytenbach himself finally experienced what it was to be cut off from the tribe — in Pretoria — where the tribe came to plead for him, castigate him, and mourn for him. If anything, his trial showed that the 'Sestigers' can only fully be appreciated in relation to the tribe. For, while Afrikanerdom has always made allowances for the aberrations of Afrikaners within the tribe, as the newspaper *Die Beeld* admitted in December 1975, immediately after Breytenbach was sentenced, Afrikaners have largely emerged as an 'oligarchy of ingrossers' and 'licensers of thought'.[32] And it is this, which reveals to what extent the 'Sestigers' were really iconoclasts or merely temporary prodigal sons, who eventually come home to roost.

The stranglehold of Afrikanerdom on culture is abundantly clear from the rather repressive censorship laws. These laws have been gaining in volume and invariably affect the blacks. If white South Africa is ever aware of it, then there is little indication that Afrikaners are disturbed. As long as Afrikaner writers play out their role, they are safe from the threat of being 'under pittance and prescription and compulsion'.[32]

Barring a few, Afrikaners generally belong to one of the Dutch Reformed Churches in South Africa. The three tiers of Language, God and People (Volk), constitute the backbone of their society. It is difficult to detect any opposition between Church and State. In fact, the Church has played a significant role in securing for the State an *Index Librorum Prohibitorum*. The very people who taught the Brinks at Potchefstroom are, in one way or another, also responsible for the banning of his book.

Let us take a closer look at some of the prohibitive laws passed in South Africa. *The Suppression of Communism Act,* which was promulgated in 1950, has more to do with the suppression of free speech and ideas than would be inferred from the name. *The*

*Riotous Assembly Act* served a similar purpose. In 1955, *The Customs Act* prohibited the distribution of literature (by post) which was objectionable, indecent or obscene. In 1958 and 1959 respectively, *The Post Office and Prisons Acts* were passed. In the various provinces there were ordinances prohibiting the distributions of indecent and profane literature. In 1960, *The Publication and Entertainment Law* was proposed. After numerous amendments, it was finally passed in 1963. Under the control of public entertainments was meant any place which admitted persons who carried membership cards or who paid contributions. The Board was, for instance, given the power to prohibit 'any film which in its opinion, inter alia, depicts matter which prejudicially affects the safety of the State, may have the effect of disturbing the peace.'[33]

A classical example of a farcical interpretation of the law was the film *Ocean's Eleven,* which was about a big bank robbery in Las Vegas. On the posters advertising the film, the face of Sammy Davis Jr. was painted white.

This then, is the crux of the 'Sestiger' movement. Its members were all Afrikaner writers who railed against the tribe, but who never really left the tribe to oppose, fully, the system of apartheid. In his open letter to André Brink, in *The Educational Journal*, the writer cuttingly comments: 'Maybe I should not be ashamed on your behalf. Maybe, you have nothing in common with us'.[34]

Nowhere does the chasm between the citizens and the non-citizens come out so clearly as in the censorship laws. Afrikaner writers protested vigorously when Brink's book was banned and Breytenbach jailed. Yet, they shed no such tears when La Guma's works were proscribed or when Nat Nakasa and Arthur Nortje died in exile. For these people do not, did not, and never will, belong to the Afrikaner tribe.

In 1963, Dr Verwoerd, the chief architect of apartheid, stated in the House of Assembly: 'We want to keep South Africa White ... "keeping it white" can only mean one thing namely white domination, not "leadership", not "guidance", but "control", "supremacy".'[35]

The Afrikaner writer generally never seriously cared for the dispossessed of the country, except in a master-servant relationship. Not even the 'Sestigers' can succeed in changing this. After all, the highest cultural organization of Afrikanerdom, which awards the 'Hertzog prize', still has difficulty accepting Petersen, Philander and Small as ordinary members because they happen to be 'coloured'.

Censorship of the idea, the application of an arbitrary power, was something which largely affected the blacks. Armed with an impressive battery of laws and institutions, the Afrikaner has, since assuming power in 1948, muffled all protests among the dispossessed. Significantly, they had useful adjuncts in cultural organizations and the Dutch Reformed Churches.

The control of publications covers items such as newspapers not published by a member of the newspaper press, books, periodicals, posters, duplicated or typed material, drawings, photographs and sound recordings. A publication is considered undesirable:[36]

> *inter alia* if it *or any part of it* is indecent . . . offensive, harmful to
> the public morals, offensive to religious convictions of any
> section of the inhabitants of the Republic, brings any section
> of the inhabitants into ridicule or contempt, is harmful to the
> relations between any sections, is prejudicial to the safety of the
> State, the general welfare, or peace and good order.

According to a leading article in *The Star*, significantly entitled 'Operasie hou jou bek' (lit. Operation shut up),[37] there are ninety-seven definitions of the term *undesirable*.

Understandably, *The Publications and Entertainments Amendment Bill* had the full support of the public committee of the Dutch Reformed Church. Speaking on behalf of the said committee, the Reverend de Beer spoke for all Afrikanerdom when he stated:[38]

> No Christian State can allow the stream of disgusting and
> unchristian books, magazines and films which are coming into
> the country, or are created here to continue to weaken and
> undermine the national morale and Christian faith with the
> inevitable result that the people are made ripe for a takeover
> by communism.

Protected by 'an oligarchy of ingrossers', as Milton called censors in his *Areopagitica* (1644), the Afrikaner writer blissfully participated in his 'culture for the few', for the poor were non-existent and, at the most, a creation of communist-inclined South Africans.

Thus, the works of black and white writers which held any danger for Afrikanerdom in particular, and white South Africa in general, were banned. At times, this process assumed such ludicrous proportions, that it was hard to explain to foreigners that one was not joking. *Black Beauty*, by Anna Sewell, which is a story about a beautiful black horse, was reported to have fallen foul of this law at one stage. Rumour also had it that Thomas Hardy's *The Return of the Native* was also banned. Could it have been that the automatic translation of the title into Afrikaans as *Die terugkeer van die Kaffers* caused all the rumpus?

Practically all black writers in exile are banned in South Africa, the enormity of which seems to bear out Milton's depiction of control boards as 'oligarchy of ingrossers . . . measured to us by the bushel'. The works of Adam Small, Petersen and Philander are readily available in South Africa. Significantly, they all write in Afrikaans. The main point is that all those writers who oppose the regime, or describe the South African reality in a way which is not acceptable to the rulers, are regarded as dangerous. And for this reason, their works are not made accessible to the South African public.

La Guma, Brutus, Mphahlele and Rive then may not be read in South Africa. Meanwhile, many of their works are included in courses on African or Commonwealth literature. The licenser has failed to ban their books into obscurity. For, neither the writers in exile, nor these dangerous books, are 'residing over the death of free enquiry, free thought and democracy, but the very state itself'.

Brink, Breytenbach and Rabie are of the tribe and will forever belong to the tribe. Again it is interesting to look at the open letter to Brink by one of the 'non-citizens' (nie Burgers) as found in the TLSA. Speaking about the banning of the book, the writer quite categorically states that he is against censorship. But he demands not only that Brink's book be read but also the works of South Africans in exile, notably La Guma, Brutus and others. The writer in the TLSA continues:[39]

Look, the people of South Africa are not free, cannot be free . . . The law of censorship, totally unacceptable as it is, is of secondary importance. The main issue is the constitution which curtails the franchise and turns the majority of the citizens into Non-Citizens . . . When I am against the banning of your book, then I don't want the privilege of White citizens for you, and certainly not the special privilege of an Afrikaner writer. Not at all. I demand for you . . . what I demand for myself and for all of us. The democratic right of writers in a democratic country to honour only in his work of art the limitations of a man's social conscience.

In a devastating final comment, the author of this open letter comments that Brink even wrote to the censor telling him what a good Afrikaner he was, how he attended that Calvinist Protestant

University of Potchefstroom, how he did all those good and healthy things that a thorough-bred Afrikaner should do. He even addressed the censor as 'Oom Jannie' — 'To emphasize that you are tribally related . . . as it behoves a good Afrikaner'.[40]

The 'Sestiger' movement will therefore always remain an Afrikaner (white) exercise, because the writers were not iconoclasts, merely nigglers, and Afrikanerdom has always been able to cope with pin-pricks. The Brinks, the Rabies and those others who styled themselves 'Sestigers', were significantly quiet during the upheavals at Soweto, Manenberg and Bonteheuwel. For, as Sartre puts it, the choice is either to stop writing or to fight for the freedom of the oppressed, which means taking a political stand, for example, renouncing the tribe, and risking exile or a term of imprisonment. For the 'Sestiger', if he is not careful, 'the very truth he holds becomes his heresie'[41] — that is, he dupes himself into thinking that he is on the side of the oppressed.

# Chapter 8

# The poor are unthinkable[1]

Anyone familiar with the South African cultural scene will immediately be struck by the dearth of non-white novelists. Somehow, the novel has appeared too arduous a literary exercise. The strains and tensions of a vigorous political climate created an atmosphere whereby it became rather difficult to distinguish fact from fantasy. The inability to grasp and come to terms with the complex whole, apparently precluded the portrayal and the delineation of the single, the individual, who in many cases sinks into the bottomless pit of the whole. White and black writers in South Africa find it extremely difficult to circumvent the all-pervading group-consciousness. Durrant, in his review of Guy Butler's *A Book of South African Verse*, writes:[2]

> What I complain of is an exaggerated concern for one self as a member of a particular group — as a Christian amongst the heathens, a white man among blacks or Coloureds, an Englishman among Afrikaners, a European in Africa, or a South African in Europe.

Unlike his European counterpart, the non-white invariably has, as his base of operation, nay origin, the semi-literate to the illiterate peasant and unsettled urban proletariat. Their disabilities are his. It is as if the creative black artist finds it impossible at times to fictionalize his nightmare, whereby it becomes the nightmare of all mankind.

The black writer cannot feign innocence when he knows that his people are living under oppressive circumstances. Nor can he only celebrate the tribe. Mphahlele has openly conceded that, within the South African context, the white absence is unthinkable. 'I personally cannot think of the future of my people in South Africa as something

135

in which the white man does not feature. Whether he likes it or not, our destinies are inseparable.'[3]

Ironically, therefore, the non-white creative artist, writing about a semi-literate public, and hoping in many cases to reach it through his works, finds himself dependent upon the urban, sophisticated European public, European critical standards, and publishing companies. The black artist will also be involved in the struggle for freedom, be committed to his people. What Kenneth Ramchand observes for the West Indies, in his book *The West Indian Novel,* is fairly true of what is now generally referred to as the 'third world': 'Since 1950, most West Indian novels have been first published in the English capital, and nearly every West Indian novelist has established himself while living there'.[4]

The choice of one's capital of exile was largely determined by the nature of colonialism and the actual colonizer himself (e.g. mostly Paris or London).

The writing of a novel in an atmosphere of political and economic prosperity is a luxury seldom afforded the 'third world' writer. The work of the black artist in South Africa has, as has been overtly clear until now, been permeated with the stench of colour. The operative words for most blacks are economic, psychological and physical survival. There was, and still is, little room for culture and creation in the accepted European sense. Mphahlele observes: 'It is not easy for the oppressed African to organize himself for the writing of a novel unless he produces the kind that panders to European "supremacy"'.[5]

Where non-white artists did write, their earliest attempts invariably found their way into print via popular newspapers and magazines, for example, *The Golden City Post* and *Drum.* One of the most influential editors of *Drum,* Anthony Sampson, has left us with a very vivid impression of the magazine, when he wrote:[6]

I looked through the first four numbers of *Drum* that had already appeared. It was a sixpenny monthly magazine, written in English, printed on cheap yellow newsprint; the bright cover showed two Africans facing each other, symbolically, across the continent: one in a Western hat and suit, the other with African skins and assegai. The first numbers contained African poems and short stories; articles on 'Music of the Tribes' and 'Know Yourselves', recounting the history of the Bantu tribes; instalments of *Cry, the Beloved Country*; features about religion, farming, sport and famous men; and strip cartoons about Gulliver and St. Paul.

There was a poem by the American negro poet, Countee Cullen . . ..
In one early number there was a Zulu poem called: 'Mlung
ungazikhohlisi' — Whiteman do not deceive yourself —

In such magazines then, many a budding young writer started off
with his poetic effusions. Sometimes, it was fashionable to encourage
talent through short story competitions. Often, black South African
artists started off as journalists. Mphahlele, Can Themba, Alf Hutchinson,
Alex La Guma and numerous others were all processed through this
unavoidable literary pipe-line.

Like many others in South Africa, these writers were also fed, in
their youth, on the works of Thomas Hardy or the Romantic poets. It
does not seem to be an accident of language that the short-story writer,
the late Can Themba, should have called his place 'The House of
Truth', thereby recalling Chaucer's 'House of Fame'. One wonders
how many poems, imitative of the English Romantic School, perhaps
never found their way into print.

The literary form which attracted most attention among black
South Africans was the short story. There are, of course, various
reasons why the short story became the desired form. The short story
is terse, to the point and 'drives the message home with an economy
of language and time'.[7] E. V. Downs comments on the short story
in English literature in the following vein:[8]

The short story-writer visualises his theme through the light
of his own personal mood. He sees it from *one* point of view,
but sees it clearly, and that clear, contracted picture on which
his mind is intensely focused, he depicts with an economy
proportionate to its vividness and definiteness.

Mphahlele writes of the short story in *The African Image:*[9]

The short story in such a multi-racial setting, in my own
experience, goes through three stages: the romantic-escapist;
the protest short story; and the ironic, which is the meeting
point between protest and acceptance.

Most African short story writers seem to move within this trinity as
outlined by Mphahlele.

One of the best exponents of the short story is Alex La Guma,
whose stories are a mixture of farce and anxiety. His handling of
the racial situation is never such that it becomes platitudinous,
moralizing or politically didactic. He seems to have grasped the essential

lesson that racial tensions 'are a part but never the whole of experience'.[10] The Cockroaches, the Joeys, the Arthurs and the Michaels, main characters in his works, are all umbilically linked to one another.

La Guma exploits the surprise ending with expertise, deftly delays and catches his reader on the wrong foot. His story, *Out of Darkness,* is just such an example of ironic detachment. The author knows his people well, realizes that the system has inculcated in them a penchant for defining each other in terms of fine colour gradations. Cockroach, his main character, is in prison for murder. His girl friend's behaviour triggered off his tragedy.[11]

'Then she began to find that she could pass for white. She could pass as white, and I was black . . . She drifted away from me, but I kept on loving her.

'I talked to her, pleaded with her. But she wouldn't take any notice of what I said . . . She said I was selfish and trying to deny her the good things of life. The good things of life. I would have given her anything *I could.* And she said I was denying her the good things of life.

'In the end she turned on me. She told me to go to hell. She slapped my face and called me a black nigger. A black nigger.'

'Then you lost your head and killed her,' I said quietly. 'That's why you're here now.'

'Oh, no,' Old Cockroach answered. 'I could never have done that to Cora. I did lose my head, but it was Joey whom I killed. He said I was a damn fool for going off over a damn play-white bitch. So I hit him, and he cracked his skull on something. Ah, here's Joey now. Hullo, Joey. I hope you've brought my book.'

Richard Rive is another short story writer of note, although he does not always succeed in avoiding the pitfalls of political pamphleteering at times. In his short story, *Dagga Smoker's Dream* (Dagga = Hash), he seems to have excelled himself. One is immediately impressed by the author's insight into his character, the undertone of irony, the strength of his dialogue and his clever exploitation of the language of the poor in Cape Town and its environment. The story is a very good illustration of the racial situation handled with poise and expertise. Unfortunately, Rive falters occasionally, as is so clear from the following extract from *The Bench,* which is a good story marred only at the beginning by his political trumpeting:[12]

We form an integral part of a complex society, a society complex in that a vast proportion of the population are denied the very basic privileges of existence, a society that condemns a man to an inferior status because he has the misfortune to be born black, a society that can only retain its precarious social and economic position at the expense of an enormous black proletariat!

Another literary form which became very popular was the autobiographical novel. Again, as in the case of the short story, there were various reasons why this happened. Most important of all was the fact that many of these writers started off their careers as journalists. Pride of place among the autobiographers goes to the Afro-American writer Richard Wright, who with his *Black Boy* (1946), paved the way for a host of similar books. Nadine Gordimer observes in *The Black Interpreters:*[13]

Almost any African who has anything to say about the condition of being African, either in the colonial past or in the independent present, is likely to find interested readers, since he or she has information to offer, an inside story or an experience over-documented from the outside, white-side.

The autobiographical novel in South Africa has done much to acquaint the outside world (and some white South Africans), with the horror of apartheid.

The most difficult transition for the black artist was from the autobiographical half-way house to the novel proper. For the problems are varied and great. In some cases poverty looms large, in others, the main issues are racism and colonialism. Often, one finds a combination of all these. One of the cardinal problems will be the role of the writer in societies of oppression and deprivation. Jean Paul Sartre, in an article on the responsibility of the writer, maintains:[14]

If the writer is a maker of literature; in other words, if he writes — it is because he is assuming the function of perpetuating, in a world where freedom is always threatened, the assertion of freedom and the appeal to freedom. A writer who does not take his stand on this ground is guilty; not only is he guilty, but he soon ceases to be a writer.

Sartre continues in the following vein:[15]

The writer, to the extent that he postulates and demands freedom, cannot furnish the governing class, nor any other class, with an ideology, except one which insists on the freedom of men who still remain oppressed. And, on the other hand, he cannot address himself to those whose freedom he desires, unless he becomes a member of a party and acts as a member of that party by becoming a propagandist, by allowing his art to become propaganda; that is, by calling for the death of literature and ceasing to be a writer.

In even stronger terms he postulates:[16]

Yet, in the name of ethical values, he must demand plainly and above all else — for otherwise he is an oppressor or a trickster — the liberation of all oppressed people, proletarians, Jews, Negroes, colonial subjects, occupied countries and so on.

For Lenin in his article on *Literature and Art* states: 'Literature cannot be a means of enriching individuals or groups; it cannot, in fact, be an individual undertaking, independent of the common cause of the proletariat'.[17]

African writers themselves have grappled with the particular role of the writer in Africa. Thus Achebe, the distinguished Nigerian novelist, observes:[18]

African people did not hear of culture for the first time from Europeans; . . . . The worst thing that can happen to any people is the loss of their dignity and self-respect. The writer's duty is to help them regain it by showing them in human terms what had happened to them, what they lost.

In an interview with the American, Bernth Lindfors, in 1970, Achebe reiterated his belief that it was 'impossible to write anything in Africa without some kind of commitment, some kind of message, some kind of protest'.[19]

Africa's foremost dramatist, Wole Soyinka, is even more forthright in his views:[20]

when the writer in his own society can no longer function as conscience, he must recognise that his choice lies between denying himself totally or withdrawing to the position of chronicler and post-mortem surgeon . . . . The artist has always functioned in African society as the record of the mores and experience of his society *and* as the voice of vision in his own time.

Ngugi, the Kenyan writer, warns of the reality that '80 per cent of the people are living in poverty and not a single step ... so far taken in fact to change the social structure.' He continues, as long as this situation has not changed: 'so long shall we continue to have impotent writers and intellectuals'.[21]

Achebe's aim, 'to help my society regain belief in itself and put away the complexes of the years of denigration and self-abasement',[22] finds its highest expression among black South African writers. Black writers are not the first to have concentrated on what is generally referred to as the social novel. Wellek and Warren remark:[23]

> Much the most common approach to the relations of literature
> to society is the study of works of literature as social documents,
> as assumed pictures of social reality. Nor can it be doubted that
> some kind of social structure can be abstracted from literature.

and,[24]

> One can argue that 'social truth', while not, as such, an artistic
> value, corroborates such artistic values as complexity and
> coherence. But it need not be so. There is great literature
> which has little or no social relevance; social literature is only
> one kind of literature and is not central in the theory of literature
> unless one holds the view that literature is primarily an
> 'imitation' of life as it is and of social life in particular. But
> literature is no substitute for sociology or politics.

While there is considerable truth in the observations of Warren and Wellek, this becomes rather academic in a situation of oppression. The American critic, Howe, is closer to reality when he avers that, 'where freedom is absent, politics is fate'.[25]

Of equal importance is the question of the medium used by the writer, for invariably it will be that of the colonizer or the oppressor. In the South African context, it will be English (Abrahams and La Guma) or Afrikaans (Petersen and Small). I have already referred to this question of language in dealing with Adam Small's special brand of Afrikaans. Again, it is worthwhile listening to Achebe when he states:[26]

> The African writer should aim to use English in a way that
> brings out his message best without altering the language to
> the extent that its value as a medium of international
> exchange will be lost. He should aim at fashioning out an

English which is at once universal and able to carry his
peculiar experience.

Achebe hints that 'the price a world language must be prepared
to pay is its submission to many different kinds of use'.[27] This is
certainly true of La Guma. From all this emerges the view that the
novel will, of necessity, be social and depending on the nature of
oppression, very often political. Max Beloff observes: 'Politics is an
aspect of human relations and like other aspects of the subject (e.g.
love-making) is better suited to the novel than the treatise. Considering
how well it is adapted for this treatment, the wonder is not that there
are so many political novels but that there are so few.'[28]

Stendhal, speaking of politics in a work of art, likened it to a 'pistol
shot in the middle of a concert, something loud and vulgar, and yet
a thing to which it is not possible to refuse one's attention'.[29]

Speaking of the political novel, in an essay on Orwell, Frederick
Karl remarked: 'The political novel at its best — *The Possessed, The
Magic Mountain, Nostromo, The Red and the Black* — requires an
imaginative projection in which characters are trapped, almost
smothered, by forces that remain inexplicable and subterranean.'[30]

The novelist's social matrix will stifle his created character, his
individual who is caught up in the system, and despite his efforts
to the contrary, he is 'doomed to walk the night'. These problems
constitute the spiritual, historical and factual inheritance of the non-
white writer in a system of racially ascribed roles and institutionalized
separation in South Africa.

Special attention will be given to three writers in this chapter,
namely, Peter Abrahams, Alex La Guma and Richard Rive. And it must
be stated quite categorically, that it is not their 'supposed colouredness'
which merits their selection, but rather the peculiar social conditions
they describe in their novels.

Peter Abrahams, the Northerner, is an interesting contrast to Alex
La Guma, the man from the Cape. This difference is also reflected in
their themes and approaches to literature. Abrahams left South Africa
before apartheid revealed its true and vicious face, although one could
argue that the covert apartheid of the late 1930s was no less obnoxious or painful. La Guma's characters find themselves in a more
specifically bi-cultural situation. Their knowledge of both English
and Afrikaans leads to language interference and the emergence of a
peculiar brand of English exploited so expertly by La Guma. Much
of the work of Abrahams refers to a pre-nationalist period, that is,

before the Afrikaners took over political control in 1948. *Dark Testament* appeared in 1942, *Song of the City* in 1945, *Mine Boy* in 1946, *The Path of Thunder* in 1948. Then followed *Wild Conquest* (1950), *Return to Goli* (1953), *Tell Freedom* (1954), *A Wreath for Udomo* (1956) and *A Night of Their Own* (1965).

By the time the 'coloureds' were beginning to exert themselves politically, Peter Abrahams was already outside the country. As we have seen in the Introduction, 1943 was a watershed in 'coloured' politics. Very little of the complex political situation is found in the early works of Abrahams. *Mine Boy* is an earlier forerunner of Paton's *Cry the Beloved Country*, possibly falling into Lewis Nkosi's categorization of 'Jim comes to Jo'burg'. It deals with the, by now, fairly familiar picture of the black man in the city. The novel is more of a collage of African life. *The Path of Thunder* falls neatly in the other South African literary tradition of miscegenation. His 'coloured' protagonist may then be more of a human being than the characters in works with a similar theme by white authors; however, he is still a stereotype.

La Guma and Abrahams represent two stages in the politics and history of South Africa. If Abrahams is still closer to the period of Hertzog and Smuts, where the 'coloured' man was very much a 'poorer' (brown) relation, then the period of La Guma was definitely shaped by the political events of the bus boycott in the 1950s, culminating eventually, in the shootings at Sharpeville in 1960. La Guma, after all, was one of the main actors in the political arena during the fifties. He was also detained during the treason trial. The works of Abrahams are still characterized by romantic idealism, whereas La Guma's prose is steeped in social realism.

In contrast, there is Richard Rive who is also from the Cape. He has several short stories to his credit and one novel, *Emergency*. Some of his fiction is banned, some available in South Africa. There are no indications that Rive ever aligned himself with any of the political movements in the Cape. Yet, his fiction is decidedly political in tone and tenor. However, notwithstanding his hostile portrayal of South Africa (from the Government's point of view), Rive has not suffered political harassment of imprisonment. A closer look at his fiction seems to reveal more about viewpoints and prejudices of the various ethnic groups, than about the overall political setup. And as such, he also moves, to my mind, more within the accepted South African literary tradition, than is apparent to the non-South African. *Emergency* is an excellent illustration of this, as will be demonstrated later on.

Abrahams was born in 1919 in Vrededorp, a ghetto for 'coloureds' and Asians in Johannesburg. His early development is at once interesting, for his writings highlight the difference between life in the North and the South. 'Colouredism' of the Cape variety does not have that special aura of differentness (*andersoortigheid*). The 'coloured' as a bi-cultural being is less noticeable in the North. On the other hand, the gulf between African and 'coloured' seems less in the North. In the Cape, the tendency to accommodate is responsible for greater frustration and confusion.

Abrahams had his reputation firmly established by the time the Ekwensis and Achebes appeared on the African literary scene. As a writer, he was most productive, producing eleven books between 1945 and 1966. The first one which will be discussed here is his autobiography, *Tell Freedom* (1954).

In *Tell Freedom* we have a beautifully told, vivid and imaginative account of his early years. Of his own family he writes:[31]

> My mother was the widow of a Cape Malay (a product of the
> East Indies' strain of the coloured community) who had died
> the previous year and left her with two children. She was
> alone except for an elder sister, Margaret. My mother and
> her two children were living with her sister Margaret when
> she met the man from Ethiopia. Margaret was the fairer of
> the two sisters, fair enough to 'pass'. Her husband was
> a Scot. He worked on the mines. They had a little girl
> with blonde hair and blue eyes. They lived in 19th Street,
> Vrededorp. And there, in the street, the two brown children,
> my brother and sister, played with their cousin, the little
> white girl with blonde hair and blue eyes. To this street
> and this house came the Ethiopian. There, he wooed my
> mother. There, he won her. They married from that house.

Here then, in a nutshell, we have all the complexities of the situation in which those classified as 'coloured' in South Africa find themselves.

*Tell Freedom* is written in simple prose and is in no way maudlin in tone. It is livened up at times with a gentle touch of humour, while the comi-tragic note is never totally absent. At an early age, Peter Abrahams is introduced to the racial hierarchy in his society:[32]

> 'Sixpence crackling, please.'
> Andries nudged me in the back. The man's stare suddenly
> became cold and hard. Andries whispered into my ear.

'Well?' the man repeated coldly,
'Please *baas* ,' I said,
'What d'you want?'
'Sixpence crackling, please.'
'What?'
Andries dug me in the ribs.
'Sixpence crackling, please *baas*.'
'What?'
'Sixpence crackling, please *baas*. '
'You new here?'
'Yes, *baas*.' I looked at his feet while he stared at me.

This was just the prelude to many similar, harrowing scenes in colour-conscious South Africa.

Now the interesting thing about this scene is the effect it subsequently has. The white man comes to Peter's Uncle Sam to tell him to teach his boy *mores* for having dared to hit back at white children. Abrahams succeeds in re-creating the nightmare of Uncle Sam, who stands for all the Uncle Sams who ever found themselves in similar positions.

Sociologically then, this passage tells us a lot about the role of the father, or the father figure, in poor 'coloured' communities. One abstracts a picture of the 'coloured' who is completely emasculated by society, humiliated, yet ironically expected to reveal himself as a voice of authority at the point where he himself is being humiliated. This is a point worth taking into consideration in deciding whether his (Abrahams') women characters are over-emphasized, as Wade wrote in his book on Abrahams in 1972. Let us, with this in mind, look at the flogging scene, for example. After his deed Sam begs of his wife Eliza:[33]

'Explain to the child, Liza', he said.
'You explain', Aunt Liza said bitterly. 'You are the man. You did the beating. You are the head of the family. This is a man's world. You do the explaining.'
'Please, Liza . . .'

And some time later in the passage, Aunt Liza explains to the boy:[34]

'It hurt him,' she said. 'You'll understand one day.'

The women are often forced to take over the man's role. Uncle Sam's behaviour is aptly depicted in O'Toole's study *Watts and Woodstock*:[35]

Coloured men are weak fathers by their own standards. It is
difficult for a man to be servile in one context and masterful
in the next. The self-demeaning role Coloured men are bound
to play in society is too demanding to allow them to
step out of the role in their homes.

In this case it is Eliza who covers for Sam and cushions the hurt.
Fieta in *The Path of Thunder* (1948), fulfils a similar role in mangled
Sam's life. Lea in *Mine Boy*, is another example of this strong breed.
That female characters are portrayed so strongly has its origin in the
very society which gave rise to them. That this factor caused bewilderment to the South African critic, Wade, should be attributed to his
non-understanding of poor 'coloured' societies. O'Toole is probably
very close to the truth when he avers in *Watts and Woodstock*: [36]

The poor women of Woodstock play instrumental roles
because of their relatively favored social and economic
position in South African society as compared with their
men . . . . The Coloured man has been carefully and expertly
taught to jump when the 'master' says jump . . . . For this
reason the Coloured man is punctillious in his deference
to whites.

Fieta and Liza are thus prime examples of a breed which endures
and endures.

Peter Abrahams is acquainted with the wider, more educated world,
through a Jewish typist. The scene is fraught with comi-tragedy.[37]

'Lee?'
I stopped and turned to her.
'That is your name, isn't it?'
'Yes, missus.'
'Miss, not missus, You only say missus to a married woman.'
Her smile encouraged me.
'We say it to all white women.'
'Then you are wrong. Say miss.'
'Yes, miss.'
'That's better . . . Tell me, how old are you?'
'Going on for eleven, miss.'
'Why don't you go to school?'
'I don't know, miss.'

The upshot is that she reads to him *Lamb's Tales from Shakespeare* —
standard fare, to my knowledge, for anyone who had grown up in

former British territories. This is how he reacts to the story of Othello: 'The story of Othello jumped at me and invaded my heart and mind as the young woman read. I was transported to the land where the brave Moor lived and loved and destroyed his love.'[38]

When the typist gives him the book as a present, he can only utter:[39]

'Thank you, miss. Thank you!'
Her eyes looked strangely bright behind the thick glasses.
'Go away!', she said. 'Go away . . . and good luck . . .'
I hesitated awkwardly at the door. Was she crying? and why?
'Yes, thank you, miss. Thank you.'

A new world was now opened to him. When Abrahams first came upon the works of black writers from America, he was similarly moved. One can only imagine what this discovery must have meant to the impressionable youngster. Reading Langston Hughes and Countee Cullen opened his eyes further to the plight of the black's in South Africa. The open note of defiance, the pride in being black and the revolutionary tone which characterized Cullen's poem, *The Dark Tower,* found willing penetration into the tortured soul of Abrahams. Here was a black man who openly stated:[40]

We shall not always plant while others reap
The golden increment of bursting fruit,
Not always countenance, abject and mute,
That lesser men should hold their brother cheap.

Here was a poet who was prepared to say that, 'we were not made eternally to weep'.[41] This, then, is the dilemma of the black artist who, in order to make his art acceptable to the white public and publisher, must perforce tone down his reality, clothe it in a cocoon of lies, or else go into exile. To 'pander to white supremacy', or to be completely absorbed and usurped by political organizations which spell an end to one's creativity. The choice for Abrahams was eventually determined by the romantic lure of England and its liberal tradition. Perhaps it is one of the banes of the non-white artist that he must first be a freedom fighter and then only an artist.

Abrahams put a very high premium on the freedom of the individual, and this is something one should at least welcome, for tension in the climate itself can so easily tempt African writers into 'dealing with men as component units of a social problem . . . [while] such tensions are a part but never the whole of experience'.[42]

In his autobiographical *Down Second Avenue* (1959), that other.

well-known novelist, short story writer and critic, Ezekiel Mphahlele, who was with Abrahams at the same school, gives the following impression of him, which is very instructive:[43]

> I remember him vividly talking about Marcus Garvey, taking
> it for granted we must know about him. And dreamily he
> said what a wonderful thing it would be if all the negroes in
> the world came back to Africa. Abrahams wrote verse in
> his exercise books and gave them to us to read . . . I remember
> now how morose the verse was: straining to justify and glorify
> the dark complexion with the I'm-black-and-proud-of-it
> theme.

Abrahams did eventually reach his destination, England, but not before he had submerged himself into what is regarded as the home of the 'Cape coloured' — Cape Town and its environment. Towards the end there is a passage in his autobiographical *Tell Freedom* which foreshadows similar lunar, barren landscape depictions by Alex La Guma.[44]

> Entering the Cape Flats was stepping into a new Dark Age. The
> earth, here, is barren of all but the hardiest shrub. It is a dirty
> white, sandy earth. The sea had once been here. In its retreat
> it had left a white, unyielding sand, grown dirty with time.
> Almost, it had left a desert. And in this desert strip, on the
> fringe of a beautiful garden city, men had made their homes.
> They had taken pieces of corrugated iron and tied them together
> with bits of string, wire and rope.

Abrahams fails generally to depict the smell of decay and degradation which is so well featured in La Guma's work, possibly because he is more of a romantic, not that La Guma is in any way devoid of this trait. It is only in Abrahams' autobiographical work that the disturbing note of odorous poverty is constant. One gets the feeling that his overwhelming desire 'to tell freedom', and his ardent desire to portray the individual, leads to insufficient characterization at times.

His novel *The Path of Thunder* (1948) deals with the oft-encountered theme of 'sex across the colour line'. The story is about Lanny Swartz, a young 'Cape coloured', who returns to his village with several degrees after a stay in Cape Town. His search in Cape Town and his contact with other people leads him to ponder on the very self-same question the little girl had asked old Johannes, the slave, in *Wild Conquest* (1971): 'What is freedom?'[45]

Lanny, one gathers, has returned with some missionary zeal to improve the lot of his people in Stilleveld. In this small micro-cosmos are to be found all the elements of an explosive racial situation. Lanny's very presence as an educated person upsets the pattern of racially ascribed roles, which dictates that 'coloureds' should be servants, fools and generally ignorant. Thus the stage is set for the inevitable orgy of violence. In fact, the operative symbol in the novel is violence — it starts off with it and ends with it. The reader is treated to a blaze of guns and false heroism.

Lanny's arrival in Stilleveld sets the tone throughout the novel:[46]

Across the way from the siding was a little coffee stall. A buxom Afrikaner lass tended it. A lorry stood a little way from the stall. Two bronze, muscular men were drinking coffee. They all looked at Lanny . . .

'Do you see what I see?' one of the men asked.

The other pursed his lips and looked doubtful.

'I'm not sure. It looks like an ape in a better Sunday suit than I have. But today's not Sunday so I'm not sure.'

'Perhaps he wears suits like that every day . . . . Besides, you are all wrong, he's too pale to be an ape. That's a city bushy.'

(The confrontation was not far off.)

'Hey! You!'

Lanny stretched himself and waited. He had discussed the colour question a lot in the National Liberation League and the Non-European United Front and now it had picked him out. It had called him.

'Come here!' It was the first man.

South Africa, Lanny thought tiredly, this is South Africa. He walked across the narrow track. At least they won't frighten this Coloured, he decided; hurt me, yes, but frighten me, no. He stopped directly in front of the man and looked straight into his face.

The man inspected him closely.

'Where you from?' the man shot at him.

'Cape Town.'

'What do you want here?'

'I live here.'

'Haven't seen you around.'

'I've been in Cape Town for seven years.'

'School?'

'Yes.'

> 'University?'
> 'Yes.'
> 'What are you?'
> 'What do you mean?'
> 'I mean what I say. Have you any fancy titles?'
> Lanny smiled. 'Yes, I have two.'
> Suddenly the man's hand shot out and cracked across Lanny's mouth.

Lanny, the main character, is different from the rest of the 'coloured' rural cast. Unlike them, he is not docile or obsequious, and this would spell his downfall in the end. Ironically, however, in this initial scene, he allows himself to be humbled by the Boers. It is as if he simply cannot help falling into his ascribed role, as dictated by white South Africa, when he hears the, 'Hey! You!'

On the night of his arrival, he is invited to the house of Gert Villier, who bluntly tells him that 'We do not like independent bastards here, *Mister* Swartz'.[47] Once more, the predator threatens the prey with violence. But Lanny is also a romantic idealist, and the scenario does not allow for such aberrations. Lanny recalls Josef Malan in Brink's novel, Jan Herold in Rabie's, Abe Hanslo in Rive's and Adam Small's 'coloured' in *Die eerste steen.*

It is this maudlin, sentimental and tug-at-the-heart portrayal which makes Lanny a character cast in the typical South African tradition. He, like all such characters in a similar position, is destined for extinction.

But *The Path of Thunder* is also about inter-racial sex, as such indulgencies are sometimes euphemistically called in South Africa. Now, it is interesting to discover that white women in such literary encounters are, as Claude Wauthier puts it, 'redeemers [who] like Desdemona ... come to a tragic end.'[48] Of the man of colour in the novel one could state that his endeavours are a 'Subjective consecration to wiping out in himself and his own mind the colour prejudice from which he has suffered so long'.[49] To that extent then, *The Path of Thunder* is about 'the sexual myth – the quest for white flesh – perpetuated by alien psyches'.[50] For, running through the entire novel, is the love of Lanny, the 'coloured', for Sarie, the Boer girl. Thus Abrahams, too, continues the South African literary tradition of thrusting white paragons of beauty into the arms of disturbed 'coloured' youths. One wonders whether André Brink was so original and revolutionary as Afrikaner critics seem to think, in his novel, *Kennis van die aand.*

Lanny's predicament is symbolically represented in Sam who was mangled by the Boers for daring to 'sleep and love white'. In between, one is confronted with vignettes of minor frustrations at different levels. In Lanny's second encounter with the Boer girl Sarie, there are already the first rumblings of what Tucker calls in his book, *Africa in Modern Literature* (1967), 'the aura of sex which no book about white women and black men has yet avoided'.[51] Lanny had just been at the receiving end of his second spell of violence. Sarie transgresses the ethics of the tribe by helping him.[52]

> He didn't behave as though he were Coloured. She had to force
> it into her mind in order to remember it all the time.
> And now, should she give him a towel to wipe his face?
> Impulsively she gave him her own hand towel. She watched him
> wipe his face, then looked curiously at the towel when he
> returned it to her. It was so strange. He thanked her, but as a
> matter of course, as though he were used to getting towels from
> white girls, but he couldn't be — or could he?
> 'There's dust on the back of your jacket,' she whispered.
> He tried to reach it but failed. Tentatively she stepped forward
> and brushed it off . . . .
> They smiled at each other.

Again, Tucker seems to be right when he observes: 'no miscegenation occurs, but its unheard music reverberates throughout the novel(s)'.[53]

Lanny's story is an exact replica of Mad Sam's, whose physically mangled body is a constant reminder of what whites are capable of doing to 'coloureds' and blacks, if they transgress the rules. Mad Sam is just another man of colour who, in the words of Geoffrey Gorer, 'is kept in [an] obsequious attitude by extreme penalties of fear and force'. Gert Villier lives out this attitude when he tells Lanny:[54]

> I'm going to kick you and kick you until you are like Sam.
> They call him Mad Sam. But he was like you. Thought he was
> good enough for a white woman . . . I made him what he
> is today. My slave! . . . I kicked him and now he moves
> like an animal. That's what's going to happen to you, *Mister*
> Swartz![54]

The three major 'coloured' characters symbolize different strata in the racial hierarchy. Lanny is the educated, defiant idealist, with a tinge of romanticism, who having dared to cross the institutionalized sexual and racial borders, is destined for extinction. The 'coloured' preacher stands for that species which retreats into religious passivity, an example of the Orwellian 'passive non-cooperative attitude'.[55] Mabel, Lanny's sister, is stereotyped, for a moment, in the English man's car, into an euphoric, all fleece and fluff character.

The white characters in the novel are the spiritual descendants of the Jansen family, as found in the historical novel about the Great Trek by Abrahams, *Wild Conquest* (1950).

It is Finkelberg, a Jewish intellectual (himself historically an underdog), who ironically explains to Mako, an African, the lowest category on the racial totem pole, what has happened between Lanny and Sarie, the Boer girl:[56]

> 'You don't understand, Mako. There are two ways of falling in love . . . You and I know one way . . . But there is another kind too. By that love people are just drawn together without looks or anything else mattering, not even the fact that this is the highveld.'
>
> 'I don't believe it, Finkelberg.'
>
> 'Yesterday I would have said the same, Mako.'
>
> 'Swartz must be a fool. Why didn't he go away?'
>
> 'You're asking why a drowning man struggles for his life.'
>
> 'This fatal, inevitable love is nonsense.'
>
> 'For you Mako, yes. But not for Swartz. I don't know what it is. I know the fact that your internal freedom is greater than his has something to do with it. You are at once freer as well as being more restricted because you have a past and a tradition whereas he has none.'

Poor Lanny, one is inclined to utter, to suffer even at the hands of Abrahams under the schmalzy excuse that he had no past! No wonder then, that an Afrikaner novelist, Brink, decided to correct this literary hiatus. But Abrahams, by putting this comment about the 'coloureds' having no past and tradition in the mouth of Finkelberg, himself seems to succumb to stereotypes whites have of 'coloureds'.

Peter Abrahams gives his novel an ironic Great Trek twist of two beleaguered individuals who go under in a display of pyrotechnics while facing a hostile crowd. His passage towards the end is reminiscent of the satirical swipe by the Nigerian novelist Chinua Achebe in his novel *Things Fall Apart*. This is how Abrahams ends his novel;[57]

> The *Eastern Post* of the next day carried a story on its
> front page in bold black letters. It told how a young
> Coloured teacher, one Lanny Swartz, had run amok, killed
> a prominent farmer, Mr Gert Villier, and then been chased
> into the house of Mr Villier.
>     Alone in the house was Miss Sarie Villier. He had found
> a gun, shot her, and then turned the gun on his pursuers. In
> the ensuing battle three other people had been killed before
> Swartz had finally been shot down . . .
>     The story ended with a strong protest against educating
> black people.

Politics and the political situation in South Africa must be a major preoccupation for the black artist – a ready-made theme. In *Wild Conquest*, one of the few historical novels written by a black South African, the author, Peter Abrahams, has an excellent opportunity to correct the farcical portrayal of 'coloureds' and blacks. Yet, sadly, he allows Boer history to predominate. The novel is remarkable for its relatively fair treatment of the Boers – a compliment not extended to Abrahams's people in Afrikaner literature. The novel also deals with the slave element in the 'coloured' people. The slaves do not emerge as docile victims, ready for slaughter. Instead, old Johannes, the slave, in defying the Boer Trekkers, becomes a spiritual ally of Boni from Surinam and Toussaint L'Ouverture from Haiti.

If the works of Abrahams are permeated with romanticism and individualism, then those of Alex La Guma are filled with the 'naturalistic' stench of decay and deprivation. Born in the Cape, he soon embarked on a literary career through the medium of journalism. La Guma has written several short stories (an art in which he excels), and some four novels, notably, *A Walk in the Night* (1962), *And a Threefold Cord* (1964), *The Stone Country* (1967) and *In the Fog of the Season's End* (1972).

Son of a redoubtable freedom fighter, Jimmy La Guma, Alex grew up in an atmosphere where politics was fate from the very inception. Theirs was a well-known household name in the Cape, especially among the politically-conscious. Alex was very active in the struggle for freedom and played an important role in preparing the congress of the people of South Africa at Kliptown, Johannesburg in 1955, where the historic Freedom Charter was drawn up. Subsequently, he was one of the persons arrested on a charge of high treason in 1956. In the post-Sharpeville period, he was once more detained for a period of five months without a trial.

In 1962, he was served with a banning order and then placed under arrest.[58] This made it impossible for him to move around, to publish or be published. The only way out was exile in England. Brief though this synopsis of La Guma's life is, it is nevertheless important for an understanding of his work. His committtedness springs from a deep-rooted personal belief, as anyone who has ever had the joy and privilege of knowing him will tell you. At a later stage, we shall see how this affected his portrayal of South African society.

La Guma is a living testimony of the novelist turned warrior, freedom fighter. His story *And a Threefold Cord* (1964) is, to quote another freedom fighter, Brian Bunting, 'drenched in the wet and misery of the Cape winter whose grey and dreary tones . . . [are] captured in a series of graphic etchings'.[59] The novel also recalls the Afrikaner author Uys Krige's lampooning of another poverty-striken wasteland inhabited by the 'coloureds' — Windermere, meer Wind dan Meer (i.e. Lake of Winds, more Winds than Lake). But let us recall La Guma's description:[60]

In the north-west the rainheads piled up, first in cottony
tufts blown up by the high wind, then in skeins of dull cloud,
and finally in high, climbing battlements, like a rough wall
of mortar built across the horizon, so that the sun had no
gleam, but a pale phosphorescence behind the veil of grey.
The sea was grey, too, and metallic, moving in sluggish swells,
like a blanket blown in a tired wind . . .
    The people of the shanties and the *pondokkie* cabins along
the national road and beside the railway tracks and in the
suburban sand-lots watched the sky and looked towards the
north-west where the clouds, pregnant with moisture, hung
beyond the mountain. When the bursts of rain came, knocking
on the roofs, working-men carried home loads of pilfered
corrugated cardboard cartons, salvaged rusted sheets of iron
and tin to reinforce the roofs. Heavy stones were heaved onto
the lean-tos and patched roofs, to keep them down, when the
wind rose.

La Guma's characters are subordinate to his physical descriptions. The terror and agony of his characters are rather felt through his finely drawn social settings and minute details, for example, the 'hesitant drip-drip onto the plank floor; then a quicker, steadier plop-plop-plopping'.[61] This concentration on external forces occurs at the expense of individual characterization.

Charlie Pauls and his family are only incidental to the setting. There is no question of the nightmare being an inner one. Instead, one is confronted with the 'smells in the room .... The smell of sweat and slept-in blankets and airless bedding . . . the smell of stale cooking and old dampness and wet metal'.[62] Occasionally, one is given a glimpse into a character's soul, for example, when Charlie tries to console his girl friend Freda after the fire death of her children: 'Like he say, people can't stand up to the world alone, they got to be together. I reckon maybe he was right.'[63]

La Guma has this naturalistic bent to portray the sound and the taste of objects and landscapes. His story is narrowed down to a particular family or category of persons, and the environment in which they find themselves. This imposes certain limitations on him, since he is more concerned with the censures of the society on the protagonist rather than what the latter is or can become in the society.

To an extent then, La Guma's characters and heroes are trapped in a vicious maelstrom of cause and effect, paralysed by forces which reduce their desires and needs to animal-like proportions. Ronnie, the sullen ghetto product, is largely impelled by primitive emotions of revenge and has no qualms about killing his girl Susie, when he suspects her of running around with other men. Even the knifing is seen in graphic, animal, sexual terms, 'the savage, enraged, cutting caresses of the blade . . . [her] . . . surrender as to another lover.'[64]

His novels are about poverty and the victims of poverty, politics and racism. His characters cannot escape from the situation in which they find themselves. La Guma's characters are doomed from the start. The author is no psychological novelist. As social novelist, he is less interested in delineating character than in the society that has infected him. His emphasis is not on the man, but on the social group and the social setting. His characters are primarily social animals, described in terms of their race and their place in the social setting. Caroline for example was seventeen 'married and great with pregnancy . . . a machine . . . wound up and set to perform an automatic function'.[65]

The novel, *And A Threefold Cord,* is rather episodically structured, but then this is true of the author's other novels too. It is full of interest and details. The experiences are external, hardly internal. The tragedy is conceived in social and not individual terms. What emerges in all the novels is a picture of crushed humanity and pitiful human beings. Seldom are they in open conflict with others. Events predominate, people are reduced to mere pawns, action is meaningless, violence is directed at each other.

Reduced to this sub-human condition, La Guma's characters can only love and hate, fight and kill with animal brutality. There is Roman for example, more anthropoid than homo sapiens, who 'beat his wife's head with faggots . . . kicked her ribs and broke her arms [who] when he became tired of beating her, whipped the children. [A person who was] as dangerous as a starved old wolf, ready to turn on anybody who got in his way.'[66]

Alex La Guma's characters are all isolated elements in an atmosphere which will eventually devour them. The author paints a landscape of annihilation without being maudlin. He uses the language of the poor, that peculiar mixture of English and Afrikaans, which I shall refer to as *Englikaans*. This type of language seems to define the oppressive circumstances as well as the tragic-comic position of the poor. There is no political rhetoric, no trumpeting of slogans with La Guma. The force of his social protest gains momentum from his rather naturalistic depiction of the physical and spiritual landscape in which his characters dwell.

White people hardly intrude, or only peripherally, for example policemen who are the representatives of the legalized brutality of the system. They don't have to intrude, for without the haunting spectre of white brutality, the Cape Flats and District Six would not exist in the form these places exist in La Guma's novels. The only white character in his novel, *And A Threefold Cord,* is George Mostert, who is a lonely soul caught up in his own spiritual waste land. He is doubly cut off from the main stream of existence. He is white, but lives outside their normative structure; he lives in a 'coloured' area, but through his skin, is largely precluded from the warmth and proletarian exuberance of the shanty towns.

In *The Stone Country* (1967), La Guma explores another ghoulish facet of South African life — that of the prisons. The novelist has an inside knowledge of South African prisons. The picture he paints is a grim one. It is a joyless existence, punctuated with an occasional, mock-humorous tone — a painful indictment against society. Prison is a place populated with 'Ragged street-corner hoodlums, shivering drunks, thugs in cheap flamboyant clothes and knowledgeable looks, murderers, robbers, house-breakers, petty criminals, rapists, loiterers and simple permit-offenders.'[67]

The narrator, George Adams, is one of the politically subversive types, possibly the author in disguise. He is a sensitive recorder of details and events — although with somewhat too detached an air. But the latter trait saves him from becoming a political commentator. The prison is described as follows:[68]

> built . . . during Victorian times, and over the years bits and pieces had been added to its interior, and alterations made here and there, a and because it could not expand outwards, it had closed in upon itself in a warren of cells, cages, corridors and yards.
>
> Outside, the facade and been brightened with lawns and flower-beds: the grim face of an executioner hidden behind a holiday mask.

The inmates are a tragic collection. There is Butcherboy Williams, animal-like in his persecution of others and who dies a violent death. There is the Casbah Kid, a mere boy waiting to be executed in Pretoria and of whom the author writes: 'to force conversation from the boy was like tackling a safe with a soft tool'.[69] John Solomons, the clown, was obsequious, pathetically playing out his role of a 'coloured' buffoon. A ragged, motley collection then, the jetsam cast up by a society which discriminates and destroys on the basis of colour. These are the derelicts of apartheid who have no raft to cling to.

In the novel, *A Walk in the Night* (1962), the setting is District Six, that ghetto which once overlooked Table Bay, with its varied population of Indians and 'coloured', Jews and Greeks (with their numerous shops). A dirty place, but like that other black ghetto in Johannesburg, once long ago, Sophia Town, a place teeming with life.

Once more, La Guma operates within his limitations. We are introduced to an atmosphere of decay, moral degradation and deracination through his graphic descriptions. 'A row of dustbins lined one side of the entrance and exhaled the smell of rotten fruit, stale food, stagnant water and general decay. A cat, the colour of dishwater, was trying to paw the remains of a fishhead from one of the bins.'[70]

Here one is confronted with the lumpen proletariat, the poor who are unthinkable. That same animality which is in his other books lurks subterraneously on every page.

H. Africa, in his unpublished MA thesis on La Guma's use of language, makes some very interesting observations. La Guma's language further serves to define and illustrate the lowly position of the poor. La Guma's exploitation of the peculiar language of the 'coloured' serves to strengthen the finely drawn and naturalistic social setting. Africa's thesis is especially concerned with the lexical, grammatical and phonological interferences in the speech patterns of the 'coloureds', as they appear in the novel, *A Walk in the Night*. He identifies four situations in which certain lexical items recur:[71]

A   Those that occur in the dialogue of skollies [thugs] and uneducated workers and refer to their own social group.

B   Those that occur in the dialogue of the skollies and uneducated workers when they refer to people outside their own social group, for example, Constable Raalt.

C   Those that occur in the speech pattern of Raalt when he deals with the people of District Six, or when he thinks of his wife whom he suspects of infidelity.

D   Those that occur in the speech of the skollies and Raalt and are common to all three groups.

Africa then proceeds to identify words and slang expressions which are frequently used in the novel. They are as follows: *baas; bedonerd* (crazy); *bliksem* (miscreant); *mos* (just); *hotnot* (hottentot); *boer* (Boer); *donder* (wretch); *oubaas* (old master); *verdomde* (damned); *volk* (people generally).[71] However, Africa fails to point out that *volk*, when applied to 'coloureds', has a much more prejorative connotation than when it is used to refer to the nation.

He also identifies the following slang expression in the novel: *juba* (a chappie); *endjie* (a cigarette stub); *blerrie* (bloody); *ching* (money); *rooker* (gangster); *bokkie* (girl friends).[71]

The language of La Guma defines his characters in terms of their social setting, their level of education, their morality. It endows his characters with a certain humour at times. Yet, it also has a comi-tragic ring to it. Whereas in *Toïings,* language is used to portray the 'farm-hand' and villagers as comic beings, in *A Walk in the Night,* language affects the entire people. This adds further to the truthfulness of La Guma's descriptions and social settings.

The political situation is never totally absent in the works of La Guma. His characters are used to reflect the iniquity of the South African society. What happens to them is, by implication, a political comment on this society. The finely drawn social settings only serve to expose the horrible system of apartheid. Very few of his earlier characters emerge as fully-fledged political heroes. However, by the time we come to *And A Threefold Cord,* his main character can state: 'like he say, people can't stand up to the world alone, they got to be together'.[72] And, 'if the poor all got together and took everything in the blerry world, there wouldn't be poor no more'.[73]

Rabkin's comment is very apt:[74]

The moral action of La Guma's characters has been described as essentially defensive. There is evidence, however, that the author has found this method increasingly inadequate, and in the succession of his leading characters can be traced a development towards an outright political posture. Thus, while Mike Adonis is shown in moral retreat, from the dignity of a factory worker to the questionable status of a petty criminal, Charlie Pauls, in *And A Threefold Cord,* is an occasional worker, in whom the roots of class-consciousness have taken a precarious hold.

The main characters in his political novel, *In the Fog of the Season's End,* Beukes, Elias Tekwane and, to a minor extent, Isaac, are all politically-conscious and motivated people. Whatever we get to know about them as human beings, by way of flash-backs, is given to show how they came to be involved in politics. We are given little insight into the individual and private struggles of the characters. References to Tekwane's youth in the Transkei are used as a commentary on, for example, the pass laws. Thus, despite La Guma's vivid evocation of scene and locale, the characters, as fully-fledged political heroes, remain largely outside the grip of the reader.

The minor characters in the novel who are involved with Beukes help him out of a peculiar loyalty. They are either semi-literate urban types, like Tommy who 'knew vaguely that Beukes's "business" involved handing out printed papers during the night, calling on people to strike, even being arrested'.[75] Or, they are middle-class teachers, like Flotman, who openly concedes: 'I'm scared . . . I don't want to go to jail and eat pap and lose my stupid job or get bashed up by the law.'[76] And then there is the doctor, towards the end, who, despite all the risks involved, treats Beukes's wound and justifies his actions pontifically: 'If the community is given the opportunity of partici-pating in making the law, then they have a moral obligation to obey it . . . . But if the law is made for them, without their consent or partici-pation, then it is a different matter.'[77]

Beukes is not a superman, but an ordinary person with ordinary desires. La Guma at least refrains from creating a super-educated hero, who can only find salvation in the arms of a white liberal woman. True to form, his heroes are practically all from the working class. The love affair between Beukes and Frances is the first normal one

159

from South Africa — the white liberal 'goddess' in the arms of the politically disturbed and sensitive 'coloured', does not intrude. Beukes muses: 'Looking at her he thought sentimentally that her face could be disfigured with a hammer and she would still look beautiful.'[78] At last, one is confronted with a relationship where the 'coloured' character is not forced to quote from Shakespeare, Pirandello, Garcia Lorca or Molière. The conversation which follows between Beukes and Frances is totally in keeping with the tone, setting and intention of the novel.[79]

'So, you saw me before, hey?'
'Yes. You interested in political things?'
'I reckon so. Help out, now and then?'
'My pa goes to meetings and stuff like that.'

The novelist leaves the reader in no doubt as to his political stance. The struggle will increasingly become an armed one. This is spelt out clearly when Beukes says farewell to some youngsters (including his friend Isaac), who are off to undergo guerrilla training abroad: 'What the enemy himself has created, these will become battlegrounds, and what we see now is only the tip of the iceberg.'[80] Yet, the 'children . . . in the sunlit yard'[81] appear to be a symbol of the future South Africa without racialism.

It is a huge step from La Guma's working class characters to Richard Rive's educated middle-class heroes. References to, and descriptions of the poor and their poverty-stricken environments do nothing to wipe out the middle-class aura which surrounds his political novel, *Emergency* (1964). The novel concentrates on the events leading up to, and including, the massacre at Sharpeville in 1960. Its theme is decidedly political. The author himself states in the prologue: 'Since to my knowledge there is no recorded history of this important and dramatic period in South African history, I have had to rely on my own compilation gleaned from newspapers at the time.' One is therefore entitled to expect, at the least, an important historical, if not political statement. Yet the novel falls far short of the author's bold statement in the prologue. On the contrary, the novel reveals, upon closer scrutiny, that the author moves very much within the accepted South African literary tradition of accommodation. The authorities may then object to his presentation of historical and political facts — they object to anything which is contrary to official government policy and nationalist ideology. In the treatment of his characters, Rive proves to be far less revolutionary.

His main character, Andrew Dreyer, is a 'coloured' school teacher, who was born in the slums of District Six, outside Cape Town. He suffers miserably at the hands of his near-white family (mother, brothers and sisters), and never seems to rid himself of his inferiority complexes. This is reflected in the descriptions of some of the major characters which cross Andrew's path. James, his brother, is described as follows: 'James was very fair like his mother, went to white cinemas and bars.'[82] Abe Hanslo, his close friend, 'had a freckled skin, green eyes and a shock of fair hair'.[83] Apparently the novelist had a special affection for Abe, for little further on we read that Abe was 'Fair, with freckles around the nose and green eyes and a mop of fair hair'.[84] Rive does not even bother to use different words to describe Abe, unless 'mop' for 'shock' is regarded as a fundamental change.

Andrew's mother was fair. 'She had always been strange in her attitude towards him . . . . He wondered whether it had anything to do with colour. She was fair, like James and Annette, whereas he was dark.'[85] His brother-in-law, Kenneth, had 'A pale, sickly-white skin and dull, expressionless, green eyes'.[86] Eldred Carollissen, his pupil, was 'good-looking with greenish-grey eyes'.[87] Florence Bailey reminded one of 'a German lass. Flaxen hair, blue eyes and apple-red cheeks . . . in the Black Forest'.[88] Only her husband, Justin Bailey, is not evaluated in terms of skin colour, possibly because the relationship between him and Andrew is not that deep.

When Andrew meets the white girl, Ruth Talbot, for the first time, he is immediately swept off his feet. She is not described in detail, but then one assumes that she is aesthetically pleasing to the eye. Andrew dislikes the cheap white girls his brother James and brother-in-law Kenneth consort with, yet objects when Mrs Carollissen, his landlady, says of Ruth: 'She's a nice girl. Pity she's white.'[89]

After reading through the physical descriptions of Rive's characters one is inclined to conclude with O'Toole: 'One comes away from such a genealogical discussion with the general impression that many Coloured people are descended by a neat biological trick from only one (white) ancestor.'[90]

Andrew Dreyer is fraught with such inconsistencies. He feels overwhelmed in the comfortable study of his friend, Abe Hanslo, which is 'pleasantly furnished with Gauguin and Utrillo reproductions . . . records of Beethoven, Mozart and Smetana'. Yet our political hero cannot refrain from reminding his friend that he has working class origins. 'Yes. I grew up somewhat differently. In a slum to be exact.'[91] When, however, he is harassed by the police and in real danger, our

161

hero calmly turns to Ruth and says: 'What would you like to hear? Britten, Purcell or Rachmaninov?'[92]

What Soyinka says of Rive's *Make Like Slaves* (1976) is perhaps also applicable to his *Emergency*. 'We are left to feel that, given a more sensitive white woman or a less abrasive (guilt-ridden) coloured man . . . a small part of the battle could be won.'[93]

Andrew Dreyer, the political hero, comes across as a confused, woolly-headed liberal and romantic. The political discussions sound more like a re-run of speeches from the early 1960s among the politically involved groups in Cape Town. In no way do they enhance the reader's understanding of the political situation. Most of the discussions highlight the contradictions in, what is referred to as the 'coloured' community. The main character, Andrew Dreyer, is closer to his 'brown' brother, Josef Malan, and like him, he refuses to run away when the opportunity presents itself. Instead, he chooses a peculiar form of martyrdom, by simply deciding to stay at Ruth Talbot's place.

Lewis Nkosi had some rather pertinent remarks to make about Rive's novel:[94]

> We find here a type of fiction which exploits the ready-made plots
> of racial violence, social apartheid, interracial love affairs which
> are doomed from the beginning without any attempts to transcend
> or transmute these given 'social facts' into artistically persuasive
> works of fiction.[94]

Commenting on Rive's use of dialogue, Nkosi writes:[95]

> Rive's use of dialogue is never to reveal his characters but to
> present argument about the political situation, which is
> his main interest. Thus the characters never use words which
> are uniquely theirs; but words and arguments which suggest
> the position of the various ethnic political groups they
> represent.

Andrew Dreyer has more in common with Brink's Josef Malan than with La Guma's Beukes. In his final discussion with Abe Hanslo, after an unbelievably bizarre scene in Langa, he simply states: 'Who me? Oh, I'm going to Ruth's flat to listen to Rachmaninov.'[96] And then he moves out to await his fate in the flat of his white girl friend. Such action points to an extreme form of naivety and a lack of political consciousness, or a misunderstanding of the political task at hand. Dreyer destroys Rive's proud boast in the prologue. 'Ruth smiled nervously at him, then Andrew started to open the French windows.'[97] Ah, well! one is inclined to exclaim. We are at least saved the embarrassment of another heart-rending death-cell scene in the style of Alan Paton or André Brink.

We have seen how the novel follows the political situation in some respects. As the political climate changed, so also did the literary idiom of the writer. If initially, it was openly accommodating, then in the early 1950s and 1960s, the tone was decidedly political. One may disagree with the way in which the novelist presents his politics, and question whether the true political novel will ever emerge from South Africa. Yet, it is an indisputable fact that the writings of many black South Africans have largely contributed to an awareness of the inhuman political situation in South Africa. The early works of Abrahams reflected some of the human disruption in South African society in the late 1930s and mid 1940s. La Guma's writings reflect increasingly the changes in the political climate in the 1950s and early 1960s. While initially, he unmasks the iniquity through his realistically drawn (naturalistic), social settings, his characters become increasingly more politically conscious. This too follows the general pattern among the 'coloureds'. Rive's novel reveals some of the pitfalls for the South African novelist. The ambiguous attitudes of the political rulers are responsible for a fair amount of ambiguity among 'coloureds' themselves. Even the novelist who chooses politics as his theme may, unconsciously, be a dupe of his own ambiguous past.

# Chapter 9

# New tenants of memory[1]

The 'Cape coloured' has been the greatest dupe of white stereotyped portrayals than any other group in South Africa. This is a phenomenon which is by no means over, as is evident from the numerous letters and debates in Afrikaans daily newspapers, such as *Die Burger,* concerning the political future of this group. In an attempt to find a way out of the problems, the government even decided to appoint a special commission under an Afrikaner Professor of sociology. In order to give the commission a further respectability, well known personalities who take pride in being classified, or referred to, as 'coloureds', for example Professor van der Ross and the Reverend Beets, were co-opted onto the body which became known as the Theron Commission.

Yet all these many lengthy debates and letters cannot hide the ambiguity which still characterizes both white and 'coloured' attitudes. Thus, when the 'coloured' leader, Sonny Leon, who, despite his ostensibly militant stand against apartheid, still moves within the white institutionalized structure, tried to sabotage the proceedings of the especially created Coloured Representative Council (CRC), the response was of a varied nature. Whites did not hesitate to accuse the 'coloureds' of ungratefulness, despite the government view that no other 'racial' group should interfere with the politics of another 'racial' group. Some of the letters bordered on verbal lynching, others were noted for their ambiguity and, at times, almost empathetic pleas to try and understand 'our brown people'.

'Coloured' readers themselves displayed a similar duality. But, as is so often the case in South Africa, many were held back from openly condemning apartheid by the uniformity of violence which generally characterizes life in this part of the world.

The stereotypes as found in South African literature and culture seem to complicate, at least for white South Africa, a truthful appraisal of the 'coloured' situation. The history of the 'coloured' reads like a re-run of the stereotypes found in Herskovits's *The Myth of the Negro Past* (1941). Colin Turnbull's observations would readily be underscored by many whites in South Africa:[2]

> It is in the past that the tribe finds its present strength, its
> present morality . . . . But, more important still, the tribe
> finds in the past the incentive to work for the future, and
> to maintain its present integrity. If the past is destroyed
> through taught disbelief, or through exposure to scorn or
> ridicule . . . the result can only be total collapse and chaos.

White legislators justify political attitudes towards the 'coloureds', precisely on the basis of such views. The 'coloured', they argue, has no glorified tribal past, or ritualized order, to sustain himself. He has no folk heroes like Piet Retief, Chaka or Toussaint L'Ouverture (see: O'Toole, 1973).

Outwardly, this may then appear damaging to the development of a group identity. Yet, in a sense, within the South African context, it can also be a blessing in disguise. The African and the white man can, after all, both fall back on a tribal myth, the 'coloureds' are asked to forge one which is all South African. Not surprisingly, many in this group reject terms such as 'kleurlinge' and 'bruinmense' and prefer to be known as South Africans.

This is clear from Edelstein's study, *What Do the Coloureds Think?* (1974), and also from the Theron Commission Report (1976). It is not the shame of identification with being 'coloured', which prompts the 'coloured' to refer to himself as a 'so-called coloured', as O'Toole (1973) would have us believe. It is rather the connotations attached to the word 'coloured', as found in the white political ethos, which cause the violent rejection. Ironically, it is the Afrikaner (Boer) past, as the sacramental fount into which members of the laager dip from time to time, in order to maintain a group unity, which may, yet, spell the greatest danger to Afrikanerdom. For it is this group unity through myth and taught belief which makes it impossible for the Afrikaners as such, to change from being a group unto themselves, into a group for others.

Part of the problem of defining people referred to in South Africa as 'coloured', is the existence of a play of contrasts. The 'coloured' position has been largely obscured by the overall black–white political confrontation, and the notion that, 'from the standpoint of the way of duty, anyone in exile from the community is nothing'.[3] Yet, there are increasing indications that 'this exile [may be] the first step towards the quest'.[4] That this quest will steer many 'coloureds' into the direction of an orphic descent is already crystal clear.

The African continent has, in the process of demythologization, seen the emergence of two significant myths in modern times. I interpret myth here as 'a directing of the mind and the heart, by means of profoundly informed figurations, to that ultimate mystery which fills and surrounds all existence'.[5] The one myth was Pan Africanism, the other, négritude. Both contributed to the freeing of the former colonized from their servile status. In the Americas, there was, of course, the emergence of soul-brotherism and black power.

One of the striking features, or by-products, of such rallying cries, was their reflection in the literature of the people concerned. A comparative analysis will bear out that the facets of négritude, Pan Africanism and soul-brotherism are increasingly being reflected in 'coloured' thinking and writing. There are similar indications that the 'no past, no myth through taught disbelief' image, as imposed on 'coloureds' by white South Africans, is also being expunged through a greater political awareness.

In the French Antillean and West African colonies, it was assimilation of the French language, culture and civilization, which partly determined one's supposed acceptance, as distinct from the South African criterion of skin colour. But the expectations created in the colonized élite in French colonies were soon to prove false. Négritude was a means of throwing off the cultural and historical legacy of the French policy of assimilation. In America, the Afro-Americans embraced soul-brotherism and black power as a means to achieve their freedom.

Balandier has sketched the colonial situation as one in which the indigenous society is subordinate to the European group politically, culturally and economically. Such a policy was to have dire consequences for the society and the respective groups in the society. Césaire, the Martiniquean, who was the first to use the term négritude in his, by now, well-known *Cahier d'un retour au pays natal*, describes the situation as consisting of a colonizer and the colonized, in which one also finds the elements of intimidation and mistrust (*méfiance*).

Yet, it is interesting to note that in both the French colonial societies and the South African situation, the whites were, and in some cases still are, able to count on a relative amount of stability. This meant, that in both societies, the dominant white groups found some legitimacy for their exercise of power. It is also significant, that their dominant scheme of values and norms was to some extent accepted within, and by, the indigenous population. Césaire cannot therefore be wholly right in stressing only the elements of intimidation and mistrust, for, quite obviously, there must have been quite a measure of trust (*confiance*), as opposed to mistrust, in order for the colonizer to have been so effective.

In both types of societies, the whites justified their dominant positions through a series of rationalizations. For example, to the French, the African and the Antillean were noble savages, passive people who had never been capable of any ingenious, intricate or profound discoveries. In the case of the 'Cape coloureds', the whites refer to them as children, indolent, ne'er do wells, happy-go-lucky, gregarious and shifty people. Statements like the following by high-ranking police officials are still the order of the day: 'The Coloured man is *by nature* [sic] lazier and more work shy than the Bantu.'[6] This statement was made by one Colonel J. H. Vorster, district police commander of Athlone, a 'coloured' suburb.

Yet, while the French attempted to establish an intimate relationship between the colonial territory and the metropolis, the policy of apartheid was designed to ensnare each group within its peculiar ethnicity. In the case of the 'coloured', the absence of a tribal heritage and an indigenous culture helped in the non-formation of a 'coloured' identity. For apartheid to be successful, it needs the tribe. And it is for this reason that the Afrikaners have tried, and are still trying, to forge a 'coloured' myth. Sadly, however, what has emerged (if anything at all) can only be classified as folklore.

The 'coloureds', while traditionally not subjected to the pass laws, have been allowed by some gentleman's agreement to live marginally in the white man's cultural and economic valhalla, without being co-sharers in the administrative process. For the 'coloured', the mother country was not situated overseas. Traditionally again, while the 'coloureds' attended separate schools, the syllabuses initially did not differ from those of the whites. The 'coloured' child was treated to similar white historical visions of South Africa. He too, was forced to regurgitate the well-orchestrated myths at the annual examinations. But under apartheid, this has undergone a radical change as the following quote from the *Primary School in Environment Study* in the Cape Province reveals:[7]

The aim of school activity is to give the child a clear idea
of himself in the socio-economic structure of his country
and, more specifically, the place taken in by the particular
section to which his family group belongs and the addition
to the economic and cultural values of his particular
section.

The group of literates in the French colonial situation was assured
of all sorts of privileges, for example, they were exempted from taxes
and did not have to take part in corvées. The 'coloureds' were also,
up to a certain point and stage, given a measure of preferential
treatment.

Western education was an important channel of mobility in the
colonial society. In West Africa and the West Indies, all this led to
an alienation from their own culture and environment. The French
colonized were expected to recite in parrot fashion, 'nos ancêtres
les Gaulois'. In the case of the 'Cape coloured', the situation was
slightly different. One could hardly speak of an alientation from
their own culture. Whatever indigenous culture the 'coloured' had
was effectively destroyed by the end of the eighteenth century. In
their case there was no ritualized order to sustain them, or constitute
the formation of a group. They lingered on, constituting what Fanon
called the 'terrified consciousness', on the fringe of white, puritan
society. Yet, as in the case of the French colonies, the educational
system was purely European-orientated. In the French colonies, the
image of France was buttressed up by the school system, the whites
present in the colonies and the Africans and Antilleans who had
visited Paris. Understandably, it was a rather distorted picture which
led to such irreverencies as an idealization of France, with Paris regarded as the mecca of culture. The African or Antillean who had been
to France, the 'been-to', was regarded as a half-god, as Fanon so aptly
indicated in his book *Black Skin, White Masks*. One finds a similar
distortion of the image of the white man and his civilization, 'die
duusman' (duus = diet = volk = people), as he is called sometimes
by the 'coloured' populace. But, while the educated black man from
French colonies in Africa and the Antilles had to go to Paris to experience his disillusion, the 'Cape coloured' stayed at home to undergo
his. In the case of both the French colonized and the 'Cape coloured',
whatever fringe benefits of white society they were allowed to enjoy,
had led them to a misguided anticipatory socialization.

In both cases the reference group was, for a very long time, the ruling group. In South Africa, there were various laws which prevented 'coloureds' from achieving full citizenship. For example, the Franchise laws, the *Group Areas Act,* the Race Classification laws, the *Job Reservation Act.* Harsh reality revealed that the term South African was only reserved for those who, according to the laws of apartheid, were *civilized* and by implication, *white.*

The Africans and the West Indians soon discovered that complete assimilation led to a negation of their own culture and an acceptance of French bourgeois values. But in actual fact, their acceptance by the French was of a circumscribed nature. In the metropolis they soon discovered that they were still looked upon as 'le nègre', by even the lowest of Frenchmen.

The 'coloured' finds himself in a similar situation. No matter how civilized or Westernized and educated, he is still ranked lower than the poor white, or the Greek and Portuguese urban proletariat or peasant turned immigrant. Both groups thus experienced a deflation of the norm which they had been led to believe in. This deflation led the French African and the Antillean students living in Paris, to an awareness of their own 'self-deception in self-definition', and culminated in the 1930s in a discovery of their brotherhood under the skin.

The eminent West Indian novelist and thinker, Wilson Harris, in a paper delivered to the Conference of Commonwealth literature at Aarhus, Denmark in May 1971, explored and discussed two particular concepts, as related to the indigenes, which are of extreme relevance in our context. Namely, 'ritual bounty or continuity on one hand – ritual bounty [being the] victor's assets or hoard of conquest – and, on the other hand, the great chain of memory expressing subtle and complex ambivalences woven through the bodies of nature and history, man with man, victor with victim.'[8] According to Wilson Harris, the total effect of ritual bounty can be gauged from the manner in which the conqueror has managed to pulverize the conquered into a 'uniform conviction so that the reality or play of contrasts is eclipsed within an order of self-deception'.[9]

He warns of the self-deception, which can play parts with both revolutionary and conservative:[10]

> without a ceaseless creative and re-creative *rapport* between
> old monuments and new windows upon the cosmos, one may mis-
> conceive the arts of genesis – one may plaster over afresh every
> break-through appearing within an old collective myth into a

new recurring monument in the name of uniform or time-less identity.

While the négritude and soul-brother writers have succeeded in becoming 'the new tenant of memory within the hollow monument'[11] [of the colonizer], and thus responsible for the 'devolution or break-down of historical premises',[12] this process is only gathering momentum among the 'coloureds'. The breaking down of old premises means destruction, even self-destruction at times. But this very act of destroying opens up the way for new perspectives. Négritude and soul-brotherism was, in essence, the 'charting of the hollowness', which remained after the destructive process, in order 'to set up a new echoing dimension of spatial resources for the liberation of community'.[12]

In the Americas, it was to lead to a rediscovery, and even glorification of Africa. The West Indian poet, Mackay, who lived in Harlem during the 1930s, sings of the 'dim regions whence my father came' and hopes 'my soul would sing forgotten jungle songs'.[13]

These ideas were an expression of the quest through exile. This would eventually climax into a self-mockery — at times even an anti-clericalism — which is so often characteristic of black poetry, in contrast to the irony of the white poet. The West Indian poet, Leon Damas, is an excellent exponent of this type of poetry.[14]

> I feel ridiculous
> in their shoes, in their dress suits
> in their starched shirts, in their hard collars,
> in their monocles and bowler hats . . .
> I feel ridiculous
> with their theories which they season
> according to their needs and passion.

In contrast, the poet, Petersen, laments his dark skin. But passivity and religious acceptance was also a trait of the earlier Afro-American poetry.[15]

> Let it then be O Lord that I
> a thousand years ago have sinned
> against man and God . . .
> then know I now at your command
> is this scabbiness laid bare . . .

There is just a hint of the plaintive and sad quality of the American spiritual in this poem.

The post-Sharpeville period (1960 onwards) produced a considerable number of exiled writers and political militants, whose influence was felt at home and abroad. At home, for example, Matthews, Thomas, and even Adam Small, seemed to be drawing on a 'more folkloristic (oral) tradition, as opposed to the more cerebral white poetry'. They drew on the language of the ghettos, like the American black poet Langston Hughes and endowed it with some literary respectability. In English, Brutus and Nortje exhibited the first stirrings of a 'ceaseless creative and recreative rapport between the old new windows upon the cosmos'. Politically, 'coloured' students joined up with blacks in SASO (South African Students' Organization for blacks).

The poetry of Matthews and Thomas, who both still live in South Africa, moved significantly closer to the soul-brotherism of the Americas, reminding one forcibly of Le Roi Jones:[16]

> we want poems
> like fists beating niggers out of Jocks
> or dagger poems in the slimy bellies . . .
> We want poems that kill.

What formerly applied to black poets from America, now also came to apply to the writings of 'coloured' South African writers. 'For a white man to read Le Roi Jones . . . is like being held in a dark room listening to an angry voice he is not expected to appreciate or understand.'[17] In the Cape too, poets like Matthews and Thomas came to fulfil the function of being 'poetry guerrilla fighters who talk Black English and ignore accepted aesthetics'.[17]

Matthews and Thomas are both inundated with their blackness (which is revealing and new, within the South African 'coloured' context). Moreover, they are concerned with the negation of the black man's humanity. In their poetry, they are closer to the négritude and soul-brother writers. One is not specifically conscious of the man or woman of 'mixed' origin in their *oeuvre,* but of the entire condition of the black man in a white-controlled world. Their poetry transcends the Liesbeek and the Vaal Rivers, and links up with that of the Niger and the Mississippi.

Matthews and Thomas seem to be moving in the direction of the two important black emancipatory phenomena, namely, négritude and soul. It was after all the concept of 'soul', which bound the American black in an all-class emancipatory struggle. Jeanpierre defined it as follows: 'Soul seems to be African négritude dressed in American clothing imbuing with an African-American hue all the encounters which have fallen within the province of blacked-lived experience in America.'[18]

Stephen Henderson looked upon soul as 'all of the unconscious energy of the Black Experience . . . primal spiritual energy . . . the expression of powerful total personality, drawing its reserve from centuries of suffering and joy.'[19] The celebration of blackness becomes a demythologization of the white myth, that black is ugly. Langston Hughes eulogizes the black woman in the following manner:[20]

> Ah,
> My black one
> Thou art not beautiful
> Yet Thou hast
> A loveliness
> Surpassing beauty . . .
>
> Ah,
> My black one
> Thou art not luminous
> Yet an altar of jewels,
> An altar of shimmering jewels,
> Would pale in the light
> Of Thy darkness
> Pale in the light
> Of Thy nightness.

In contrast Senghor's black woman is more specifically sensuous:[21]

> Naked woman, dark woman
> Firm-fleshed ripe fruit, sombre raptures of black wine,
> mouthmaking lyrical my mouth . . .
> Pearls are the stars on the night of your skin . . .

All these echoes are to be found in the poetry of James Matthews, who writes:[22]

> Look upon the blackness of my woman
> and be filled with the delight of it
> her blackness a beacon among the insipid
> faces around her
> proudly she walks, a sensuous black lily
> swaying in the wind
> This daughter of Sheba . . .
> my woman wears her blackness like a queen

a robe
This daughter of Sheba.

The resuscitation of the black woman was, and is, an important act in the black man's effort to liberate himself from Euro-centric myths. Matthews and Thomas see themselves not specifically as the muses of the 'Cape coloured'. Their anthology, *Cry Rage* (1972), is therefore an important literary event, in that there is definite indication of a black orphic descent. It is this fundamental realization by the 'coloured' that, while his language may be Western, his idiom is non-Western (black if one wishes). White attempts to define and come to grips with 'coloured' political aspirations may founder precisely because they think that they understand the 'coloured' *language*, whereas in essence, they miscomprehend the 'coloured' *idiom*.

The black writer cannot shirk his responsibility to attack a political system which denies him his freedom. Through his art, he does not only give vent to his own frustration, but also to that of his entire people. The poems of Matthews and Thomas form an indictment, a litany of protest against the system of apartheid, bearing out the American black poetess Nikki Giovanni's belief that 'there is no difference between the warrior, poet and the people'.

Matthews and Thomas mistrust words like democracy, liberalism, dialogue and reconciliation, which are only employed to ensnare the black man in his status of inferiority. The Europeans may then be shocked by these raw emotions. Whites in South Africa simply banned the anthology.

The title of the anthology *Cry Rage* already signifies the impotency, the rage, the hysteria, the comi-tragic lurking everywhere. For the black artist, South Africa is a frustrating place — he is cut off from other artists of a different pigmentation; he cannot even go to a proper theatre; he is, ironically, dependent on white publishers and white critical evaluations. Writing about, and presumably for, his semi-literate people, he is in the anomalous position of reaching only the ritual proprietors of his distorted universe. Matthews is bitter and will brook no altruism under the guise of Christian Nationalism and Western Humanitarianism.

In one of his poems he writes of these hypocrites:[23]

> they speak so sorrowfully about the
> children dying of hunger in Biafra
> but sleep unconcerned about the rib-thin
> children of Dimbaza . . .

Literature *engagée* can, however, be harmful to the poetic element, as the following poem so aptly shows:[24]

> poverty is my cross
> My colour binds me to it
> charity offices the stations
> on the road to Golgotha.

This is an example of protest writing at its worst, and what Stephen Spender called 'poetry conscripted for the victims'. Yet, to Matthews and Thomas, such niceties are trivial in the South African context. Reality after all indicates:[25]

> Fear is the knock
> at the fourth hour after midnight
> when the house is hushed in sleep.

In a foreword to this anthology, Matthews spelt out his credo quite clearly: 'For blacks, to be born and to live in South Africa is like living through a nightmare where words have different connotations because of pigmentation.'[26] Only occasionally does Matthews allow himself an ironic stance, for example, when he lampoons the patronage and patronizing attitudes of South Africa's white liberal culture vultures:[27]

> the occasion is to honour
> missus marshall's latest discovery
> a painter who paints in the manner
> of picasso
> that was before picasso produced works
> which missus marshall found rather strange.
>
> I am invited to view the works of her protégé
> another in her collection that numbers a singer, a sculptor,
> and me
> to be displayed when missus marshall
> flaunts her liberality
> in presenting her cultured blacks.

Gladys Thomas is one of the few 'coloured' women, if not the only hitherto, who has seen fit to give expression to her unfreedom poetically. No doubt there are very real reasons why the 'coloured' woman in South Africa has not yet announced her presence on the literary scene. They are, after all, the nursemaids of the white kids, they are the ones who have to supply rational explanations to their own children as to why they cannot enjoy certain privileges. They are the ones who give birth to a generation of the enslaved. Morbid and sad is her *Haunted Eyes*:[28]

> A Beautiful land
> with beautiful mountains
> and beautiful seas
> But not for me
>
> Come take my hand
> Stop touring and go slumming with me
> Look! before your eyes
> You see a jungle
> See the white cages
> with thousands of animals running wild
> look at their eyes
> Haunted eyes
> That's why you see wire fences . . .

Nadine Gordimer, the novelist, says: 'I do not fear the Blacks, but many whites do. My message to the self-appointed guardians of our culture is: There can be no such thing as South African Literature if it excludes Black Literature — and it does at the moment.'[29] Matthews's *cri de coeur* echoes through three hundred years of rapine and despoliation and finds support in the poems of Langston Hughes, Nikki Giovanni, Le Roi Jones (Baraka) and Eldridge Cleaver, when he writes:[30]

> Can the white man speak for me?
>
> Can he feel my pain when his laws
> tear wife and child from my side
> and I am forced to work a thousand miles away,
>
> does he know my anguish
> as I walk his streets at night
> my hand fearfully clasping my pass?
>
> is he with me in the loneliness
> of my bed in the bachelor barracks
> with my longing driving me to mount my brother?

> will he soothe my despair
> as I am driven insane
> by scraps of paper permitting me to live?

> Can the white man speak for me?

Matthews and Thomas both still live in South Africa. The extent
to which their messages have, however, penetrated the disenfranchised
of South Africa may be largely underestimated by whites. One has
only to read Mongane Wally Serote's tribute to James Matthews, in
*Black Literature and Arts Congress* (vol. 2, 1974), to realize this. I
recall how deeply Serote spoke of his brother Jimmy Matthews in
Amsterdam in May 1976.

But the struggle is fought on two fronts, that is at home by people
like James Matthews, and abroad, by poets like Dennis Brutus. He
too is a practical illustration of the poet-cum-warrior. Opposed to
the regime, he soon fell foul of it and was imprisoned on Robben
Island. *Letter to Martha* are poems which record his experiences and
feelings on the island. As is the custom in South Africa, Brutus was
banned on release from prison. This not only severely restricted his
freedom of movement, but worse still, made it impossible for him to
publish. These poems were written as letters to his sister-in-law Martha.

Brutus first attracted attention with the publication of the anthology, *Sirens, Knuckles, Boots* (1963). In 1955, Daniel Abasiekong
wrote in *Transition:* 'It is natural that a South African poet with an
open sensibility should react to the horny regime that operates in his
country.'[31] Yet, it is an indisputable fact that the strength of his poetry
lies precisely in the political attitude of the poet. He deliberately uses
an imagery and an idiom which is suggestive of the terror of the landscape: 'jackboots'; 'bones'; 'spirits crunch'; 'Sharpevilled to spear-
points'.

In exile, Brutus has become the focal point of many activities.
In America, in particular, where Black Studies and African Depart-
ments are plentiful, his political role as a poet is not insignificant. One
wonders, however, whether Abasiekong was so completely right when
he argued that 'these political poems ... [are] ... not so much a
political attitude'. It is difficult at times to abstract the poetic man
from the political man. Obviously, for Brutus, the creative act is a
political act. And the man himself has not been slow to respond to
this challenge. Occasionally, for me at least, one is afforded a peep
into his soul:[32]

I remember rising one night
after midnight
and moving
through an impulse of loneliness
to try and find the stars.

And through the haze
The battens of fluorescents made
I saw pinpricks of white
I thought were stars. ·

Only to be rudely reminded of the harsh reality of 'anxious boots', 'machine-gun post' and the 'brusque inquiry' lingering longer than the 'stars'. But there is just a hint of poems conscripted for the victims.

Whatever qualms one may have about ethno-inspired poetry, as a reaction against white domination, it remains a fact that phenomena such as négritude and soul have functioned as a 'cultural concept which has gone far to unite the community and prepare it for more important changes'. Ironically, again, the whites in South Africa have always insisted on the development of group consciousness and a deep-rooted pride in one's own ethnic identity. Yet, in practice, they are afraid of the concepts of soul and black power. When, for instance, blacks started wearing T-shirts with the slogan, 'Black is beautiful', this was immediately translated as a threat to the establishment, and, therefore, banned. Afrikaner intellectuals and political scientists hastened to act as apologists for apartheid, by pointing out that the slogan was inflammatory, detrimental to good race relations and revolutionary.

Some 'coloureds' are increasingly referring to themselves as blacks. African leaders are also beginning to reassess the role of the 'coloured' group. Thus, Mr Ramusi, the leader of the opposition party in Lebowa, a Bantustan, commented in *Die Burger:* 'There is a movement to group the coloured with the whites in order to reinforce the numbers of the whites. But we are watching whether you are trying to be white.'[33]

The 'coloured' ghetto inhabitants of Manenberg and Bonteheuwel are fast discovering their counterparts in Soweto, Gugulethu and Langa. Nowhere does this come out more clearly than in the statement of one of the teenagers sentenced to a long term of imprisonment during the upheavals of 1976:[34]

> Separate education which was unsatisfactory made me
> think even more. All institutions should be open to all.
> Because of the lack of facilities it appears that Blacks
> do not have the necessary qualifications to occupy higher
> posts. Bodies like the C. R. C., the Indian Council and
> Bantu Administration are fruitless because they can never
> remove our frustration. Our people feel they are a waste
> of time . . . I asked myself what was to be done to bring to
> the Government's attention the dissatisfaction and what
> changes should be made. Perhaps the way I did it was wrong
> but to date I have still not found any other way to bring
> my dissatisfaction to light.

This nineteen-year-old was sentenced to six years in prison.

The proposed new deal which was recently made known by the South African government, envisages a white, 'coloured' and Indian parliament. Some 'coloureds', Indians and whites may dupe themselves into believing that they have found a solution to the country's problems. No solution can exclude the majority of the people, the Africans. Even the Reverend A. Hendrickse, the new leader of the 'coloured' Labour party, was forced recently, at their annual conference, to speak out in favour of the African National Congress. His motives may be unclear or even impure. Yet, it is an indication of the type of reflection in 'coloured' society. Nothing, however, has been solved and nothing will be solved, as long as the 'coloured' is seen as a separate problem, which must be solved separately. In the language of Joseph Campbell, 'everyone of us shares the supreme ordeal — not in the brightest moments of the tribe's great victories, but in the silences of his personal despair'.[35]

# Appendix I

# Dr Abdurahman—pioneer

The most formidable figure in 'coloured' politics was undoubtedly Dr Abdurahman. He was born in the rural village of Wellington in the Cape in 1872. He studied at the Old South African College (the forerunner to the present-day University of Cape Town) and then proceeded to study medicine at Glasgow. Dr van der Ross, commenting on Abdurahman, says: 'Although his grandparents were slaves, they were not ordinary slaves; they were said to be "worthy of respect".'[1]

The young and brilliant Abdurahman returned to Cape Town as only the second man of colour to practise medicine in the Cape (van der Ross points out that the first one came from the West Indies). In 1904 he became the first 'coloured' to be elected to the Cape Town City Council and in 1919 he won a seat on the Cape Provincial Council.

Abdurahman became associated with the African People's Organization in 1905, a relationship which was to last for about forty years. This organization, first called the African Political Organization, was started in 1902–3 to help the 'coloureds' in the Northern Provinces who had no civic rights.

The inaugural meeting of this organization, which came to be referred to, generally, as the APO, was held in March 1903. A scrutiny of the main aims as propounded at this meeting is very illuminating:[2]

1   The APO was set out 'to create a unity among us'.
2   Education was seen as the key to success: 'a poor education will always keep us poor'.
3   The APO did not seek social integration with white people: 'we don't want to get into company where we have no business, we do not crave social intercourse'.
4   The APO would not fight other political organizations:

'since we have been so often sold and re-sold, we cannot
afford to support any particular party.'

5   Class legislation (i.e. descriminatory colour legislation) was
opposed: 'it is unjust, as it is unfair.'

6   The people were ever to be elevated, and so: 'Let us fight
the drink traffic, it has wrought havoc amongst our people.'

Once more van der Ross comments as follows: 'To a great extent
the political history of the Coloured people, of the APO and of
Dr Abdurahman, to the time of his death, were inextricably interwoven, although the influence of the APO diminished after the
mid–1930s.'[3] Abdurahman was president of the APO from 1905 until
his death in 1940. The activities of Abdurahman and his APO to have
a race-free South African constitution in 1910, are of great historical
importance.

There were three important non-white conferences held to discuss
the Draft Constitution of South Africa. First, there was the South
African Native Convention held at Bloemfontein between 24 and 26
March, 1909 under the presidency of Rubusana. The APO held its
annual conference in April 1909. The third conference was held
under the presidency of John Tengu Jabavu. On 5 June 1909, the
APO took the following resolutions, that in order for 'Union to be
enduring [it] should be founded upon the eternal rule of order and
justice'. It went on to say that, 'conference has read with inexpressible
disappointment the introduction of a colour line in the Draft S.A.
Act' and 'That the franchise of the Coloured races of the Cape
Colony should be permanently protected.' It continued 'That provision be made for the extension of the franchise to all qualified
coloured persons in the contemplated Union, and that the Native
territories should not be transferred to the Union except upon
conditions satisfactory to the Chiefs and Councillors.' Commenting
on the stipulation that only whites were eligible to become members
of Parliament the APO called it 'the foulest work that ever South
African Statesmen attached their names to . . . . It is an injustice
and cannot be tolerated by any self-respecting man . . . . We feel sure
that the Coloured people and natives will never cease to agitate until
injury is repaired and peace and mutual goodwill once more restored.'[4]
Even at this stage, the main aim was still to strive for peace and
goodwill. The early writings of 'coloured' leaders are interesting as an
index of the type of attitudes held by this group.

On the first Union Day celebrations, Dr Abdurahman made a
statement to the 'Coloured People of South Africa' in which he
exhorted 'every individual to prove by his life and conduct that he
values his political rights and privileges, and both knows how to
and actually does, discharge his duties faithfully and fearlessly.'[5]

Abdurahman was a child of his times and still believed that he could persuade the whites to undergo a change of heart. Blacks also believed in consultation. In the 1930s it led to the 'toy telephone' stage — that is, blacks were allowed to phone white government institutions, but the final outcome was still detrimental to their interests. Even the, now militant, TLSA, gestated as it was by the APO, was more renowned for the fact that 'members of rival church denominations could actually drink tea and dance together'.[6] The major concern was with the education of the 'Bruin Africander', a term actually used during the years 1915–16. Largely, it was a teachers' body of diverse social plumage, and with very little, if any, political orientation. This change would only come about in 1943.

## Nascent protest movements

The first Non-European conference held at Kimberley during June 1927 which was attended by the APO, the Cape Native Voters Association, the ANC and the South African Indian Conference, produced no great revolutionary decisions. The year 1935 saw the birth of the All African Convention (AAC). From the point of view of political developments in the Cape, the birth of the AAC was important. The journal of the TLSA comments that it was 'born out of a country-wide reaction against the Hertzog trinity, it was brought into the world by various left-overs from the political period'.[7]

Following the founding of the AAC, came the emergence of the New Era Fellowship (NEF) which according to the TLSA journal, 'initially started as a sorting house of ideas and later developed into a political force which played a major part in changing the whole basis and outlook of the liberatory movement. It was out of the NEF, for example, that there came the ideas and many of the people, who beginning in 1940, challenged the old regime in the TLSA.'[8]

The efforts of the Smuts regime to establish a Coloured Advisory Council (CAC) which would later become a fully-fledged Coloured Affairs Department (CAD)[9] led to one of the most significant events in 'coloured' politics. As a direct consequence, the TLSA advocated a boycott of the institution. Totally in conformity with the pattern of ambiguity and near-kinship, some individuals (e.g. Golding) decided to co-operate with the Government. This led to the formation of another 'coloured' teachers' body, the Teachers Educational and Professional Association (TEPA).[9] Members of this organization came to be branded as quislings, traitors and collaborators. In Government eyes however, they found solace and official recognition. Some of these people even started a political wing known as the Coloured Peoples National Union (CPNU).[9] At the end of 1943, the Non-European Unity Movement (NEUM) came into being. From now onwards, the TLSA,[9] the Anti-Coloured Affairs Department (Anti-CAD)[9] and the Non-European Unity Movement (NEUM), were to shape 'coloured' intellectual and political life in the Cape to a very considerable extent. Whatever the faults of the Movement (as these three bodies were sometimes collectively called), there are few 'coloureds' who have not, at one stage or another, undergone its influence.

The once meek and mild Teachers League now became a militant and politically conscious organization, fighting for the education of the children, always prepared to expose the 'Herrenvolk' ideology.

Not surprisingly, it was an Afrikaner Member of Parliament who correctly assessed the danger inherent in the League and the Movement. For, if there is anything the Afrikaner understands, it is the nature of power and the nature of the threat to power. Having fought the English for so long, the Afrikaner was not prepared to make a similar mistake with the blacks. Thus Cas Greyling, a prominent nationalist in Parliament, said as follows:[10]

> After the establishment of the Coloured Advisory Council in 1943, the then T.L.S.A. of South Africa held their annual conference at Kimberley where the establishment of the so-called CAC was discussed. There it came to a split because a certain extremist section or wing would not reconcile themselves with a Coloured Advisory Council while the more moderate group did. There was thus an extremist or leftist group and a more moderate group. From this division resulted the Teachers Educational and Professional Association, the so-called TEPA which under the leadership of Golding represents the moderate wing. They also established a political front, the Coloured People's National Union . . . . By way of opposition against the establishment of the Coloured Council, one had the development of the Anti-Cads. The Coloured Council was consistently opposed by the Anti-Cads. . . . These two groups, the Anti-Cads and the TLSA are the people who through the years have been closely allied with the Non-European Unity Movement, and they have drawn their sword against all moderates amongst the Coloureds in this country . . . they are the ones who in their ten-point programme fight segregation and apartheid measures tooth and nail. They are the ones who preach absolute equality and who militate against apartheid in Schools.

That the impact of the Movement has not been greater is largely due to a fundamental political miscalculation during Sharpeville and before, and also the tenacious clinging to the principle of the boycott. Moreover, the Movement has never broadened its scope to become a mass organization, objections which have been raised as early as 1944 by Hoseah Jaffe in the *Worker's Voice*.

# Appendix II

# Thomas Pringle

The poetry and prose of Thomas Pringle, one of the most outstanding figures among the 1820 settlers, contrast strongly with the
emergent Afrikaans fiction of the late eighteenth and early nineteenth
centuries. While Pringle himself is worthy of more than a mere
Appendix — he was the main actor in the struggle for the freedom
of the press, the major opponent of the then Governor, Lord Charles
Somerset — our interest is in his writings concerning the Khoisan and
'coloured' peoples, as well as in his anti-slavery activities. Pringle
became secretary of the anti-slavery movement upon his return to
England in July 1826.

His observations of the inhabitants of colour within South Africa
are illuminating and harrowing at times. His first visit to Bethelsdorp,
a mission station for 'Hottentots', singularly disturbed his peace
of mind. Here, he was confronted with 'God's Step-children',

> groups of woolly-haired, swarthy complexioned natives,
> many of them still dressed in the old sheep-skin mantle or
> caross; the swarms of naked or half-naked children . . . the
> strange words of the evening salutation (*goedenavond*) . . . the
> uncouth clucking sounds of the Hottentot language [all of
> which served to remind him that he was] at length in the Land
> of the Hottentot.[1]

Pringle's description of the conditions of the jail which he visited
while on his way to Cape Town in 1822, to me is still one of the great
passages against tyranny.[2]

> The tronk consisted of a single apartment, of about twenty feet
> by twelve or fourteen broad; and for the purposes of light and
> ventilation, had only one small grated opening, in the shape of
> a loop-hole, at a considerable height in the wall. Into this
> apartment were crowded about thirty human beings, of both sexes,

184

of all ages, and of almost every hue, — except white . . .. The condition of the gaol was dreadful. On the door being opened, the clergyman requested me to wait a few minutes until a freer ventilation had somewhat purified the noisome atmosphere within — for the effluvia on the first opening of the door, was too horrible to be encountered.

This factual account is in stark contrast to the poetry and prose of the early Afrikaans tradition. Pringle gives other such examples of the horror of slavery. There is, for example, his encounter with a Malay slave from Cape Town, in the village of Graaff-Reinet in the Eastern Cape, who bewailed his miserable lot and related how he was tricked and then sold into slavery. In the words of Pringle:[3]

But such occurrences as these were, at no remote period, of almost every-day occurrence, and sink into insignificance when compared with the revolting cases which stain the judicial records of the colony.

Of the purported mildness of slavery at the Cape, he observes:[4]

I had long been convinced, from sad observation, of the utter fallacy of the allegation then so constantly heard both in the colony and in England, that slavery at the Cape was 'so mild as to be nominal'. I had seen it, on the contrary, continually overflowing with misery, cruelty and debasement.

Pringle was particularly concerned with the de-humanizing effect the pernicious system of slavery had on the slave-holder. He considered 'European countrymen, who thus made captives of harmless women and children . . . in reality greater barbarians than the savage natives of Caffraria.'[5]

His preoccupation with the South African virus of colour was to find reflection in his poetry and his prose. His *Narrative of a Residence in South Africa,* initially published as part II of *African Sketches* (1834), which included his poems, translated into German and Dutch, becomes a very important first-hand account of life on the eastern frontier, of the 'coloured' people and the fauna and flora of South Africa.

Considering the Afrikaans view of the Khoisan as comical, and the total absence in Afrikaans writings of the brutalizing effect of slavery, the poems of Pringle become even more remarkable. But then it must be added, that he was an exponent of the liberal, Christian Humanitarianism of the Abolitionist Movement. His hatred of oppression comes out very strongly in his sonnet *To Oppression*, written in 1826:[6]

I swear, while life-blood warms my throbbing veins,
Still to oppose and thwart with heart and hand
Thy brutalising sway — till Afric's chains
Are burst, and Freedom rules the rescued land,—
Trampling Oppression and his iron rod.
— Such is the vow I take — So help me God:

One of the most impressive poems on the subject of slavery and the slave-holder is *The Slave Dealer*. In it, Pringle gives a picture of Africa swaying under the yoke of tyranny. His slave dealer is consumed with doubt and fear. The poem is Macbethian in parts, with an ancient Mariner-like quality that fascinates and abhors:[7]

There's blood upon my hands! he said
    Which water cannot wash;
It was not shed where warriors bled —
    It dropped from the gory lash,
As I whirled it o'er and o'er my head,
    And with each stroke left a gash.

With every stroke I left a gash
    While Negro blood sprang high;
And now all ocean cannot wash
    My soul from murder's dye;
Not e'en thy prayer, dear Mother, quash
    That Woman's wild death-cry!

His sonnet on *Slavery*, written in 1823, portrays the slave-holder as the victim and not the victor in this trade in human flesh:[8]

Oh Slavery! thou art a bitter draught!
And twice accursed is thy poisoned bowl,
Which taints with leprosy the White Man's soul,
Not less than his by whom its dregs are quaffed.
The Slave sinks down, o'ercome by cruel craft,
Like beast of burthen on the earth to roll.
The Master, though in luxury's lap he loll,
Feels the foul venom, like a rankling shaft,
Strike through his veins. As if a demon laughed,
He, laughing, treads his victims in the dust —
The victim of his avarice, rage or lust.
But the poor Captive's moan the whirlwind waft
To Heaven — not unavenged: the Oppressor quakes
With secret dread, and shares the hell he makes!

Pringle gives us some of the best, and most race-free depictions of the early and original inhabitants of South Africa, which in Afrikaans

literature is either absent or an object of comic embellishment, scorn
and ridicule. This becomes even more striking in view of the image of
the Khoisan as it unfolds in *Jakob Platjie* and the first Afrikaans
Language Movement in chapter 1. Within the Afrikaner ethos, there
was no room, as yet, for the non-white as a full-blooded character,
or even as a noble savage, with all its implications of lost innocence.
There was no social criticism of Christian barbarity and white
encroachment. The anti-slave trade lobbyist, with his abolitionist
rhetoric, also contributed to the African being enshrined as a 'good
negro', as is so clearly illustrated in the anti-slave trade poem, *The
Dying Negro,* written by Thomas Day and John Blicknell in London
in 1773.

Pringle, too, employs the noble savage to portray the Khoisan. In
*The Brown Hunter's Song* he sketches a picture of idyllic bliss in the
best noble savage tradition:[9]

> Under the Didima lies a green dell,
> Where fresh from the forest the blue waters swell;
> And fast by that brook stands a yellow-wood tree,
> Which shelters the spot that is dearest to me.
>
> Down by the streamlet my heifers are grazing;
> In the pool of the guanas the herd-boy is gazing;
> Under the shade my Amána is singing —
> The shade of the tree where her cradle is swinging.
>
> When I come from upland as daylight is fading,
> Though spent with the chase, and the game for my lading,
> My nerves are new-strung, and my fond heart is swelling,
> As I gaze from the cliff on the wood-circled dwelling.
>
> Down the steep mountain, and through the brown forest,
> I haste like a hart when his thirst is the sorest;
> I bound o'er the swift brook that skirts the savannah,
> And clasp my fist-born in the arms of Amána.

The Khoi becomes someone who is 'mild and melancholy and
sedate', the white man a person who is harsh and oppressive:[10]

The Hottentot

> Mild, melancholy and sedate, he stands,
> Tending another's flock upon the fields,
> His father's once, where now the White Man builds
> His home, and issues forth his proud commands.
> His dark eye flashes not; his listless hands
> Lean on the shepherd's staff; no more he wields

> The Libyan bow — but to th' oppressor yields
> Submissively his freedom and his lands.
> Has he no courage? Once he had — but, lo!
> Harsh Servitude hath worn him to the bone.
> No enterprise? Alas! the brand, the blow,
> Have humbled him to dust — even hope is gone!
> 'He's a base-hearted hound — not worth his food' —
> His Master cries — 'he has no gratitude!'

In his poem *The Bushman,* there is a picture of lost innocence as opposed to civilized barbarity not encountered in early Afrikaans literature:[11]

> The Bushman sleeps within his black-browed den,
> In the lone wilderness. Around him lie
> His wife and little ones unfearingly —
> For they are far away from 'Christian-Men'.
> No herds, loud lowing, call him down the glen:
> He fears no foe but famine; and may try
> To wear away the hot noon slumberingly;
> Then rise to search for roots — and dance again.
> But he shall dance no more! His secret lair,
> Surrounded, echoes to the thundering gun,
> And the wild shriek of anguish and despair!
> He dies — yet, ere life's ebbing sands are run,
> Leaves to his sons a curse, should they be friends
> With the proud 'Christian-Men' — for they are fiends!

By enshrining the 'Bushman' as a noble savage in *The Song of the Wild Bushman,* the 'coloured' inhabitants are salvaged from the anthropoid, homo ludens categories:[12]

> Let the proud White Man boast his flocks,
> And fields of foodful grain;
> My home is mid the mountain rocks,
> The Desert my domain.
> I plant no herbs nor pleasant fruits,
> I toil not for my cheer;
> The Desert yields me juicy roots,
> And herds of bounding deer.

The last two lines in particular recall those by Chaucer in *The Former Age:*[13]

> A Blysful lyf, a paisible and a swete,
> ledden the peples in the former age.
> They held hem payed of the fruites that they ete,
> Which that the feldes yave hem by usage.

Compare for instance the poem *Jan Bantjies,* during the period of the first Language Movement, about a Khoi who often goes to the races, and is then actually responsible for one of the horses winning. But it all goes to his head and he ends up drinking heavily. The same comic note is struck when the 'coloured' character in Du Toit's poem *Hoe die Hollanders die Kaap ingeneem het*[14] (How the Dutch got hold of the Cape) relates the story of this take-over.

Rightly, then, Pringle is accorded the honour of being the first South African poet, and his name lives forth in the prize for English Literature. Nowhere in Dutch Afrikaans during the early to mid-or-late nineteenth century, does one find the indigenous Khoisan so beautifully portrayed.

# Appendix III

# Race classification and definitions in South Africa: what 'coloured' is or is not in South Africa

This appendix is largely based on the definitions as laid out in the very useful and instructive booklet by Arthur Suzman entitled *Race Classification and Definition in the Legislation of the Union of South Africa 1910–1960* (Johannesburg, 1960).

The Constitution (Grondwet) of the South African Republic of 1858, Article 9

1   'Het volk will geene gelijkstelling van gekleurden met blanke ingezetenen toestaan, noch in de Kerk noch in Staat'.
(The people would tolerate no equality between coloured and white inhabitants either in Church or State). Suzman comments that the term 'coloured' as used here is not defined and includes all people of colour.

2   *The Precious and Base Metal Act, No. 35, sec. 3. of 1908.* Here 'coloured' means 'any African or Asiatic native or any other person who is manifestly a coloured person'.

3   Section 8 of Law 8 of 1893 in the Orange River Colony. Here a 'coloured' is defined as 'a man or woman . . . of any native tribe in South Africa and also all coloured persons and all who in accordance with the law or custom, are called coloured persons or are treated as such, of whatever race or nationality they may be'.

4   *The Native Urban Areas Act, No, 21 of 1923, sec. 29.* 'Any person of mixed European and native descent and shall include any person belonging to the class called Cape Malays'.

5   *The Pensions Act No. 22 of 1928* (see amendments of this Act, No. 34 of 1931 and 1934). In the Act of 1928 the definition of a 'coloured' is as follows.
A 'coloured' is neither:
a.  a Turk or a member of a race or tribe in Asia nor

b. a member of an aboriginal race or tribe in Africa nor
c. a Hottentot, Bushman or Koranna nor
d. a person residing in a native location . . . nor
e. an American negro.

6 *The Asiatic (Transvaal Land and Trading) Act No. 29 of 1939 sec. 7.* 'Coloured' here is defined as 'Any person other than a European or Asiatic'.

7 *The Coloured Persons Settlement Act No. 7 of 1946.* 'Coloured' here is defined as 'Any person other than a European, an Asiatic as defined by section 11 of the Asiatics (Land and Trading) Amendment Act (Transvaal), 1919, or a native as defined by section 35 of the Native Administrative Act, 1927'.

8 The *Disability Grants Act No. 36 of 1946, sec. 1.* Here 'coloured' is defined as 'Any person other than a white person, a native, a Turk, or a member of a race or tribe whose national or ethnic home is Asia and includes a member of the race or class commonly called Cape Malays, or of the race or class commonly called Griquas'.

9 *The Prohibition of Mixed Marriages Act, No. 55 of 1949.* Here, the legislators were obviously more cautious and resorted to the rather general definitions of European and non-European with appearance playing a prominent part. One suspects that such caution was exercised more to protect the European who looked non-European rather than vice versa. Marriages between European and non-Europeans were considered to be not valid under this act provided that such a marriage was deemed valid if:

I 'it has been solemnized in good faith by a marriage officer and neither of the parties concerned has knowingly made any false statement to the marriage officer relating to the question whether such party is a European or a non-European and

II any party to such a marriage professing to be a European or a non-European, as the case may be, is in appearance obviously what he professes to be, or is able to show, in the case of a party professing to be a European, that he habitually consorts with Europeans as a European or, in the case of a party professing to be non-European, that he habitually consorts with non-Europeans as a non-European.'

10 The various Immorality Acts. In the *Immorality Act, No. 5 of 1927* which forbade sex across the colour line, the basic terminology resorted to was 'European and Native'. (The first term was left undefined and 'native' was understood to be 'any member of any aboriginal race or tribe in Africa'). In the *Immorality Amendment Act No. 21 of 1950,* the term

'Native' was replaced by the term 'non-European', which was defined as:
'a person who in appearance obviously is or who by general acceptance and repute is a non-European'. The term 'European' meant:
'a person who in appearance obviously is or who by general acceptance and repute is European'.

11 *The Population Registration Act of 1950.* Here 'coloured' means: 'a person who is not a white person or a native'.

12 *The Industrial Conciliation Act, 1956.* The definition of 'coloured' is the same as in 11.

13 The *Nursing Act of 1957.* The definition of 'Coloured' is the same as in 11 and 12.

14 The *Group Areas Act No. 77 of 1957 which is a consolidation of the Group Areas Act of 1950* (the numerous amendments) interprets the 'Coloured Group' as being neither White nor 'Native'.

15 *Proclamation 46 of 1959* was declared invalid by the High Court because of its vagueness, as if the other definitions were so crystal clear. Here the basis for the division of the 'coloured' into seven different categories (see 16) was laid.

16 *Proclamation 123 of 1967* divided 'coloured' people into the following categories, namely: (1) Cape Coloured; (2) Malay; (3) Griqua; (4) Chinese; (5) Indian; (6) 'other' Asiatic; (7) 'other' Coloured.

*Postscript:* In order to grasp fully the horror of these laws the following examples as described in Venter (1974) are cited:

a. Here it concerns a young man who was obviously white but re-classified as 'coloured'. This interfered with his marriage plans to an Afrikaner girl. The letter he received from the Race Classification Board read as follows:[1]

> Sir, I have to advise you that this office has at its disposal certain information contradictory to your statement on your census forms: viz. that you are a White person. After careful con-sideration of the available information I am inclined to the view that your race description as reflected on the census form should be amended to read 'Coloured' instead of 'White'.

The young man in question was eventually re-classified as white but the damage was done and he is now considering emigration (or has already left the country).

Another case in which a man was declared Indian in Cape Town cost the taxpayer, according to Venter,[2] R5000. The man was later declared Cape Malay by the Appeal Board (of the Race

Classification Board) and by the Supreme Court. He is still without a 'race' card and therefore does not exist officially, such being possible only after due classification.

A famous case was that involving Sandra Laing, who at the age of eleven, was declared 'coloured', and therefore forced to leave her 'White parents' and family, to live in a 'coloured' area. She then went to live with an African, and was later again re-classified as white, although by general acceptance and repute, she was by now non-white.

In some instances, people have committed suicide. The white Boxing Champion of the Cape, Ronnie van der Walt, who suddenly found himself re-classified as 'coloured', and therefore stripped of his privileges and titles (apart from becoming a criminal because he lived in a white area), simply chose exile and anonymity in England.

b. Apparently the division of people into European and non-European was dropped, because American visitors unwittingly used the non-European entrances, which they naïvely thought were erected for people who did not geographically come from Europe.

# Appendix IV

# Constitutional blueprint

The official blueprint of the Government's new constitutional proposals, which appears below, was released to the *Cape Times* yesterday by sources close to the CRC executive.

This is the first time the detailed plan has been published, and expands on the bare outline given by Mr Vorster at a public meeting in Cape Town two weeks ago.

Here is the document in full:
Memorandum re. proposals for a new constitutional dispensation:

As intimated in the interim memorandum of the government on the report of the Theron Commission, the government agreed with both the majority views of the commission, as expressed in recommendation 178, that the Westminster-founded system of government does not necessarily have to be followed slavishly in the RSA, and consequently committed itself to a thorough and authoritative investigation into the necessary organizational and statutory adjustments of the system in view of the problems and considerations set forth in chapters 17 to 20 of the report of the commission.

In accordance with a decision of the Cabinet, this investigation had been assigned to a special Cabinet committee in August 1976. The committee had been instructed to investigate simultaneously the political dispensation for the Indians and had been authorised to obtain advice from extra-parliamentary experts.

In accordance with its assignment, the committee concentrated exclusively on the political situation of the whites, coloured and Indians.

The following proposals of the committee had been approved by the Cabinet for discussion with the leaders of the population groups concerned:

## A.  EXECUTIVE GOVERNMENT

1.  State President:
    The State President shall be elected for five years by an electoral college composed for this purpose on a fair and representative basis by the white, coloured and Indian Assemblies. Fifty whites; 25 coloureds; 13 Indians.

    The State President shall be the chairman of the Cabinet Council (or Council of Cabinets). His duties further include the opening of sessions of the Assemblies and meetings of the President Council and the approval of the legislation on matters of mutual interest to all three population groups.

2.  Cabinet Council (or Council of Cabinets):

    The Cabinet Council (or Council of Cabinets) shall be composed of the State President, as chairman, the three prime ministers and the number of ministers from each Assembly agreed upon. (White Prime Minister plus five ministers; coloured Prime Minister plus three ministers; Indian Prime Minister plus one minister.)

    The State President nominates a member of this council as his permanent substitute for those occasions when he is absent and this person also serves as Acting State President in the absence of the former.

    The Cabinet Council shall initiate and draft all legislation on joint matters and its members may address the different Assemblies. The Cabinet Council shall further arrange the order papers of the various Assemblies in consultation with the Leaders of the Assemblies.

3.  Cabinets:

    The State President shall appoint for each Assembly as prime minister a person whom he deems capable of mustering a majority in the Assembly and on the advice of the latter, a number of ministers. The State President shall also have the power to remove ministers from office.

195

## B. LEGISLATIVE GOVERNMENT

1. Assemblies:

Each population group shall have an equally paid, elected assembly with exclusive legislative powers in respect of the matters which affect that population group and it shall be co-responsible for joint matters. The matters affecting only the coloured and Indian Assemblies and vesting presently in the white Assembly, shall be transferred gradually.

Each Assembly shall have full powers in respect of suitable taxes and loans.

The powers with regard to the assent to legislation presently vesting in the State President, shall, in connection with legislation in respect of which each Assembly has exclusive powers, be exercised by the prime minister of the Assembly concerned.

White Parliament: 165 elected, 20 nominated.
Coloured Parliament: 82 elected, 10 nominated.
Indian Parliament: 46 elected, 5 nominated. There is no Senate.

2. Joint Advisory Committees:

Whenever conflicting decisions are taken during the committee stages in the various Assemblies in respect of legislation on matters of mutual interest, such matters shall, on the advice of the Cabinet Council, be referred to joint advisory committees of the three governments to settle these conflicts. Such matters may also be referred to the President Council for consideration and recommendations. Should the joint advisory committees fail to settle such conflicts, the final decision rests with the State President. These joint advisory committees shall be constituted ad hoc whenever necessary.

## C. THE PRESIDENT COUNCIL

A non-parliamentary prestige body, the President Council, shall be established. The members of the President Council shall be elected by the different Assemblies in proportion to population figures, while the State President shall nominate a number. Only persons of exceptional quality and knowledge shall be qualified to become members of the President Council. A member of an Assembly or a provincial council shall not simultaneously be a member of the President Council. The State President appoints the chairman of the President Council from among its members.

The President Council advises the Cabinet Council at the latter's request on matters of national interest and may discuss such matters of its own initiative.

Composition: 20 appointed by white Parliament; 10 appointed by coloured Parliament; 5 appointed by Indian Parliament.

Provincial and Regional Administrations:

1.  For coloureds and Indians there shall be a system of regional administrations without legislative bodies. In control of each region shall be a Regional Administrator. (For this purpose provincial borders shall be used, but for effective administration the Cape Province shall be divided into three regions for coloureds and Transvaal and Natal each into two regions for Indians.)

2.  As for whites the provincial authorities concerned may decide themselves to follow the proposed division.

Local Government:

1.  Each population group shall elect its own councils with full local authority in cities and towns under an electoral system developed on the basis of the electoral lists of Assemblies and other practical qualifications.

2.  Rural communities of each population group shall be linked on a regional basis.

3.  Where necessary, an organization for liaison between white, coloured and Indian local authorities should be established.

# Notes

## Introduction

1 'Not a race of slaves'. The phrase is culled from Mercia MacDermott's portrait of Vasil Levsky. The original quote reads: 'For what does it profit the tyrant, if after five hundred years of captivity and humiliation, a land brings forth not a race of slaves, but men like Vasil Levski'. M. MacDermott, *The Apostle of Freedom* (London, 1967), 390.

2 'Coloured' is placed in inverted commas to express the author's rejection of this racist term.

3 'Hottentot' is similarly placed in inverted commas for the very same reason. Sometimes its use is unavoidable. See further, note 2, Chapter 1.

4 Khoi and San are the terms generally preferred for the autochthonous people of South Africa. See further, note 2, Chapter 1.

5 S. G. Millin, *Adam's Rest* (London, 1922), 40.

6 C. Dover, *Half-Caste* (London, 1937), 13.

7 Since colour plays such an important role in South Africa, some 'coloureds' often try to cross the colour line and pass themselves off as whites. They are generally referred to as 'play-whites' or people who are 'trying for white'. There is a term known as *'venstertjies kyk'* (lit. looking in the windows, pretending to window shop). This happens when coloured friends or relatives see other 'coloureds' approaching who are 'play-whites'. They pretend to do window-shopping in order not to embarrass the person(s) or relative(s) in question.

8 A. Suzman, *Race Classification and Definition in the Legislation of South Africa* (Johannesburg, 1960), 354.

9 Ibid., 348.

10 M. G. Whisson & H. W. van der Merwe, *Coloured Citizenship in South Africa* (Cape Town, 1972), 77.

11  Al Venter, *Coloured: A Profile of Two Million South Africans*
    (Cape Town, 1974), 4–5.
12  M. Edelstein, *What Do the Coloureds Think?* (Johannesburg, 1974),
    77.
13  N. P. van Wyk Louw, the poet, in a foreword to D. P. Botha's
    book, *Die opkoms van ons derde stand* (Cape Town, 1960).
14  L. Thompson, *The Cape Coloured Franchise* (Johannesburg, 1949),
    9.
15  Ibid., 10.
16  Ibid., 21.
17  *Die Burger,* 18 June 1925.
18  L. Thomson, *The Cape Coloured Franchise* (Johannesburg, 1949),
    25.
19  Ibid., 28.
20  E. Theron, *Verslag van die kommissie van Ondersoek na
    Aangeleenthede rakende die Kleurlingbevolkingsgroep* (Pretoria,
    1976), 525.
21  Ibid., 505.
22  Ibid., 506.
23  M. Horrell, *Action, Reaction and Counter-action* (Johannesburg,
    1971), 125.
24  *Star,* 17 July 1976.
25  *The Educational Journal* (Cape Town, June 1976), 47:8–12.

**Chapter 1 Untroubled things**

1  'Untroubled things'. The phrase is culled from the novel, *Die
   Meulenaar,* in which the white woman, Betta, refers to the
   'coloured' workers as, *'onbekommerde goed'* (lit. untroubled
   things), 38.
2  Re the terms 'Hottentot and Bushman', Dr Robert Ross observes
   in an unpublished paper, *The Changing Legal Position of the
   Khoisan in the Cape Colony, 1652–1795* (Leiden, 1978,
   Werkgroep Geschiedenis Europese Expansie), footnote 1: 'The
   Khoi or Khoikhoin used to be known as Hottentots, while
   "Bushmen" are often called San. When no distinction is made
   between the two groups – and it is often meaningless to make
   any – they are known as Khoisan.'
3  Dian Joubert, *Met iemand van 'n ander kleur* (Cape Town, 1974),
   12.
4  Ibid., 12.
5  J. L. M. Franken, 'Die taal van slawekinders en fornikasie met
   slavinne', in: D. F. Malherbe (ed.), *Tydskrif vir wetenskap en kuns*
   (Bloemfontein, 1927), 6.1: 22.
6  Otto Mentzel, *A Geographical and Topographical Description of*

*the Cape of Good Hope* (Cape Town, 1952), V.R.S. 6:125.

7   H. P. Cruse, *Die opheffing van die kleurling bevolking* (Kaapstad, 1947), 251–4.

8   C. Dover, 1937, 74–5.

9   D. P. Botha, *Die opkoms van ons derde stand* (Kaapstad, 1960), 60.

10   Ibid., 60–1.

11   G. S. Nienaber, 'The Origin of the Name "Hottentot"', in *African Studies* (Johannesburg, 1963), 66–90.

12   O. Dapper, *Naukeurige Beschryvinge der Afrikaensche Gewesten* (Amsterdam, 1668), 652.

13   G. S. Nienaber, 1963, 76.

14   Ibid., 89.

15   Jahnheinz Jahn, *Wir Nannten Sie Wilden* (München, 1964), 30–1.

16   Godéé Molsbergen, *Reizen in Zuid Afrika in de Hollandse tijd* ('s-Gravenhage, 1916), 10.

17   G. P. Rouffaer and J. W. Ijzerman (eds), *De eerste schipvaart der Nederlanders naar Oost Indië onder Cornelis de Houtman, 1595-1597. 1. D'Eerste boeck van Willem Lodewijcksz* ('s-Gravenhage, 1915), 6.

18   Ibid., 7.

19   Ibid., 8.

20   Jahnheinz Jahn, *Wir Nannten Sie Wilde* (München, 1964). See also: *Reisebeschreibungen von Deutschen Beamten Und Kriegsleuten Im Dienst Der Niederländischen West-Und Ost-Indischen Kompagnien* (1602-1792), Den Haag, 1930–1.

21   A. Hulshof (ed.), *H. A. van Rheede tot Drakensteyn. Journaal van zijn verblijf aan de Kaap* (Utrecht, 1941), 36.

22   D. B. Bosman, *Oor die ontstaan van Afrikaans* (Amsterdam, 1928[2]), 16.

23   Aya, normally written as *aia* in Afrikaans, is a term denoting a nurse-maid. It is, however, generally used in the South African context to refer to an older, 'coloured' woman. In Afrikaner eyes, it is looked upon as a term of respect (see: F. Malherbe, 1958, 78). 'Coloureds' regard it as a term of abuse.

24   This example is culled from the notes compiled by J. du P. Scholtz for his Nederlands en Afrikaans class at U.C.T. during 1959–60. The example was recorded in 1672.

25   This is from Kolbe (1710).

26   M. Valkhoff, *Studies in Portuguese and Creole with special reference to South Africa* (Johannesburg, 1966), 218.

27   Ibid., 219.

28   Ibid., 5–6.

29   Ibid., 38, n.36.

30   H. J. Lubbe, 'Valkhoff en die ontstaan van Afrikaans veral n.a.v. sy

New light on Afrikaans and "Malayo-Portuguese", in: *Tydskrif vir Geesteswetenskappe* (Kaapstad, 1974), 14, 2:89.

31 Valkhoff, 1966, 243.

32 For the term 'kaffer-boetie', i.e. a negrophilist, see note 29, Chapter 7.

33 Kalfachter. The Afrikaans dictionary gives a word for Kalfakter, meaning a 'lay-about', 'a gossip', a 'trouble-maker'. Toiings can be translated as Ragamuffin (Rags).

34 F. C. L. Bosman, *Drama en toneel 1652-1855, deel 1* (Amsterdam, 1928), 312.

35 Ibid., 318.

36 Ibid., 314.

37 Ibid., 318.

38 E. B. Dykes, *The Negro in English Romantic Thought* (Washington, 1942), 43.

39 P. S. du Toit, 'Waarom hulle getrek het', in: *Die Huisgenoot* (Kaapstad, 1938), Gedenkuitgawe, 45.

40 Ibid., 45.

41 Grietjie Drilbouten. It has been suggested by J. Voorhoeve (Leiden), that Drilbouten might, possibly, have a sexual connotation.

42 The 'tot system' is one whereby 'coloured' farm-hands are rewarded right through the day with tots of wine or brandy, presumably to keep up productivity. It also keeps the poor worker in a constant state of inebriation and makes him a willing partner to his own degradation. It is literally labour through alcoholism. The earliest reference to this *tot of brandy* (croessje brandewijn) is found in the writings of Jan van Riebeeck. The system has been heavily criticized.

43 F. C. L. Bosman, 1928, 308.

44 Ibid., 313-14.

45 G. R. von Wielligh, *Jakob Platjie, egte karaktersketse uit die volkslewe van Hotnots, Korannas en Boesmans* (Pretoria/ Amsterdam, 1918). The book first appeared in instalments in *Ons Klijntji* (1896). L. van Niekerk, who wrote her thesis in 1916, uses the earlier instalments of *Jakob Platjie*. I have used the 1918 edition of *Jakob Platjie* in this manuscript. This accounts for the apparent disparity in dates at times.

46 Ibid., 4.

47 Ibid., 5.

48 Ibid., 16.

49 Ibid., 35.

50 Ibid., 37.

51 Lydia van Niekerk, *De eerste Afrikaanse taalbeweging en zijn Letterkundige voortbrengselen* (Amsterdam, 1916), 190.

52  Jan Frans Willems (1793–1846) was the main force behind the Flemish language and cultural struggle. I have purposely used the Afrikaans and/or Dutch terms. 'Die taal' (i.e. the language) and 'de taal is gansch het volk' (i.e. the language is the entire people), a phrase used during the Flemish movement, have a mystique which is missing in the English equivalents. Language played a significant role in the shaping of Afrikaner and Flemish nationalism. Compare the Afrikaans–English struggle with the Flemish–Walloon opposition. Volk usually refers to people and used in this sense in South Africa, means white people in general and Afrikaners in particular. 'Volkies', in its diminutive form only refers to 'coloureds' and in particular, farm-hands.

53  D. J. Opperman, *Groot Verseboek* (Kaapstad, 1964[6]), 6.

54  Ibid., 7.

55  Lydia van Niekerk, 1916, 99. Note the terms 'Rooi-nekke' and 'geel-bekke' in the poem. The first refers to the English, because of their supposed ability to roast red like turkeys in the sun. It harks back to the Anglo-Boer war; the second is a reference to the Khoi, or more generally, the 'coloureds'. These terms are used negatively.

56  D. J. Opperman, 1964[6], 9–10.

57  James Matthews and Gladys Thomas, *Cry Rage* (Johannesburg, 1972), 5.

58  P. Edwards (ed.), *Equiano's Travels* (London, 1967), 28.

59  'Bruinmens' and 'kleurling' (lit. brownman and coloured) are terms used by whites to refer to the "coloured' population.

60  F. E. J. Malherbe, 'Die Kleurprobleem en die letterkunde', in: *Afrikaanse Lewe en Letterkunde* (Stellenbosch, 1958), 76.

61  'Outa', like aia (aya, see note 23 above), is used to refer to an older 'coloured' man, who is invariably from the rural areas. Again, 'coloureds' regard it as a derogatory term.

62  The word used in Afrikaans is 'oorlams'. It is generally applied to a 'coloured' who, in Afrikaner eyes, is too clever and who does not stick to his ascribed role.

63  C. M. van den Heever, *Somer* (Pretoria, 1930), 30.

64  Ibid., 47.

65  Ibid., 47.

66  Ibid., 123.

67  D. F. Malherbe, *Die Meulenaar* (Bloemfontein, 1930[5]), 35.

68  Ibid., 151.

69  Ibid., 160.

70  Ibid., 161.

71  Ibid., 135.

72  Ibid., 57.

73  Ibid., 35.

74  Ibid., 97.
75  Ibid., 38.

## Chapter 2 You taught me language

1  'You taught me language' (and my profit on't is, I know how to curse), see W. Shakespeare, *Complete Works,* Tudor Edition (ed. P. Alexander, 1951) especially, *The Tempest*, Act 1, scene 2,6. Caliban is the speaker.
2  P. J. Nienaber, *Afrikaanse Skrywers aan die woord* (Johannesburg, 1947), 211.
3  'K'ben een Africaander', see J. L. M. Franken, *Taalhistoriese bydraes* (Amsterdam, 1953), 102. Incidentally, Bibault's life with the slave, Diana, and their slave child is seldom recalled (see: Valkhoff, 1966, 212–13).
4  Allan Hall, 'The African Novels of Joyce Cary', in: *Standpunte* (Kaapstad, 1958), 12, 2:49.
5  Nienaber, 1947, 211.
6  Review of *Toiings* by Fransie Malherbe in *Die Huisgenoot*, 20 July, 1934, 33.
7  'Meid' generally has a derogatory connotation when applied to a 'coloured' female. In translation, however, it loses its sting and racial connotation.
8  The way in which terms are used in South Africa gives a clear indication of ethnic inter-relationships. The terms 'baas' (master), 'jong' (boy), 'meid' (see note 7), 'skepsel' (thing), express the subordinate position of the 'coloured' in white South Africa. See also the parallel with the Latin word 'creare' (thing/house-hold slave), Afrikaans *skepsel.*
9  G. Beukes and F. Lategan, *Skrywers en Rigtings* (Pretoria, 1959[3]), 254.
10  E. Mphahlele, *The African Image* (London, 1962), 107–8.
11  Jochem van Bruggen wrote some novels in which he realistically portrayed the poor-white via his main character, Ampie. The Hobson brothers wrote a novel called *Skankwan van die duine* (Skankwan of the dunes), which has, as its main character, one of the original inhabitants of South Africa, a San. He is portrayed as being half-animal, half-human.
12  Allan Hall, 1958, 47–8.
13  C. Fyfe, 'The Colonial Situation in Mister Johnson', in: *Modern Fiction Studies*, 9 (London, 1963), 226–30.
14  Joh. Volkelt, *System der Aesthetik, 11* (München, 1910), 400.
15  Mikro (pseudonym of C. H. Kühn), *Toiings* (Pretoria, 1944[11]), 97.
16  Joyce Cary, *Mister Johnson* (London, 1952), 62.
17  A. Hall, 1958, 52.

18  E. Mphahlele, 1962, 161.
19  Cary, 1952, 86.
20  F. E. J. Malherbe, 'Die kleurprobleem en die letterkunde', in: *Afrikaanse Lewe en Letterkunde* (Stellenbosch, 1958), 81.
21  Ibid., 82.
22  Ibid., 82.
23  'Vaaljapie' is a cheap wine drunk especially by the farm labourer and the urban proletariat. The educated 'coloured' sometimes frenchifies the word in jocular fashion to 'vaeldzdpi'.
24  J. Cary, 1952, 204.
25  Mikro (C. H. Kühn), *Toiings* (Pretoria, 1944[11]), 13.
26  Ibid., 33.
27  F. R. Karl, *The Contemporary English Novel* (London, 1963), 139.
28  G. Beukes and F. Lategan, 1958, 253.
29  Arnold Kettle, *Introduction to the English Novel* (London, 1955), 2:183.
30  A. Hall, 1958, 54.
31  F. R. Karl, 1963, 179.

## Chapter 3 Smelling strangeness

1  'Smelling strangeness' is a phrase from C. Dover's book, *Half-caste* (London, 1937), 13.
2  S. G. Millin, *The Measure of My Days* (London, 1955), 265.
3  For Derozio see C. Dover, *Half-caste* (London, 1937), 145–62.
4  C. Dover, *Half-caste* (London, 1937), 201.
5  Ibid., 13.
6  Ibid., 14.
7  Ibid., 13.
8  S. G. Millin, *Adam's Rest* (London, 1922), 40.
9  C. Dover, 1937, 17.
10  S. Howe, *Novels of Empire* (New York, 1949), 61.
11  Njai is a concubine; nonna, a young lady; djongos are house-boys or male servants; liplappen are said to be called thus, because they lisp when speaking. All these terms abound in colonial literature concerning the Dutch East Indies.
12  For these terms see Chapter 1, notes 23 and 61, Chapter 2, note 7.
13  *Krontjong* music is a popular, romantic type of music, associated with the Indo. The guitar as an instrument is also associated with the 'coloured'. See, in this respect, the symbolism in Adam Small's *Kitaar my kruis* (Guitar My Cross).
14  R. Nieuwenhuys, *Oost-Indische Spiegel* (Amsterdam, 1973), 297.

15  Ibid., 297.
16  Ibid., 194–5.
17  Ibid., 300.
18  S. G. Millin, *God's Step-children* (London, 1952), 71.
19  S. Howe, 1949, 59–60.
20  S. G. Millin, *The South Africans* (London, 1926), 195.
21  Ibid., 206.
22  S. G. Millin, *Adam's Rest* (London, 1922), 40.
23  Ibid., 65.
24  Ibid., 116.
25  S. G. Millin, *God's Step-children* (London, 1952), 34.
26  Ibid., 57.
27  Ibid., 63.
28  Ibid. 64.
29  Ibid., 71
30  Ibid., 107.
31  Ibid., 128.
32  Ibid., 306.
33  S. G. Millin, *King of the Bastards* (London, 1950).
34  *The Star* (Johannesburg, 1950).
35  S. G. Millin, *King of the Bastards* (London, 1950), 26.
36  Ibid., 2.
37  Ibid., 339.
38  Slagtersnek Rebellion — see the refusal of Bezuidenhout on the
    frontier to answer to the charge that he man-handled a Khoi
    servant, Walker, in *A History of South Africa* (London, 1947[2]),
    160.
39  Stuart Cloete, *The Mask* (Boston, 1957), 122–3.
40  Stuart Cloete, *Gazella* (Boston, 1958), 372–3.
41  Stuart Cloete, *The African Giant* (Boston, 1955), 372–3.
42  Mittelholzer, the Guianese novelist, wrote four books dealing with
    the question of miscegenation within one Dutch family, the van
    Groenwegels in the Guianas. They are fascinating and awe-
    inspiring. These books are: *Kaywana Heritage* (1952), *Children
    of Kaywana* (1952), *Kaywana Stock* (1954) and *Kaywana
    Blood* (1958).
43  Dian Joubert, *Met iemand van 'n ander kleur* (Kaapstad, 1974),
    6:56.
44  S. G. Millin (London, 1926), 195.
45  Gerald Gordon, *Let the Day Perish* (London, 1952).
46  Ibid., 252.
47  Martin Tucker, *Africa in Modern Literature* (New York, 1967),
    226.
48  Athol Fugard, *The Blood Knot* (Johannesburg, 1963), 130.

## Chapter 4 Little sorrow sits and weeps

1 'Little sorrow sits and weeps': see *The Cradle Song* by William Blake in: *The Oxford Book of English Verse* (ed. A. Quiller-Couch, Oxford, 1961), 578.

2 L. Hughes & A. Bontemps, *The Poetry of the Negro* (New York, 1970), 232.

3 C. Dover, *Half-caste* (London, 1937), 13.

4 S. G. Millin, *Adam's Rest* (London, 1922), 40.

5 K. Ramchand, 'Terrified Consciousness', *The Journal of Commonwealth Literature* (London, 1969), 7:8–19.

6 J. Rhys, *Wide Sargasso Sea* (New York, 1966), 46.

7 See Marianne Brindley, *Western Coloured Township, Problems of an Urban Slum*, 1976, 40–50:

> A large number of Western Township wives felt embarrassed about having sexual intercourse with their husbands because their children have to sleep in the same room. The whole situation requires caution, for as Aston and Dobson have found: 'Where the mother in the family was in some way inhibited or anxious about her sexual relationship with her husband', she would tend to 'turn to her child for attention.'

8 *Guardian,* 16 July 1974.

9 N. Gordimer and L. Abrahams, *South African Writing Today* (Penguin, 1967), 186.

10 Ibid., 187.

11 E. Muller, *Die vrou op die skuit* (Kaapstad, 1958), 149.

12 N. Gordimer and L. Abrahams, *South African Writing Today* (Penguin, 1967), 37.

13 Ibid., 38.

14 'Voertsek' is a term generally used in South Africa when chasing away a dog. When applied to a human being, it is a term of abuse.

15 'Tokoloshe', in Afrikaans *tokolosie*, is, according to the dictionary, a small, hairy apparition, instilling fear into children; it is also said to be a watersprite. I have known people who attribute strange and magical powers to the tokoloshe. I have known of a case where a man swore that his wife was impregnated by a tokoloshe.

16 N. Gordimer and L. Abrahams, *South African Writing Today* (Penguin, 1967), 46.

17 Ibid., 46.

18 Ibid., 47.

19 Richard Rive, *Modern African Prose* (London, 1964), 162–3.

20 Ibid., 169.
21 *Sandra Laing.* This is a true story with a particularly bizarre twist of a South African girl born to white parents, and who later turned out to be so dark that she was reclassified as 'coloured'. This had severe implications for the little girl who at that stage, was only eleven or twelve years old. It meant living in a 'coloured' neighbourhood, leaving her natural parents, her school and environment. All these activities were suddenly criminal in terms of various South African laws, e.g. the *Population Registration Act, the Group Areas Act* etc. From time to time her name still crops up in newspapers. Recently, there was a documentary on Western television, entitled 'In Search of Sandra Laing'. She is now married to an African.
22 Kenneth Ramchand, *The West Indian Novel and its Background* (London, 1970), 225.
23 Ian McDonald, *The Humming-Bird Tree* (London, 1974), 181.

## Chapter 5 Sons of Hagar

1 Sons of Hagar — see Genesis (16:1–16).
2 St Clair Drake, 'An Approach to the Evaluation of African Societies', in: *Africa as Seen by American Negroes* (Paris, Présence Africaine), 34.
3 G. Dekker, *Afrikaanse Literatuurgeskiedenis* (Bloemfontein, 1947), 161.
4 G. Beukes and F. Lategan, *Skrywers en rigtings* (Pretoria, 1959[3]), 259–60.
5 N. Gordimer, *The Black Interpreters* (Johannesburg, 1973), 55.
6 W. Plomer, *Turbotte Wolfe* (London, 1965), 30.
7 Ibid., 31.
8 Ibid., 41.
9 L. Nkosi, *Home and Exile* (London, 1965), 4–5.
10 E. Mphahlele, *The African Image* (London, 1962), 67.
11 S. V. Petersen, *As die son ondergaan* (Kaapstad, 1971[4]), 1.
12 G. Moore, *Seven African Writers* (London, 1962), 94.
13 E. Mphahlele, *Down Second Avenue* (London, 1959), 45.
14 Ibid., 159.
15 Ibid., 159.
16 *Die Huisgenoot,* 28 January 1935.
17 S. V. Petersen, *As die son ondergaan* (Kaapstad, 1971[4]), 3.
18 Ibid., 6.
19 Ibid., 24.
20 Ibid., 44.
21 Ibid., 47.

22   Ibid., 201.
23   L. Nkosi, *Home and Exile* (London, 1965), 134.


## Chapter 6 A voice in the wilderness

1   A voice in the wilderness: see Isaiah (40:3), Matthew (3:3), Mark (1:3), Luke (3:4), and John (1:23).
2   V. E. Rylate (or 'Very late') was the pseudonym adopted by Hoseah Jaffe who was a very active member of the movement. Born of Jewish (Eastern European) parents, he married a 'coloured' woman and then became one of the driving forces in the movement in the Cape during the 1950s. See also in this respect, his articles on the NEUM and the Anti-CAD, in: *Worker's Voice*, 1, 3 (July, 1945) and *Worker's Voice* (September, 1946).
3   *Educational Journal* (Cape Town, 1956), 28, 5:10.
4   Ibid., 28, 5:12.
5   *Christian National Education* (shortened to CNE), and generally referred to in Afrikaans as, *Christelike Nasionale Onderwys* (shortened to CNO), constitutes one of the pinnacles of Afrikaner nationalism. *The Educational Journal* of the *Teachers League of South Africa* (TLSA) saw fit to reprint articles 14 and 15 of CNE policy, which is rather revealing; *The Educational Journal* (Cape Town, October to November 1976), 5.

   (a)   God has willed separate nations and peoples and has given each separate nation and peoples its vocation.
   (b)   Each nation has its own unique identity or *eiesoortigheid*.
   (c)   Every nation is different and has its own alien identity or *andersoortigheid*.
   (d)   The education of the 'native' is to be firmly grounded in the philosophy of the Whites, especially of the Boer nation as the senior White trustee of the native.

6   *Educational Journal* (Cape Town, 1956), 28, 3:4.
7   Ibid., 28, 3:5.
8   F. Fanon, *Black Skin, White Masks* (New York, 1967), 18.
9   J. O'Toole, *Watts and Woodstock* (New York, 1973), 23.
10   Fanon, 1967, 17.
11   G. Jonker, *The Educational Journal* (Cape Town, 1969), 3 (11).
12   For a clever exploitation of Surinamese-Dutch, see Edgar Cairo, the Surinamese novelist's book, *Kollektieve Schuld* (lit. Collective Guilt, Amsterdam, 1975). Adam Small is the prime exponent of this type of Afrikaans in his poetry.
13   Adam Small, *Kitaar my kruis* (Kaapstad, 1974$^2$).

14  J. Voorhoeve and U. Lichtveld, *Creole Drum* (Yale, 1975), 139.
15  Uys Krige, in: *Groote Schuur* (Cape Town, 1960).
16  Adam Small, in: *Newscheck* (12 March 1965), 15
17  'The Undaunted Pursuit of Fury', in: *Time Magazine* (6 April 1970), 69.
18  H. P. Africa, *A Study of Language in Fictional Realism* (Leeds, 1969), 3. Unpublished MA thesis in linguistics. My attention was drawn to it by Alex La Guma.
19  Ibid., 4.
20  Ibid., 3.
21  Adam Small, *Kitaar my kruis* (Kaapstad, 1974²), 12.
22  G. Jonker, *The Educational Journal* (Cape Town, 1969), 7 (1).
23  Ibid., 7 (1).
24  Adam Small, *Die eerste steen* (Kaapstad, 1961), 47–8.
25  G. Jonker, *The Educational Journal* (Cape Town, 1969), 8.
26  A. Small, *Die eerste steen* (Kaapstad, 1961), 23.
27  G. Jonker, *The Educational Journal* (Cape Town, 1969), 8.
28  A. Small, *Die eerste steen* (Kaapstad, 1961), 18.
29  Ibid., 20.
30  D. J. Kotze, 'Swartbewustheid, Swart Teologie en Swart mag', in: *Tydskrif vir geesteswetenskappe* (Goodwood, 1977), 17, 3:222.
31  *Rand Daily Mail*, 13 July, 1971.
32  Ibid., 27 June 1973.
33  A. Zijderveld, *Sociologie van de zotheid, de humor als sociaal verschijnsel* (Meppel, 1971), 23.
34  J. O'Toole, 1973, 25.
35  A. Zijderveld, 1971, 158.
36  Adam Small, *Kitaar my kruis* (Kaapstad, 1974²).
37  F. Karl, *The Contemporary English Novel* (London, 1963), 176.
38  Ibid., 176.
39  Ibid., 176.
40  A. Small, *Sê Sjibbolet,* Afrikaanse Persboekhandel, Johannesburg, 1963.
41  I cite these poems in the translations as found in G. R. Coulthard, *Race and Colour in Caribbean Literature* (1962). For the poem, *The New Negro Sermon* by Jacques Roumain, see Coulthard, 50 and 134. For the poem, *Je n'aime pas l'Afrique,* by Paul Niger, see 51 and 131.
42  Ibid., 50.
43  A. Small, *Kitaar my kruis,* 1974², 27. I cite from the poem, *Die Here het gaskommel.*

        Lat die wêreld ma' praat pêllie los en vas
        'n sigaretjie en 'n kannetjie Oem Tas

en dis allright pêllie dis allright
ons kannie worrie nie
'n sigaretjie en 'n kannetjie Oem Tas
en ' lekker meid en lekker anner dinge
oe!
lat die wêreld ma' praat pêllie los en vas
wat daarvan
wat daarvan
wat maak dit saak
soes die Engelsman sê it cuts no ice
*die Here het gaskommel*

*en die dice het verkeerd geval vi' ons*
*daai's maar al*

so lat hulle ma' sê skollie pêllie
nevermind
daar's mos kinners van Gam en daar's kinners van Kain
ons moenie worrie nie

44  I cite from the poem, *Lydensweg* (Small, *Kitaar my kruis*, 1974[2],
17–18):

Ons het lankal in plekke
soes Windermere
al ons verlangens
afgeleer

O Here djy kan maar lyster
na ons lied
sonner worrie, ons is lankal
verby vadriet

altyd as ek na die
oeg toe gaan
dan dink ek aan die brylof
by Kana

maar ons het lankal in plekke
soes Windermere
al ons verlangens
afgeleer

en as tussen die shanties
hier die wet

my soek vlug ek altyd
deur Nasaret

maar Here djy kan maar lyster
na ons lied
sonner worrie, ons is lankal
verby vadriet

so moenie worrie nie Here
ek is opgafix
ek is my eie Here
en dan's ons twie kiets

prik 'n anner gêng se manne
my eendag vol snye
gaat ek sterwe aan my eie
krys vi' myne

o lankal in plekke
soes Windermere
het ons al ons verlangens
afgeleer

al lankal in plekke
soes Windermere
al ons verlangens
afgaleer

45  A. Small, *Kitaar my kruis*, 1974², 19 (excerpt from *Groot Krismisgabet*).

ons ken sulke plekke Here
dja ons ken hulle
ons het duplicates van hulle allover
in die Windermere
in die Distrik Ses
in die Blouvlei hierso annerkant die Wynberg by die Ratreat

46  A. Small, *Sê sjibbolet*, 1963, 21. This excerpt is from the poem, *Second Coming 1*.

47  G. R. Coulthard, *Race and Colour in Caribbean Literature*, 1962, 51 & 131.

48  A. Small, *Kitaar my kruis*, 1974², 43, excerpted from the poem, *Vryheid:* 'o God, U hoogste proef is nie die vuur maar die vernedering!'

49  A. Small, *Sê sjibbolet*, 1963, 10, excerpt from the poem, *Liberalis Gahêkkel*.

211

50  H. Sergeant (ed.), *Commonwealth Poems of Today* (London, 1967), 221.
51  A. Small, *Kitaar my kruis*, 1974², 32.

> Please mêrim
> kamaan smile
> kyk net
> ons tentjies is vol happiness gepaail
>
> ag hoe lyk die mêrim dan so suur
> foei foei
> is die lewe dan asyn
> en waar kœp die mêrim dit
> lyk's nogal boenop duur
>
> nai, mêrim
> toe, toe smile
> kyk daar
> ons tentjies is vol happiness gepaail . . .
>
> Ma' mêrim, pô-pô, pô-pô en banana
> en juicy drywe yt die hartjie van die Kanaän
> of hoe fancy die mêrim so 'n vy
> kyk net hoe lekker uitgaswel is hy
> van bo tot onder ytgady
> moenie blush nie mêrim
> ons het die blaar daarby . . .
>
> jou, jou koelie
> ek sal nou die polisie!
>
> Die vrugtevent se stem trek agterna
> polisie, polisie?
> ag nai mêrim, moet nou nie so spiteful wies nie
> sê tog decently goodbye . . .

52  Gerald Moore, *Wole Soyinka* (London, 1971), 11.
53  *Die Burger* (12 July 1974), 10.
54  Ibid., 10.
55  K. Armah, *Fragments* (London, 1974), 223–4.
56  D. Cooke, 'Of the Strong Breed', in: *Transition* (Kampala, 1964), 3, 13:39.
57  *Die Burger* (12 July 1974), 10.
58  J. O'Toole, *Watts and Woodstock*, 1973, 40.
59  *Die Burger*, 13 September 1973.

60  J. Polley (ed.), *Verslag van die simposium oor die Sestigers* (Kaapstad, 1973), 141.
61  Ibid., 147-8.
62  A. Small, *Kitaar my kruis,* 1974², 28. This excerpt is from his poem, *Via Dolorosa.*

> bruinman
> hoekom kommer?
> jy't die kitaar
> oor jou skouer
> — die strop trek nouer en nouer-
> maar jy't die kitaar oor jou skouer,
> bruinman
> hoekom kommer?

## Chapter 7 My brother's keeper

1  My brother's keeper, see Genesis (4:9).
2  J. Polley (ed.), *Verslag van die simposium oor die Sestigers* (Kaapstad, 1973), 7.
3  E. Mphahlele, *The African Image,* 1962, 108.
4  J. Polley (ed.), *Die Sestigers,* 1973, 161.
5  Ibid., 161-2.
6  Abraham Fischer, or Bram, as he was affectionately called by freedom fighters, came from a distinguished Afrikaner family. He was an excellent lawyer who defended, among others, the leader of the African Nationalist Congress (ANC), Nelson Mandela, at the Rivonia Trial. Bram was an ardent communist and an indefatigable opponent of the apartheid regime. Eventually, he was forced to go underground and live like a real pimpernel in South Africa. He was caught after some time and sentenced to life imprisonment. He died while still serving his sentence. Today, Bram Fischer is looked upon by black and white freedom fighters in exile as a hero.
7  Breyten Breytenbach, 'Vulture Culture', in: A. La Guma (ed.), *Apartheid, A Collection of Writings on South African Racism* (London, 1972), 138.
8  Ibid., 142.
9  Breyten Breytenbach, 'The Fettered Spirit', in: *Unesco Courier* (March 1967), 27.
10  This is an extract from the poem, *Die Beloofde Land* (Breytenbach, *Skryt,* 1972, 20):

> God die Buro vir Staatsveiligheid
> God met 'n helm op,
> in die een hand 'n aktetas vol aandele en goud
> en in die ander 'n sambok.

Sjambok, more often sambok, is an instrument for beating (whipping), fashioned out of thick animal skin or hide.

11  *Die Burger,* 9 May, 1974. See: 'Breyten bedreig die Afrikaner.'
12  Breyten Breytenbach, *Skryt* (Amsterdam, 1972), 62.
13  Breyten Breytenbach, *Kouevuur* (Kaapstad, 1969), 63.
14  Ibid., 67–9.

> binne staan ma se hart stil
> (en waar is die bril?)
> pa skrik wakker verdwaas so deur die wind
> maar mammie is reeds buite
> met 'n kamerjas en rooi wange
> en daar staan ek lewensgroot
> op die lawn naby die sementdammetjie
> waar die nuwe buitekamers aangebou is
> effens verweer deur die verre reis
> 'n keil op
>
> 'n deftige pak
> angelier in die baadjie
> nuwe Italiaanse skoene vir die okkasie
> my hand vol presente
> 'n liedjie vir my ma 'n bietjie trots vir mý pa . . .
>
> ek het gedog ek sal sommerso daar wees
> soos 'n Kleurlingkoor met Kersoggend
> mammie
> ek het gedog hoe ons dan sal huil
> en tee drink

*Die hand vol vere* (lit. a handful of feathers) is the title of a popular song in the Boland — a rural area outside Cape Town. It is rather witty and generally sung by 'coloureds'. The Afrikaans version runs as follows:

> Die hand vol vere
> die hand vol vere
> die Boland se volkies
> dra geleende klere
> en jy't verniet gestry
> en jy't verniet gestry
> so lank as die kind
> in die tjalie lê
> dan lyk hy net soos jy.

The translation, which does not do justice to the original, reads:

> A hand full of feathers
> a hand full of feathers
> the workers from the Boland
> walk round in borrowed clothes
> and it won't help to deny
> and it won't help to deny
> for as long as the baby
> is wrapped in the shawl
> he looks just like you.

15  Wim Ramaker, *Literama* (Hilversum, 1975), 394.
16  *Die Burger*, 31 January 1974.
17  *Die Burger*, 7 August 1974.
18  *Die Burger*, 6 August 1974.
19  *Times Literary Supplement*, 15 November 1974.
20  André Brink, *Kennis van die aand* (Kaapstad, 1974), 39.
21  F. Fanon, *Black Skin, White Masks*, 1967, 71.
22  A. Brink, *Kennis van die aand*, 1974, 39.
23  Ibid., 366.
24  Ibid., 272.
25  Ibid., 301.
26  *Educational Journal*, 1974, 5:4–6.
27  Jan Rabie, *Ons die afgod* (Kaapstad, 1958), 15.
28  J. Polley (ed.), *Die Sestingers*, 1973, 162.
29  A 'kafferboetie' is a negrophilist, and is generally used for white South Africans who are more concerned about the interests of the black man. It contains a suggestion of betrayal.
30  J. Rabie, *Ons die afgod*, 1958, 176.
31  A. La Guma (ed.), *Apartheid*, 1972, 147–8.
32  'Oligarchy of ingrossers' and 'licensers of thought' are from Milton's *Areopagitica*, written in 1644 against censorship in England; also, 'under pittance and prescription and compulsion'.
33  Muriel Horrell (ed.), *A Survey of Race Relations in South Africa* (Johannesburg, 1963), 70.
34  *The Educational Journal*, 1974, 45, 5:6.
35  A. La Guma (ed.), *Apartheid*, 1972, 28.
36  M. Horrell, *Survey of Race Relations in South Africa*, 1963, 69.
37  *Star*, 3 February 1971, 10.
38  *Star*, 6 February 1971.
39  *Educational Journal*, 1974, 5:4–6.
40  Ibid., 4–6.
41  J. Milton, *Areopagitica*, 1644.

## Chapter 8 The poor are unthinkable

1  The poor are unthinkable. The reference here is to the poor who are never explicitly mentioned in E. M. Forster's *A Passage to India,* yet always present, and with the realization that the great mass is beyond art. They are 'unthinkable'.
2  E. Mphahlele, *The African Image* (London, 1962), 108.
3  Ibid., 66. He is back in South Africa after 20 years, exile.
4  K. Ramchand, *The West Indian Novel and its Background* (London, 1970), 63.
5  E. Mphahlele, *The African Image* (London, 1962), 37.
6  A. Sampson, *Drum* (London, 1956), 15–16.
7  E. Mphahlele, *The African Image* (London, 1962), 37.
8  G. Beukes and F. Lategan, *Skrywers en rigtings* (Pretoria, 1959[3]), 271.
9  E. Mphahlele, *The African Image* (London, 1962), 37.
10  A. Hall, 'The African Novels of Joyce Cary', in: *Standpunte,* 1958, 12, 2:41.
11  Richard Rive, *Quartet* (London, 1965), 38.
12  Richard Rive, *African Songs* (Berlin, 1963), 93.
13  N. Gordimer, *The Black Interpreters* (Johannesburg, 1973), 7.
14  H. M. Block and H. Salinger (eds), *The Creative Vision* (New York, 1960).
15  Ibid., 179.
16  Ibid., 181.
17  V. Lenin, *On Literature and Art* (Moscow, 1970[2]), 23.
18  G. D. Killam, *The Novels of Chinua Achebe* (London, 1969), 8.
19  B. Lindfors, 'Achebe on commitment and African writers', in: *Africa Report,* 15, 3:18.
20  P. Wästberg, *The Writer in Modern Africa* (Uppsala, 1968), 21.
21  Ibid., 26.
22  Chinua Achebe, *Morning Yet on Creation Day* (London, 1975), 44.
23  R. Wellek and A. Warren, *Theory of Literature* (New York, 1955[2]), 7, 91.
24  Ibid., 98.
25  N. Gordimer, *The Black Interpreters* (Johannesburg, 1973), 33.
26  C. Achebe, *Morning Yet on Creation Day* (London, 1975), 61.
27  Ibid., 61.
28  N. Gordimer, *The Black Interpreters* (Johannesburg, 1973), 13.
29  Ibid., 33.
30  F. R. Karl, *The Contemporary English Novel* (London, 1963), 159–60.
31  P. Abrahams, *Tell Freedom* (London, 1954), 11.
32  Ibid., 35.

33  Ibid., 40.
34  Ibid., 41.
35  J. O'Toole, *Watts and Woodstock* (New York and London, 1973), 42.
36  Ibid., 42.
37  P. Abrahams, *Tell Freedom* (London, 1954), 149.
38  Ibid., 149.
39  Ibid., 151.
40  Ibid., 196.
41  Ibid., 196.
42  A. Hall, 1958, 41.
43  E. Mphahlele, *Down Second Avenue*, 1959, 128–9.
44  P. Abrahams, *Tell Freedom* (London, 1954), 287.
45  P. Abrahams, *Wild Conquest* (New York, 1971), 28.
46  P. Abrahams, *The Path of Thunder* (London, 1952), 18–20.
47  Ibid., 65.
48  Claude Wauthier, *The Literature and Thought of Modern Africa* (New York, 1967), 196.
49  F. Fanon, *Black Skin, White Masks,* 1967, 71.
50  Ibid., 81.
51  M. Tucker, *Africa in Modern Literature*, 1967, 35.
52  P. Abrahams, *The Path of Thunder* (London, 1952), 67.
53  M. Tucker, *Africa in Modern Literature*, 1967, 36.
54  P. Abrahams, *The Path of Thunder* (London, 1952), 258.
55  F. R. Karl, *The Contemporary English Novel*, 1963, 165.
56  P. Abrahams, *The Path of Thunder* (London, 1952), 162–3.
57  Ibid., 262.
58  'House arrest'. Under this law, political opponents can be confined to their houses for 12 or 24 hours a day.
59  Brian Bunting in a foreword to La Guma's *And a Threefold Cord* (Berlin, 1964), 15.
60  A. La Guma, *And a Threefold Cord* (Berlin, 1964), 17–18.
61  Ibid., 20.
62  Ibid., 20–1.
63  Ibid., 168.
64  Ibid., 145.
65  Ibid., 73.
66  Ibid., 104.
67  A. La Guma, *The Stone Country* (Berlin, 1967), 19.
68  Ibid., 17.
69  Ibid., 66.
70  A. La Guma, *A Walk in the Night and other Stories* (London, 1967), 21.
71  H. P. Africa, *A Study in Fictional Realism* (Leeds, 1969), 14–16.
72  A. La Guma, *And a Threefold Cord* (Berlin, 1964), 168.

73  Ibid., 83.
74  D. Rabkin, 'La Guma and Reality in South Africa', in: *The Journal of Commonwealth Literature* (London, 1973), 8, 1:59.
75  A. La Guma, *In the Fog of the Season's End* (London, 1972), 31.
76  Ibid., 87.
77  Ibid., 161.
78  Ibid., 41.
79  Ibid., 41.
80  Ibid., 180.
81  Ibid., 181.
82  Richard Rive, *Emergency* (London, 1970), 37.
83  Ibid., 24.
84  Ibid., 68.
85  Ibid., 45.
86  Ibid., 60.
87  Ibid., 138.
88  Ibid., 187.
89  Ibid., 148.
90  J. O'Toole, *Watts and Woodstock* (New York and London, 1973), 21.
91  Richard Rive, *Emergency* (London, 1970), 71.
92  Ibid., 84.
93  Wole Soyinka, *Myth, Literature and the African World* (London, 1976), 73–4.
94  Lewis Nkosi, 'Fiction by Black South Africans', in: *Black Orpheus* (Ibadan, 1966), 19:49.
95  Ibid., 53.
96  Richard Rive, *Emergency* (London, 1970), 230.
97  Ibid., 233.

## Chapter 9 New tenants of memory

1  This phrase was culled from the paper read by the West Indian novelist, Wilson Harris, at the conference on Commonwealth Literature at Aarhus, Denmark, 1971. The paper was entitled, 'The Native Phenomenon'.
2  Colin Turnbull, *The Lonely African* (London, 1963), 222.
3  Joseph Campbell, *The Hero with a Thousand Faces* (Princeton, 1949), 385.
4  Ibid., 385.
5  Ibid., 267.
6  Colonel J. H. Vorster, in: *Cape Herald* (23 November 1976).
7  Quoted in: J. O'Toole (1973), 18.
8  Wilson Harris, *The Native Phenomenon* (Aarhus, 1971), 2.

9   Ibid., 2.
10  Ibid., 2.
11  Ibid., 2.
12  Ibid., 2.
13  Claude McKay, *Selected Poems of Claude McKay* (New York, 1953), 41.
14  G. R. Coulthard, *Race and Colour in Caribbean Literature* (London, 1962), 44–5.
15  D. J. Opperman, *Groot Verseboek* (Kaapstad, 1964), 297.
16  LeRoi Jones, *Black Art,* in: *Understanding the New Black Poetry* (Stephen Henderson, 1973), 213.
17  See: *Time Magazine* (6 April 1971).
18  W. A. Jeanpierre, 'African Negritude — Black American Soul', in: *Africa Today* (Denver, 1967), 14, 6:10–11.
19  Mercer Cook and Stephen Henderson, *The Militant Black Writer in Africa and the United States* (Madison, 1969), 124.
20  Langston Hughes, *The Weary Blues* (New York, 1926), 58.
21  John Reed and Clive Wake, *Senghor Prose and Poetry* (London, 1965), 105.
22  James Matthews and Gladys Thomas, *Cry Rage* (Johannesburg, 1972), 69.
23  Ibid., 6.
24  Ibid., 28.
25  Ibid., 36.
26  See: Foreword *Cry Rage*.
27  Ibid., 50.
28  Ibid., 79.
29  Nadine Gordimer, *The Black Interpreters* (Johannesburg, 1973).
30  James Matthews and Gladys Thomas, *Cry Rage* (Johannesburg, 1972), 9.
31  D. Abasiekong, 'Poetry pure and applied', in: *Transition* (5, 23, 1965, 45–8), Kampala.
32  Dennis Brutus, *Letters to Martha* (London, 1970), 19.
33  See: *Die Burger* (6 January 1976).
34  See: *Cape Herald* (23 November 1976).
35  Joseph Campbell, *The Hero with a Thousand Faces*, 391.

### Appendix I Dr Abdurahman — pioneer

1   R. van der Ross, *The Founding of the African Peoples Organization in Cape Town in 1903 and the Role of Dr Abdurahman* (California, 1975), 17.
2   Ibid., 12.
3   Ibid., 13.
4   *The Educational Journal* (Cape Town), 1960, 31, 8:5.

5  Ibid., 6.
6  *The Educational Journal* (Cape Town), 1961, 32, 7:6.
7  *TheEducational Journal* (Cape Town), 1961, 32, 8:18.
8  Ibid., 20.
9  For persons not familiar with South African by-ways, the numerous abbreviations of various political organizations can be very confusing indeed. Yet, a knowledge of these organizations is imperative if one is to have any pretension of an understanding of aspects of South African life. These abbreviations have taken on such a life of their own that no South African would use the full title. In order to initiate the non-South African into these maze of organizations, a list is given below in which the organization's full name is first noted down, and then the generally accepted abbreviation.

| *Organization* | *Abbreviation* | *Founded* |
|---|---|---|
| African Peoples Organization (initially: African Political Organization) | APO | 1902–3 |
| Teachers League of South Africa (official magazine: *Educational Journal*) | TLSA | 1913 |
| African National Congress (re-named thus in 1923) (first called South African Native Congress) | ANC | 1912 |
| All African Convention | AAC | 1935 |
| New Era Fellowship | NEF | 1937 |
| Coloured Advisory Council | CAC | 1943 |
| Coloured Affairs Department | CAD | ditto |
| Anti-Coloured Affairs Department | Anti-CAD | ditto |
| Non-European Unity Movement (the basis of the NEUM was the ten point programme) magazine: *The Torch* | NEUM | 1944 |
| Coloured Peoples National Union | CPNU | 1944 |
| South African Coloured Peoples Organization | SACPO | 1950 |
| Coloured Representative Council (succeeded the Council for Coloured Affairs created in 1959) | CRC | 1969 |
| Christelike Nasionale Onderwys: a policy of education propounded by Afrikaner nationalists. In English it was known as Christian National Education | CNO (Afrikaans) CNE (English) | policy enuncia- ted at con- gress in Bloem- fontein in 1948. |

10  *The Educational Journal* (Cape Town), 1958, 30, 2:13.

## Appendix II Thomas Pringle

1   Thomas Pringle, *Narrative of a Residence in South Africa* (Cape Town, 1966), 14–15.
2   Ibid., 167–8.
3   Ibid., 218.
4   Ibid., 217.
5   Ibid., 16.
6   Thomas Pringle, *Poems Illustrative of South Africa* (Cape Town, 1970), 108.
7   Ibid., 86.
8   Ibid., 98.
9   Ibid., 62–3.
10  Ibid., 95.
11  Ibid., 97.
12  Ibid., 13.
13  G. Chaucer, *The Complete Works of Geoffrey Chaucer* (ed. F. N. Robinson, London, 1957[2]), 534.
14  D. J. Opperman, *Groot Verseboek* (Kaapstad, 1964[2]), 9–10.

## Appendix III Race classification and definitions in South Africa

1   A. Venter, *Coloured, a Profile of Two Million South Africans* (Cape Town, 1974), 120.
2   Ibid., 127.

# Bibliography

Abasiekong, Daniel, 1965, 'Poetry pure and applied', in: *Transition* (5, 23:45–8) (Kampala).

Abrahams, Peter, 1946, *Mine Boy* (London, Dorothy Crisp; Faber, 1954).

Abrahams, Peter, 1952, *The Path of Thunder* (London, Faber & Faber, first published Harper, New York, 1948).

Abrahams, Peter, 1954, *Tell Freedom* (London, Faber).

Abrahams, Peter, 1971, *Wild Conquest* (New York, Anchor Books, first published Faber, London, 1950).

Achebe, Chinua, 1958, *Things Fall Apart* (London, Heinemann).

Achebe, Chinua, 1975, *Morning Yet on Creation Day: Essays* (London, Heinemann).

Africa, H. P., 1969, 'A Study of Language in Fictional Realism' (unpublished MA Thesis, Leeds University).

Anthony, Michael, 1976, *The Year in San Fernando* (London, Heinemann, first published Deutsch, 1965).

d'Arbez (ps. of J. F. van Oordt), 1896, *Mooi Annie*. See: 'De Zuid-Afrikaansche historie bibliotheek' series.

Armah, Ayi Kwei, 1974, *Fragments* (London, Heinemann).

Bain, A. G., 1846, *Kaatjie Kekkelbek; or Life among the Hottentots* (Cape Town).

Barnouw, A. J., 1934, *Language and Race Problems in South Africa* (The Hague, Martinus Nijhoff).

Bastiaanse, J., 1956, 'Moedertaal-onderwys: Afrikanerizing instrument', in: *Educational Journal* (Cape Town), 28, 3:4–6.

Beukes, G. and Lategan, F., 1959[3], *Skrywers en rigtings* (Pretoria, J. L. van Schaik Beperk).

Block, Haskell M. and Salinger, H. (eds), 1960, *The Creative Vision. Modern European Writers on their Art* (New York, Grove Press).

Blom, Jan (ps. of Breyten Breytenbach), 1970, *Lotus* (Kaapstad, Buren Uitgewers).

Boerneef (ps. of I.W.v.d. Merwe), 1938, *Boplaas* (Kaapstad, Nasionale Pers).

Boerneef (ps. öf I.W.v.d. Merwe), 1938, *Van my kontrei* (Kaapstad, Nasionale Pers).

Boerneef (ps. of I.W.v.d. Merwe), 1956, *Teen die helling* (Kaapstad, Nasionale Boekhandel).

Boniface, E. C., 1832, *De nieuwe ridderorde; of de Temperantisten: kluchtig blijspel in vier bedrijven* (Kaapstad, P. A. Brand).

Bosman, D. B., 1928², *Oor die ontstaan van Afrikaans* (Amsterdam, Swets & Zeitlinger).

Bosman, F. C. L., 1928, *Drama en toneel − 1652-1855*, deel 1 (Amsterdam, De Bussy).

Botha, D. P., 1960, *Die opkoms van ons derde stand* (Kaapstad, Human & Rousseau).

Botha, Graham C., 1926, *Social Life in the Cape Colony in the 18th Century* (Cape Town, Juta).

Breytenbach, Breyten, 1964, *Die Ysterkoei moet sweet* (Johannesburg, Afrikaanse Boekhandel).

Breytenbach, Breyten, 1967, 'The Fettered Spirit', in: *The Unesco Courier* (March), 27–9.

Breytenbach, Breyten, 1969, *Kouevuur* (Kaapstad, Buren Uitgewers).

Breytenbach, Breyten, 1972, 'Vulture Culture', in: A. La Guma (ed.), *Apartheid, a Collection of Writings on South African Racism* (pp. 137–48) (London, Lawrence & Wishart).

Breytenbach, Breyten, 1972, *Skryt* (Amsterdam, Meulenhoff).

Breytenbach, Breyten, 1976, *Het huis van de dove* (it contains the following anthologies: *Die Ysterkoei moet sweet; Die huis van die dowe; Kouevuur*) (Amsterdam, Meulenhoff).

Brindley, Marianne, 1976, *Western Coloured Township. Problems of an Urban Slum* (Johannesburg, Ravan Press).

Brink, André, 1974, *Kennis van die aand* (Kaapstad, Buren Uitgewers) (translated as *Looking on Darkness* by the author himself, London, 1974, Wyndham publications).

Bruggen, Jochem van, 1924, *Ampie* (1) (Amsterdam, Swets & Zeitlinger).

Brutus, Dennis, 1963, *Sirens, Knuckles and Boots* (Ibadan, Mbari).

Brutus, Dennis, 1968, *Letters to Martha* (London, Heinemann).

Brutus, Dennis, 1973, *A Simple Lust* (selected poems including *Sirens, Knuckles and Boots; Letters to Martha; Poems from Algiers; Thoughts Abroad*) (London, Heinemann).

Busken Huet, C., 1946⁸, *Het land van Rembrandt. Studiën over de Noord Nederlandsche beschaving in de zeventiende eeuw* (Haarlem, Tjeenk Willink & Zoon).

Cairo, Edgar, 1975, *Kollektieve Schuld* (Amsterdam, In de Knipscheer).

Campbell, Joseph, 1949, *The Hero with a Thousand Faces* (Princeton University Press).

Cartey, Wilfred, 1969, *Whispers from a Continent* (New York, Random House).

Cary, Joyce, 1944, *The Case for African Freedom* (London, Secker & Warburg).

Cary, Joyce, 1946, *Britain and West Africa* (London, Longmans & Green).

Cary, Joyce, 1950, 'The Novelist at work', in: *Adam International Review* (November to December), 212–13.

Cary, Joyce, 1951, *The African Witch* (London, Michael Joseph, first published in 1936).

Cary, Joyce, 1952, *Aissa Saved* (London, Carfax ed., first published in 1932).

Cary, Joyce, 1952, *Mister Johnson* (London, Mermaid Books, first published in 1939).

Césaire, Aimé, 1969, *Return to my Native Land* (London, Heinemann, first published in French under title: *Cahier d'un retour au pays natal,* Paris, Volonté, no. 20, 1939).

Chaucer, Geoffrey, 1957[2], *The Works of Geoffrey Chaucer* (ed. F. N. Robinson) (London, Oxford University Press).

Cilliers, S. P., 1963, *The Coloureds of South Africa* (Cape Town, Banier).

Cipolla, Elizabeth, 1968, 'The Last Years – A Personal Impression and a Valedictory', in: *Lantern* (18, 2:49–55) (Pretoria).

Clarke, Austin, 1965, *Among Thistles and Thorns* (London, Heinemann).

Cloete, Stuart, 1937, *The Turning Wheels* (Boston, Houghton Mifflin).

Cloete, Stuart, 1939, *Watch for the Dawn* (London, Collins).

Cloete, Stuart, 1941, *The Hill of Doves* (Boston, Houghton Mifflin).

Cloete, Stuart, 1952, *The Curve and the Tusk: A Novel of Change among Elephants and Men* (Boston, Houghton Mifflin).

Cloete, Stuart, 1955, *The African Giant* (Boston, Houghton Mifflin).

Cloete, Stuart, 1957, *The Mask* (Boston, Houghton Mifflin).

Cloete, Stuart, 1958, *Gazella* (Boston, Houghton Mifflin).

Cloete, T. T., 1974, 'Breytenbach bedreig die Afrikaner', in: *Die Burger,* 9 May (Kaapstad).

Coetzee, Abel, 1940, *Waarheen Vader?* (Bloemfountein, Nasionale Pers).

Commelin, 1646, *Begin ende voortgang van de Oost Indische Compagnie* (exact reprint of the original in Gothic print in 1969 in Amsterdam). See also Joris van Spilbergen in *Commelin,* 1969, 2:12; Wybrandt van Warwijck: *Commelin,* 1969, 2:52; Paulus van Caerden: *Commelin,* 1969, 3:48; Seygher van Rechteren: *Commelin,* 1969, 4:23.

Cook, Mercer and Stephen Henderson, 1969, *The Militant Black Writer in Africa and the United States* (Wisconsin University Press).

Cooke, D., 1964, 'Of the Strong Breed', in: *Transition*, 3, 13:38–40 (Kampala).

Cottenje, Mireille, 1973, *Het grote onrecht* (Antwerpen, Standaard Uitgeverij).

Coulthard, G. R., 1962, *Race and Colour in Caribbean Literature* (London, Oxford University Press).

Cruse, H. P., 1947, *Die opheffing van die Kleurling bevolking* (Kaapstad, Citadel Pers).

Dapper, O., 1668, *Naukeurige beschryvinge der Afrikaensche Gewesten* (Amsterdam, van Meurs).

Dekker, G., 1947, *Afrikaanse literatuurgeskiedenis* (Kaapstad/ Bloemfontein, Nasionale Pers).

Domingo, Eddie, 1955, *Okkies op die breë pad* (Johannesburg, Afrikaanse Pers).

Dover, C., 1937, *Half-Caste* (London, Secker & Warburg).

Drake, St Clair, 1958, 'An Approach to the Evaluation of African Societies', in: *Africa as Seen by American Negroes* (Paris, Présence Africaine).

Drayton, Geoffrey, 1959, *Christopher* (London, Collins).

Driver, C. J., 1974, 'Mixing the Colours', in: *TLS* (15 November), London.

Dykes, Eva Beatrice, 1942, *The Negro in English Romantic Thought* (Washington, Associated Publishers).

Edelstein, M., 1974, *What Do the Coloureds Think?* (Johannesburg, Labour & Community Consultants).

Edwards, P. (ed.), 1967, *Equiano's Travels – The Interesting Narrative of the Life of Olaudah Equiano or Gustavus Vassa the African* (London, Heinemann, first published in 1789).

Fabricius, Jan, 1915, *Totok en Indo: Een plantage idylle* ('s-Gravenhage, L. A. Dijckhoff).

Fabricius, Jan, 1916, *Sonna: Indisch toneelspel* ('s-Gravenhage, L. A. Dijckhoff).

Fairchild, Hoxie, 1927, *The Noble Savage, A Study in Romantic Naturalism* (New York, Russell & Russell).

Fanon, F., 1967, *Black Skin, White Masks* (New York, Grove Press, first published as *Peau Noire, Masques Blancs* in 1952).

Franken, J. L. M., 1927, 'Die taal van slawekinders en fornikasie met slavinne', in: *Tydskrif vir wetenskap en kuns* (ed. D. F. Malherbe), 6:21–40 (Bloemfontein, Nasionale Pers Beperk).

Franken, J. L. M., 1953, *Taalhistoriese bydraes* (Amsterdam, Balkema).

Fugard, Athol, 1963, *The Blood Knot* (Johannesburg, Simondium Publishers).

Fyfe, Christopher, 1963, 'The Colonial Situation in Mister Johnson', in: *Modern Fiction Studies,* 9:226–230 (London).

Godéé Molsbergen, E. C., 1916, *Reizen in Zuid Afrika in de Hollandsche tijd* (deel 1 & 11) ('s-Gravenhage, Martinus Nijhoff).

Godéé Molsbergen, E. C., 1937, *Jan van Riebeeck en zijn tijd* (Amsterdam, P. N. van Kampen & Zn).

Gordimer, N. and L. Abrahams, 1967, *South African Writing Today* (Penguin Books).

Gordimer, Nadine, 1973, *The Black Interpreters* (Johannesburg, Sprocas Publications).

Gordon, Gerald, 1952, *Let the Day Perish* (London, Methuen).

Grové, A. P., 1974, 'Kenners gee hul menings oor *Kennis van die aand*' in: *Die Burger* (6 August) (Kaapstad).

Hall, A., 1958, 'The African Novels of Joyce Cary', in: *Standpunte,* 12, 2:40–55 (Kaapstad, Nasionale Boekhandel Bepk).

Hansen, P. C. C. (ps. Boeka), 1902, *Een koffieopziener* (Amsterdam, F. van Rossem).

Harris, Wilson, 1971, 'The Native Phenomenon' (Aarhus, Denmark).

Hay, William (ed.), 1912, *Thomas Pringle: His Life, Times and Poems* (Cape Town, Juta).

Heever, C. M. van den, 1930, *Somer* (Pretoria, J. L. van Schaik).

Henderson, Stephen, 1973, *Understanding the New Black Poetry* (New York, William Morrow & Co).

Herskovits, M. J., 1941, *The Myth of the Negro Past* (New York, Harper).

Hervey, H. C., 1950, *Barracoon* (New York, Putnam).

Hesseling, D. C., 1899, *Het Afrikaansch* (Leiden, E. J. Brill).

Hesseling, D. C., 1916, 'Africana I: de naam Hottentot', *Tijdschrift voor Nederlandsche Taal- en Letterkunde* (Leiden), 35.

Hobson, G. C. and S. B. Hobson, 1930, *Skankwan van die duine* (Pretoria, J. L. van Schaik).

Hondius, Jodocus, 1652, *Klare besgryving van Cabo de Bona Esperanca.* Amsterdam (translated by L. C. van Oordt with an introduction by Prof. P. Serfontein, 1952, Kaapstad, Komitee vir Boekuitstalling van die van Riebeek fees).

Hooijer, G. B., 1921, *De eerste schipvaart naar Oost Indië onder Cornelis de Houtman door Willem Lodewycksz in opdracht van Beheer van het Koloniaal Instituut* (Amsterdam, de Bussy).

Horell, Muriel (ed.), 1963, *A Survey of Race Relations* (Johannesburg, Institute of Race Relations).

Horrell, Muriel, 1971, *Action, Reaction and Counter-action* (Johannesburg, Institute of Race Relations).

Horell, Muriel (ed.), 1972, *A Survey of Race Relations* (Johannesburg, Institute of Race Relations).

Howe, Susanne, 1949, *Novels of Empire* (New York, Columbia

University Press, reprint; Kraus, New York, 1971).

Hughes, Langston, 1926, *The Weary Blues* (New York, A. Knopf).

Hughes, Langston and Bontemps, Arna (eds), 1970, *The Poetry of the Negro* (New York, Doubleday).

Huizinga, J., 1956², *Nederland's beschaving in de 17ᵉ eeuw* (Haarlem, H. D. Tjeenk Willink & Zoon N. V).

Hulshof, A. (ed.), 1941, *H. A. van Rheede tot Drakensteyn: Journaal van zijn verblijf aan de Kaap* (Utrecht, Kemink & Zoon).

Jacobson, Dan, 1967, *Beggar My Neighbour*, in: N. Gordimer and L. Abrahams (eds), *South African Writing Today* (Penguin Books).

Jaffe, Hoseah, 1945, 'A political history of the Anti-CAD', in: *Worker's Voice*, 1, 3.

Jaffe, Hoseah, 1946, 'The petty-bourgeois nature of the Unity Movement tops "Pondokkie' politics"', in: *Worker's Voice*.

Jahn, Jahnheinz, 1964, *Wir nannten sie Wilde, Abenteuer in alten und neuen reisebeschreibungen* (München, Erenwirth Verlag). See especially *Vasco da Gama*, 27–32; *Wurffbain*, 32–3; *Merklein*, 33–4; *Herport*, 34–6; *Hoffmann*, 36–9; *Schweitzer*, pp. 39–41. See also: *Reisebeschreibungen von Deutschen Beamten Und Kriegsleuten im dienst der Niederländischen West-und Ost Indischen Kompagnien.* See especially: *Merklein* (111), 1930; *Herport* (V), 1930; *Hoffmann* (VII), 1931; *Wurffbain* (VIII & IX), 1931; *Schweitzer* (XI), 1931 ('s-Gravenhage, Martinus Nijhoff).

Jeanpierre, W. A., 1967, 'African Negritude — Black American Soul', in: *Africa Today*, 14, 6:10–11 (Denver University).

Jonker, G., 1969, 'Politieke versies van Adam Small', in: *Educational Journal* (Kaapstad), October to November (7–9). 'Die bitterheid van 'n bruin Afrikaner', in: *Educational Journal* (Kaapstad), October to November (7–9).

Jordan, A. C., 1957–58, 'The Language Question', in: *Educational Journal* (Cape Town), 29, 3:6–8; 29, 5:10–12.

Joubert, Dian, 1974, *Met iemand van 'n ander kleur* (Kaapstad, Tafelberg-Uitgewers).

Karl, Frederick, 1963, *The Contemporary English Novel* (London, Thames & Hudson). See especially: 'Joyce Cary: The Moralist as Novelist', 131–47; 'The World of Evelyn Waugh: The Normally Insane', 167–82.

Katzew, H., 1969, 'Politics and Pain', in: *Die Beeld* (Johannesburg), 5 October.

Kettle, Arnold, 1955, *An Introduction to the English Novel* (2 vols) (London, Hutchinson's University Library).

Kiewiet, C. W. de, 1957⁶, *A History of South Africa. Social and Economic* (London, O.U.P., first published in 1941 by the Clarendon Press).

Killam, G. D., 1969, *The Novels of Chinua Achebe* (London, Heinemann).

Knuvelder, G., 1964, *Handleiding tot de geschiedenis der Nederlandse Letterkunde* ('s-Hertogenbosch, L. C. G. Malmberg).

Kotze, D. J., 1977, 'Swartbewustheid, Swart Teologie en Swart Mag', in: *Tydskrif vir Geesteswetenskappe* (Goodwood, K. P., Nasionale Boekdrukkery).

Krige, Uys, 1960, *Groote Schuur* (see especially the foreword) (Cape Town, University of Cape Town).

La Guma, Alex, 1964, *And a Threefold Cord* (Berlin, Seven Seas).

La Guma, Alex, 1965, 'Out of Darkness', in: *Quartet: New voices from South Africa*, ed. R. Rive (London, Heinemann).

La Guma, Alex, 1967, *The Stone Country* (Berlin, Seven Seas).

La Guma, Alex, 1967, *A Walk in the Night and other stories* (London, Heinemann, first published in 1962).

La Guma, Alex, 1972, *Apartheid: A Collection of Writings on South African Racism* (London, Lawrence & Wishart).

La Guma, Alex, 1972, *In the Fog of the Season's End* (London, Heinemann).

Lamming, George, 1953, *In the Castle of my Skin* (London, Michael Joseph).

Lenin, V., 1970[2], *On Literature and Art* (first published in 1967 from the *Collected Works* of Lenin) (Moscow, Progress Publishers).

Lindfors, B., 1966, 'Form and Technique in the novels of Richard Rive and Alex La Guma', in: *Journal of New African Literature,* 2:10–15.

Lindfors, B., 1970, 'Achebe on commitment and African writers', in: *Africa Report,* 15, 3:16–18.

Louw, W. E. G., 1974, 'Kanna 'n onvergeetlike toneelervaring', in: *Die Burger* (Kaapstad), 25 November.

Louw, N. P. van Wyk, 1937, *Berigte te velde* (Pretoria, J. L. van Schaik).

Lubbe, H. J., 1974, 'Valkhoff en die ontstaan van Afrikaans n.a.v. sy *New Light on Afrikaans'* and 'Malayo-Portuguese', in: *Tydskrif vir Geesteswetenskappe* (Elsies Rivier, K. P., Nasionale Boekdrukkery), 14, 2.

MacDermott, Mercia, 1967, *The Apostle of Freedom* (London, George Allen & Unwin).

MacMillan, W. M., 1927, *The Cape Colour Question* (London, Harper).

MacMillan, W. M., 1929, *Bantu, Boer and Briton. The Making of the South African Native Problem* (London, Faber).

Mahood, Molly, 1964, *Joyce Cary's Africa* (London, Methuen).

Maingard, L. F., 1935, 'The origin of the word Hottentot', in: *Bantu Studies,* 9:63–67.

Malherbe, D. F., 1928, *Hans die skipper*. Bloemfontein, Nasionale Pers Bepk.

Malherbe, D. F., 1930[5], *Die Meulenaar* (Bloemfontein, Nasionale Pers, see also Tafelberg Uitgewers, Kaapstad, 1978[15]).

Malherbe, F. E. J., 1932[2], *Humor in die algemeen en sy uiting in die Afrikaanse Letterkunde* (Amsterdam, Swets & Zeitlinger).

Malherbe, F. E. J., 1934, ' 'n Roman van Kleurlinglewe', in: *Die Huisgenoot* (20 July).

Malherbe, F. E. J., 1958, 'Die kleurprobleem en die letterkunde', in: *Afrikaanse Lewe en Letterkunde* (Stellenbosch, Universiteitsuitgewers).

Marais, J. S., 1957[2], *The Cape Coloured People. 1652–1937* (London, Longmans, Green & Co., first published in 1939).

Marks, Shula, 1972, 'Khoisan Resistance to the Dutch in the Seventeenth and Eighteenth Centuries', in: *Journal of African History*, 13, 1:55–80.

Matthews, James, 1964, *The Park*, in: *Modern African Prose* (London, Heinemann).

Matthews, J. and G. Thomas, 1972, *Cry Rage* (an anthology) (Johannesburg, Sprocas Publications).

McDonald, Ian, 1974, *The Humming-Bird Tree* (London, Heinemann).

McKay, Claude, 1953, *Selected Poems* (New York, Harcourt, Brace & World).

Meiring, Jane, 1968, *Thomas Pringle: His Life and Times* (Cape Town/ Amsterdam, Balkema).

Mentzel, O. F., 1924, *A Geographical and Topographical Description of the Cape of Good Hope* (translated from the German by H. J. Mandelbrote in V. R. S. no. 6, 1952, Cape Town). Originally published 1785–7 as: *Vollständige beschreibung des Afrikanischen Vorgebirges der Guten Hoffnung* (Glogau, Günther).

Mikro (ps. of C. H. Kühn), 1944[11], *Toiings* (Pretoria, J. L. van Schaik, first published in 1934).

Mikro (ps. of C. H. Kühn), 1942, *Huisies teen die heuwel* (Kaapstad, Nasionale Pers Bepk).

Mikro (ps. of C. H. Kühn), 1944, *Vreemdelinge* (Johannesburg, Afrikaanse Pers).

Mikro (ps. of C. H. Kühn), 1936, *Die ruiter in die nag* (Bloemfontein, Nasionale Pers Bpk).

Millin, Sarah Gertrude, 1919, *The Dark River* (London, Collins).

Millin, Sarah Gertrude, 1922, *Adam's Rest* (London, Collins).

Millin, Sarah Gertrude, 1924, *God's Step-children* (London, Constable). The edition used in this manuscript is from 1951.

Millin, Sarah Gertrude, 1926, *The South Africans* (London, Constable).

Millin, Sarah Gertrude, 1941, *The Herr Witchdoctor* (London, Heinemann).

Millin, Sarah Gertrude, 1950, *King of the Bastards* (London, Heinemann).

Millin, Sarah Gertrude, 1955, *The Measure of My Days* (London, Faber & Faber).

Milton, John, 1940, *Areopagitica* (London, O.U.P., first published in 1644).

Mittelholzer, Edgar, 1952, *Children of Kaywana* (London, Peter Neville Ltd, published in Corgi, 1976).

Mittelholzer, Edgar, 1954, *The Harrowing of Hubertus* (London, Secker & Warburg, published as *Kaywana Stock* in Corgi, 1976).

Mittelholzer, Edgar, 1958, *Kaywana Blood* (London, Secker & Warburg).

Mnguni, 1952, *Three Hundred Years* (Cape Town).

Mofolo, Thomas, 1971, *Chaka. An Historical Romance* (London, O.U.P., first published in 1931).

Mollema, J. C., 1936, *De eerste schipvaart der Hollanders naar Oost Indië, 1595–7* ('s-Gravenhage, Martinus Nijhoff).

Moore, Gerald, 1962, *Seven African Writers* (London, O.U.P.), Three Crowns Book.

Moore, Gerald, 1971, *Wole Soyinka* (London, Evans Bros).

Mphahlele, Ezekiel, 1959, *Down Second Avenue* (London, Faber & Faber).

Mphahlele, Ezekiel, 1962, *The African Image* (London, Faber & Faber, reprint in 1974).

Mulder, C., 1974, 'Oor: *Kennis van die aand*', *Die Burger* (Kaapstad) 31 January.

Muller, E., 1958, *Vrou op die skuit* (Kaapstad, Balkema) (see especially: *Die Peertak* and *Twee Gesigte*).

Multatuli (ps. of Douwes-Dekker), 1955, *Max Havelaar of de koffie-veilingen der Nederlandsche handel-maatschappij* (Amsterdam, Elsevier, first published in 1859).

Munger, Edwin S., 1974, *The Afrikaner as Seen Abroad* (California, Munger Library).

Naipaul, Vidia, 1961, *A House for Mr Biswas* (London, André Deutsch).

Neser, Regina, 1950, *Kinders van Ishmaël* (Kaapstad, Nasionale Pers Bepk).

Niekerk, Lydia van, 1916, *De eerste Afrikaanse Taalbeweging en zijn Letterkundige voortbrengselen* (Amsterdam, Swet & Zeitlinger).

Nienaber, G. S., 1963, 'The origin of the name Hottentot', in: *African Studies*, 22:65–90 (Johannesburg, Witwatersrand University Press).

Nienaber, P. J., 1947, *Afrikaanse skrywers aan die woord* (Johannesburg, Afrikaanse Persboekhandel).

Nienaber, P. J., 1960, *Perspektief en Profiel* (Johannesburg, Afrikaanse Boekhandel).

Nieuwenhuys, R., 1973, *Oost Indische Spiegel, wat Nederlandse schrijvers en dichters over Indonesië geschreven hebben vanaf de eerste jaren der compagnie tot op heden* (Amsterdam, Querido).

Nkosi, Lewis, 1965, *Home and Exile* (London, Longmans, Green and Co.).

Nkosi, Lewis, 1966, 'Fiction by Black South Africans', in: *Black Orpheus* (Ibadan), 1966, 19:48-55.

Opperman, D. J., 1953, *Digters van dertig* (Kaapstad, Nasionale Boekhandel Bepk).

Opperman, D. J., 1964[6], *Groot Verseboek* (Kaapstad, Nasionale Boekhandel).

Orwell, George, 1962, 'The Prevention of Literature', in: *Inside the Whale* (Penguin Books), 159-74.

O'Toole, J., 1973, *Watts and Woodstock* (New York/London, Holt, Rinehart & Winston).

Paton, A., 1948, *Cry the Beloved Country* (London, Jonathan Cape).

Paton, A., 1953, *Too Late the Phalarope* (London, Jonathan Cape).

Patterson, S., 1953, *Colour and Culture in South Africa* (London, Routledge & Kegan Paul).

Petersen, S. V., 1971[4], *As die son ondergaan* (Kaapstad, Maskew Miller, first published in 1945).

Plaatje, S., 1975, *Mhudi* (Johannesburg, Quagga Press, first published by The Lovedale Press in 1930).

Plomer, William, 1927, *I Speak of Africa* (London, Hogarth Press).

Plomer, William, 1965, *Turbotte Wolfe* (London, Hogarth Press, first published in 1925).

Polley, J. (ed.), 1973, *Verslag van die simposium oor Die Sestigers* (Kaapstad, Human & Rousseau).

Price, J. L., 1974, *Culture and Society in the Dutch Republic During the 17th Century* (London, Batsford Ltd).

Pringle, T., 1966, *Narrative of a Residence in South Africa* (introduction, biographical notes by A. M. Lewin Robinson) (Cape Town, Struik). This is a reprint of the original account which first appeared in 1834 as part II of *African Sketches,* part I containing *Poems Illustrative of South Africa.* The 1835 edition published by Moxon included a biographical sketch of the author by Josiah Conder. A German edition appeared in 1836, and in 1837, *Narrative* was re-worked and published at Leipzig. In 1837 it appeared in Groningen. Other editions appeared in 1840 and 1842 (Moxon, London), 1844 (William Smith), 1851 (Tegg, London).

Pringle, T., 1970, *Poems Illustrative of South Africa: African Sketches: Part One* (edited with an introduction and notes by J. R. Wahl)

231

(Cape Town, Struik). The poems first appeared as part I of *African Sketches* in 1834. See also the anthology prepared by Haynes (Cape Town, Juta, 1912).

Prins, J., 1967, *Die beknelde kleurling* (Assen, van Gorcum).

Quiller-Couch, A. (ed.), 1961, *The Oxford Book of English Verse* (London, O.U.P.).

Rabie, J., 1958, *Ons die afgod* (Kaapstad, Balkema).

Rabkin, D., 1973, 'La Guma and Reality in South Africa', in: the *Journal of Commonwealth Literature*, 8, 1:54–61 (London, O.U.P.).

Ramaker, W. (ed.), 1975, *Literama*, 10, 8. Hilversum, N.C.R. uitgawe.

Ramchand, K., 1969, 'Terrified Consciousness', in: the *Journal of Commonwealth Literature*, 7:8–19 (London, O.U.P.).

Ramchand, K., 1970, *The West Indian Novel and its Background* (London, Faber & Faber).

Raven-Hart, R., 1967, *Before van Riebeeck, Callers at South Africa from 1488 to 1652* (Wynberg, Cape, Rustica Press).

Raven-Hart, R., 1971, *Cape of Good Hope, 1652–1702. The First Fifty Years of Dutch Colonization as seen by Callers* (Cape Town).

Reed, John and Clive Wake, 1964, *A Book of African Verse* (London, Heinemann).

Reed, John and Clive Wake, 1965, *Senghor Prose and Poetry* (London, Heinemann).

Rhys, Jean, 1966, *Wide Sargasso Sea* (New York, Popular Library).

Rive, Richard, 1963, *African Songs* (Berlin, Seven Seas).

Rive, Richard, 1964, *Modern African Prose* (London, Heinemann).

Rive, Richard, 1964, *Emergency* (London, Faber & Faber, edition used here 1970, Collier-Macmillan).

Rive, Richard, 1965, *Quartet* (London, Heinemann).

Rodenwaldt, E., 1930, 'Die Indo europäer', in: *Archiv für Rassen und Gesellschaftsbiologie*, 23:102–120.

Ross, R., 1978, 'The Changing Legal Position of the Khoisan in the Cape Colony' (Werkgroep Geschiedenis Europese Expansie, Rijks Universiteit, Leiden).

Ross, R. van der, 1975, *The Founding of the African Peoples Organization in Cape Town in 1903 and the Role of Dr. Abdurahman* (California, Munger Africana Library).

Rouffaer, G. P. and J. W. Ijzerman (eds), 1915, *De eerste schipvaart der Nederlanders naar Oost Indië onder Cornelis de Houtman, 1595–1597. 1. D'Eerste boeck van Willem Lodewijcksz* ('s-Gravenhage, Martinus Nijhoff).

Rouffaer, G. P. and J. W. Ijzerman (eds), 1925, *De eerste schipvaart der Nederlanders naar Oost Indië onder Cornelis de Houtman 1595–1597. De oudste journalen der reis verhael (1597) journael (1598) van der Does* ('s-Gravenhage, Martinus Nijhoff).

Roskam, K. L., 1960, *Apartheid and Discrimination* (Leyden, Sijthof).

Rylate, V. E., 1956-7, 'A Short History of the Language Question in South Africa', in: *The Educational Journal*, 28, 4:6–8; 28, 5:10–13; 28, 6:14–16; 28, 7:11–13 (Cape Town).

Sachs, Wulf, 1947, *Black Hamlet* (Boston, Little Brown & Co. (first published as *Black Anger* in 1947).

Sampson, Anthony, 1956, *Drum* (London, Collins).

Schapera, I., 1930, *The Khoisan Peoples of South Africa* (London, Routledge & Sons).

Schreiner, Olive, 1883, *The Story of an African Farm* (London, Hutchinson & Co.).

Segal, R., 1967, *Childhood*, in: *South African Writing Today*, ed. N. Gordimer and L. Abrahams (Penguin Books).

Sergeant, H. (ed.), 1967, *Commonwealth Poems of Today* (London).

Shakespeare, W., 1951, *The Complete Works* (ed. P. Alexander) (London).

Small, Adam, 1961, *Die eerste steen* (Kaapstad, H.A.U.M.).

Small, Adam, 1963, *Sê sjibbolet* (Johannesburg, Afrikaanse Pers Bepk).

Small, Adam, 1965, 'Focus on Adam Small', in: *Newscheck* (12 March).

Small, Adam, 1965, *Kanna Hy Kô Hystoe* (Kaapstad, Tafelberg-Uitgewers).

Small, Adam, 1971, Small on Racism, in: *Rand Daily Mail* (13 July).

Small, Adam, 1973, 'We don't want to be Afrikaners' in: *Rand Daily* Mail (27 June).

Small, Adam, 1974, 'Wilna se Makiet 'n kragtoer', in: *Die Burger* (12 July).

Small, Adam, 1974[2], *Kitaar my kruis* (Kaapstad, H.A.U.M.).

Smith, Pauline, 1925, *The Little Karroo* (London, Jonathan Cape).

Smith, Pauline, 1935, *Platkops Children* (London, Jonathan Cape).

Snyman, J. P., 1968, 'The Writings of Sarah Gertrude Millin', in: *Lantern*, 18, 2:36–46 (Pretoria).

Soyinka, Wole, 1969, *Three Short Plays* (includes: *The Swamp Dwellers; The Trials of Brother Jero; The Strong Breed*) (London, O.U.P.).

Soyinka, Wole, 1976, *Myth, Literature and the African World* (London, Cambridge University Press).

Steen, Marguerite, 1941, *The Sun is my Undoing* (Toronto, Collins).

Suzman, Arthur, 1960, *Race Classification and Definition in the Legislation of the Union of South Africa, 1910–1960* (Johannesburg, Institute of Race Relations).

Swart (Ds), 1974, 'Dis my besware teen *Kennis van die aand*', in: *Die Burger* (31 January) (Kaapstad).

# Bibliography

Teenstra, M. D., 1830, 'Zamenspraak of uittreksel van een door mij gehouden gesprek met een boer, deszelfs vrouw en hunne slaven, te Caledon, kolonie de Goede Hoop', in: Teenstra, M. D. *De Vruchten Mijner Werkzaamheden, gedurende mi jne Reize, over de Kaap de Goede Hoop, naar Java, en terug, over St. Helena, naar de Nederlanden* (Groningen, H. Z. Eekhoff).

Theron, Erika, 1976, *Verslag van die kommissie van ondersoek na aangeleenthede rakende die Kleurlingbevolkingsgroep* (Pretoria, Staatsdrukkery).

Thompson, L., 1949, *The Cape Coloured Franchise* (Johannesburg, Institute of Race Relations).

Toit, P. S. du, 1938, 'Waarom hulle getrek het', in: *Die Huisgenoot* (gedenkuitgawe) (Kaapstad).

Toynbee, A. J., 1935, *A Study of History*, 3 vols (London, O.U.P.).

Tucker, M., 1967, *Africa in Modern Literature* (New York, Fred Ungar Publishing Company).

Turnbull, Colin, 1963, *The Lonely African* (London, Chatto & Windus).

Valkhoff, Marius, 1966, *Studies in Portuguese and Creole with special reference to South Africa* (Johannesburg, Witwatersrand University Press).

Venter, Al, 1974, *Coloured, a Profile of Two Million South Africans* (Cape Town, Human & Rousseau).

Volkelt, Joh, 1910, *System der Aesthetik* (München, Beck).

Voorhoeve, J. and U. Lichtveld (eds), 1958, *Suriname: spiegel der vaderlandsche kooplieden* (Zwolle, Tjeenk Willink).

Voorhoeve, J. and U. Lichtveld (eds), 1975, *Creole Drum* (New Haven, Yale University Press). English translations by V. A. February.

Wade, Michael, 1972, *Peter Abrahams* (London, Evans Bros).

Wall, Hans van der (ps. Victor Ido), 1915, *De Paupers* (Amersfoort, Valkhoff & Co.).

Walker, E. A., 1947[2], *A History of South Africa* (London, Longmans, Green & Co., first published in 1928).

Warnsinck, J. C. M. (ed.), 1930, *Reizen van Nicolaus de Graaff naar alle gewesten des werelds beginnende 1639 tot 1687* ('s-Gravenhage, M. Nijhoff).

Wästberg, Per (ed.), 1968, *The Writer in Modern Africa* (Uppsala, Scandinavian Institute of African Studies).

Waugh, Evelyn, 1932, *They Were Still Dancing* (New York, Farrar & Rinehart).

Wauthier, Claude, 1967, *The Literature and Thought of Modern Africa* (New York, Praeger). Translated from the French by Shirley Kay.

Weinreich, Uriel, 1954, *Languages in Contact*, Humanities Press.

Wellek, Rene and Austin, Warren, 1955[2], *Theory of Literature* (New York, Harcourt, Brace & World Inc.).

Whisson, M. G. and H. W. van der Merwe, 1972, *Coloured Citizenship in South Africa* (Rondebosch, The Abe Bailey Institute of Interracial Studies, The University of Cape Town).

Whitney, George, 1586, *Choice of Emblems* (Leiden).

Wielligh, G. R. von, 1918, *Jakob Platjie, egte karaktersketse uit die volkslewe van Hotnots, Korannas en Boesmans* (Pretoria/Amsterdam, de Bussy. Originally appear in *Ons Klijntji* 1896).

Wilcocks, R. W., 1932, 'The psychological report: The Poor White', in *The Poor White Problem in South Africa* (Carnegie Commission) (Stellenbosch, Pro Ecclesia Drukkery), pt II (see also pts I, II, IV and V).

Wilson, M. and L. Thompson, 1968, *Oxford History of South Africa* (vols I and II) (London, O.U.P.).

Wright, Andrew Howell, 1958, *Joyce Cary: a preface to his novels* (London, Chatto & Windus).

Wyk, T. J. van, 1974, 'Blanke beeld veragtelik', in: *Die Burger*, 7 August (Kaapstad).

Younghusband, Peter, 1974, 'Mirror Image', in: *Newsweek*, 2 December (New York).

Zijderveld, Anton, 1971, *Sociologie van de zatheid, de humor als sociaal verschijnsel* (Meppel, Boom).

# Index

# Index

Mandela, Nelson, 213 n.6
Manenberg township, 111; 'coloured' ghettoes, 177; police brutality, 89, 134
Mansfield, Katherine, on Millin's *Dark River*, 58
Marais, J. S., *The Cape Coloured People*, 1, 15, 124
Matthews, James (Jimmy), 171, 174; 'Can the white man speak for me?', 175–6; *The Park*, 73, 77
Matthews, James and Thomas, Gladys, *Cry Rage* (anthology), 34, 172–6
Mentzel, Otto, 13
Mikro (ps. of C. H. Kühn), Calvinist background, 40; didactic purpose, 44; new treatment of 'coloureds', 40–2; *Huisies teen die heuwel*, 41, 48; *Pelgrims*, 41; *Stille Uur*, 41, 48; *Toiings*, 45, 124, 126; 'Cape coloured' hero, 44, 122; character, 45–6, 47, 48, 49; 'coloureds' re-actions, 47, 48, 51; comic supremacy, 40, 41, 44, 49; compared with *Mister Johnson*, 47, 48; reviewed by Malherbe, 42–3; *Vreemdelinge*, 41
Millin, Sarah Gertrude, 58, 67, 125; and 'colour', 2, 51, 54, 60–1, 71; miscegenation theme, 52, 59, 60–3, 84; Mphahlele's criticism, 43; racial preoccupation, 9, 52, 58, 60; 'smelling strangeness' symbolism, 60, 71; *Adam's Rest*, 2, 52, 54, 60–1, 71; *The Dark River*, 52, 58, 60; *God's Step-children*, 41, 52, 54, 57, 61–3; *The Herr Witchdoctor*, 52, 63; *King of the Bastards*, 52; fictionalizes Coenraad Buys, 64–5; *The Measure of My Days*, 52; *The People of South Africa*, 52; *The South Africans*, 59
Milton, John, *Areopagitica*, 132, 133, 215 nn.32, 41
Mittelholzer, Edgar (W. Indian writer), 66–7
Moore, Gerald: on Mphahlele's prose, 85; on social role of drama, 110
Moore, John, *Zeluco*, 25
Morand Paul, *Magie Noire*, 54
Mossel Bay, Dutch-Khoi encounter, 18
Movement, the (Anti-CAD; NEUM; TLSA), 182–3
Mozambique, 12, 14, 53

Mphahlele, Ezekiel, 85, 119, 136; on Cary's *Mister Johnson*, vii, 46; exiled, 121; and humour, 51; assessment of Mikro, Millin, etc., 43–4; on the short story, 137; on the white man, 135–6; *The African Image*, 116, 137; *Down Second Avenue* (autobiographical), 85, 148
Muller, Elise, *Die Peertak*, 73, 74–5; *Twee Gesigte*, 75–6; *Die Vrou op die Skuit* (anthology), 74
Multatuli (ps. of Douwes-Dekker), *Max Havelaar*, 25

Naipaul, Vidia, *A House for Mr Biswas*, 72
Nakasa, Nat, death in exile, 131
'natives': abolition of franchise, 8; definition, 5; statutory term, 3; Western terminology, 15
National Government (1948), 142–3; new constitutional proposals, 194–7
National Liberation League, 149
négritude, 170; first use, 166; modern myth, 166; reflected in 'coloured' thinking and writing, 166, 171; white fear, 177
negrophilism, 23, 26; in *Kennis van die aand*, 129
Neser, Regina, 53, 66, *Kinders van Ishmaël*, vii, 67
New Era Fellowship (NEF), 181, 220
*Newscheck*, on Adam Small, 96
Ngugi (Kenyan writer), 141
Niekerk, Lydia van, and 'Jakob/Platjie' image, 29–30, 201 n.45; use of terms 'rooi-nekke' and 'geel-bekke', 32
Nienaber, G. S., 'Origin of Name Hottentot', 16, 17
Nieuwenhuys, Rob, *Oost-Indische Spiegel*, 56
Niger, Paul (Guadeloupe poet), *Je n'aime pas l'Afrique*, 107–8
Nigeria, 40; *see also* Lugard
Nkosi, Lewis: 'Jim come to Jo'Burg syndrome', 83, 143; on Rive's use of dialogue, 162; on vernacular English novels, 83, 88; 'Fiction by Black S. Africans', 218 n.94; *Home and Exile*, 83
'noble savage' concept, 47, 58, 64, 187; French image, 167, 169

244

247